CREATING COMMUNITY

HISPANIC MIGRATION TO RURAL DELAWARE

KATHERINE BO

CREATING COMMUNITY
Hispanic Migration to Rural Delaware

By Katherine Borland, Ph.D.

Copyright © 2001

A DELAWARE HERITAGE PRESS BOOK

First Printing, June, 2001

ISBN: 0-924117-19-2

Library of Congress Control Number: 2001091612

The Delaware Heritage Commission
Carvel State Office Building
820 North French Street, 4th Floor
Wilmington, DE 19801

Delaware
• • • • • • ◆ • • • • • •
Freedom's First

About the Author

Katherine Borland has been an assistant professor in the Division of Comparative Studies in the Humanities at Ohio State University–Newark since 1999. She has published in the subject areas of folklore, festival, oral narrative and literacy. She has also conducted public sector research for the Historical Museum of Southern Florida, the Delaware Folklore Program, and the Delmarva Folklife Project. After presenting a dissertation on the Politics of Culture in Nicaragua, Dr. Borland received a Ph.D. in Folklore from Indiana University in 1994. One month later she moved to Wilmington, Delaware to help create a nonprofit organization dedicated to helping inner city youth prepare for college. During the following five years, she met and admired many community workers throughout the state including those working with Hispanic immigrants in Sussex County. Her current research assesses the impact of ten years of neoliberal reform and continuing outmigration on the cultural life of a working community in Masaya, Nicaragua.

Photo Front Cover: *Poultry Worker's Clothing – Emilia Alvarez with her children Johnny and Josue (Courtesy of Allison Burris)*

Acknowledgements

Always in a project of this type, the end product represents the contributions of many people. I thank all of the wonderful residents of Sussex County who shared their time, expertise and commitments with me. I particularly thank Pilar Gomez, Gonzalo Martinez, and Nancy Soriano, who made it possible for me to meet many of those whose stories are contained in this volume. This project was first inspired by fieldwork conducted for the Delmarva Folklife Project, through a grant from the National Endowment for the Arts. The Delaware Department of Parks and Recreation, the Delaware Heritage Commission, and Ohio State University– Newark have provided additional financial support for the project. Finally, I thank editors Deborah Haskell and Paul Bauernschmidt for their wonderful support and feedback.

Table of Contents

Preface vii
Introduction 1
The Community Organizers
    Gonzalo Martinez 23
    Rev. Jim Lewis 36
    The Carmelite Sisters:
        Sister Ascension Benegas 53
        Sister Rosa Alvarez
        Sister Maria Mairlot

The Workers
    Esteban Perez 79
    Fernando Natareno 107
    Ticha Roblero 117
    Yanitza Delgado 125
    Carmen Garcia 135
    Chavez Family 145
    Colon Family 157
    Nevy Matos 173

The Entrepreneurs
    Wilson Hidalgo 187
    Rosario Hernandez 197
    Zenon Perez 215
    Margarita Gonzalez 227

Community Workers
    Pilar Gomez 249
    Maria Lopez 277
    Maria Martinez 295
    Maria Mendoza 313
    Juan Perez 333
    Olegario Capriel 367

List of Illustrations 387
Bibliography for Further Reading 389

Children dressed in traditional clothing for a festival
(Courtesy of Rocio Flores)

Preface

The story of Delaware is a history of people seeking a better life for themselves and their families. From the Swedes to the Finns to the English, from the Irish to the Italians to the Eastern Europeans and more recently the Asians and many others, Delaware has experienced great waves of immigration that have shaped our identity and heritage. These immigrants along with Native Americans and African Americans, who prior to 1865 arrived in slavery, have combined their strengths and talents to build our State. Each new group eventually finds its way, almost always with great effort and courage. Today, the American Dream and its unending promise still attracts new immigrants to our shores.

After each new wave of immigration ends, historians assemble documents, data, and photographs to try to reconstruct what happened. More recently, historians have gathered oral histories—often conducting interviews in the participant's twilight years as memories may have begun to fade. Seldom have historians had the foresight to gather oral histories while events are still unfolding.

In 1999, the Delaware Heritage Commission discovered a manuscript written by Katherine Borland for the Delmarva Folklife Project. Ms. Borland's collection of interviews with Hispanics in Sussex County from January through July 1999 chronicled the challenges faced by this newest wave of immigrants. The Commission realized that it had a unique opportunity to capture an oral history of Delaware immigration as it was happening. The Commission approached Ms. Borland to enlarge the project, conduct more interviews, and prepare a manuscript for the Delaware Heritage Press. The result was upwards of 50 interviews the text of which you are holding in your hands or viewing on your computer terminal.

Creating Community: Hispanic Migration to Rural Delaware is a window into the largest and newest group of immigrants to the United States. The Hispanic community's

vii

growth in Delaware has been both extensive and rapid. Like the groups that preceded them, they have gone about finding their way in a new and strange environment. Like immigrant groups of the past, they are a sizeable labor pool that helps to fuel Delaware's economic growth. Yet, like immigrant groups of the past, they are viewed as new and strange. In these interviews, many of us will be reminded of the achievements and struggles of our forebears who came to these shores. We will be reminded that our ancestors and their ethnic community ultimately prevailed against the challenges of language, housing, poverty, and crime.

  This is a valuable book because it speaks to every one of us about change. It reminds us of Delaware's diversity and our unity. It reminds us that America's heritage is that of "E Pluribus Unum" —"Out of Many—One."

The Delaware Heritage Commission

Introduction

In the past decade Sussex County has suffered a sea change. A settled rural community, where residents had known their neighbors for generations, suddenly experienced an influx of a large, unfamiliar, non-English speaking people, who were mostly but not exclusively Hispanic. In 1990, county residents were much more accustomed to the idea of out-migration than to the introduction of new peoples and new cultures within their very midst. Although Sussex communities had depended upon seasonal workers for decades to harvest crops, seafood, and assist in other productive enterprises, these non-native residents had remained largely separate from and invisible to the settled population. So, communities were understandably surprised at the influx of a new, highly visible, non-English speaking group of mostly male workers, who sought housing, not in the traditional labor camps, but in homes that were in convenient walking distance from the other growing presence in Sussex towns, the poultry processing plants. Tensions were inevitable, yet the Hispanic communities in Selbyville, Georgetown, Lincoln, Milford, and Seaford have grown. And if some Sussex neighbors have observed the transformation with dismay, others have embraced these, our newest immigrants, with open arms.

This volume is an attempt to overcome some of the barriers that have impeded our understanding of one another. It is an attempt to answer the question: Who are these newest neighbors? The volume offers a series of oral narratives from Hispanic residents that reveal who each is and how each found him or herself in lower Delaware. The answers, of course, are as varied as the people who have so generously shared their lives with me, and now with you. The volume is also intended to highlight the important work that individual community members are doing right now to create a strong, vibrant community out of what might otherwise be a population aggregate. This Sussex Hispanic community is in the process of formation. While it is in some ways separate from the established Sussex community–by

1

language, custom, and circumstance–it is not inherently antagonistic to it.

Growth

Impressionistically, Georgetown seems the center of growth for the Hispanic population in Sussex County with Hispanics making up about 40% of the overall population and nearly doubling the size of the town in a decade.[1] The 2000 census figures show a slightly different picture.[2] According to this census, Georgetown city attracted 911 new people for a total of 4,643 people, just a 24% increase. However, the growth in the number of Hispanics from 75 in 1990 to 1,398 in 2000 represents an increase of 1,864%. Hispanics now make up 32% of the population of the city of Georgetown, up from 2% in 1990.[3] This means that as Hispanics have moved into the area, other non-Hispanic residents have moved out. A native Georgetown resident and civil servant has watched the town change rapidly from twenty years ago when he was a boy.[4] He says that although some of the old timers have died off, others have felt invaded, and have sold out in order to find communities in which they feel more comfortable.

For Georgetown and the surrounding area, there was a 51% overall population increase and a 1,343% increase in the number of Hispanics. Hispanics make up 18% of the greater Georgetown population. Compare this with Selbyville-Frankford, another area

---

[1] These are the general figures that have been used by newspaper reporters, city officials and community organizers before the census data were published.

[2] Census data for Hispanics in Delaware can be accessed at the University of Delaware website: http://www.cadsr.udel.edu.

[3] We can assume that the real figures for Hispanics are somewhat greater than those reported in the census, because many immigrants resist participating in such counts. However, the figures give us some measure with which to gauge the extent of the transformation this area is experiencing. Nevertheless, it is interesting to note that Georgetown has surpassed New York City, the traditional center for immigration, in proportion of foreign born (32% to 28%).

[4] The interviewee prefers to remain anonymous.

that has seen a dramatic rise in Hispanic residents of 1,571% in the last ten years. Only 4% of the area is Hispanic with 1,053 Hispanics in 2000. Milford reports 789 Hispanics, a growth of 1,653%, or a total of 5% of the area population. For Sussex County as a whole the Hispanic population has grown from 1,476 people in 1990 to 6,915 people in 2000, a 368% increase, while the overall population has grown only 38%. In fact, the Delaware Population Consortium estimated that Sussex County Hispanics numbered 7,932 in 1995, a figure substantially higher than the 2000 census.

Like most immigrant groups, Hispanics tend to settle in pockets with others from their place of origin. Thus, the Georgetown Hispanic population is largely Guatemalan, with a large percentage of these residents from the Northwestern region of San Marcos, close to Mexico's southern border. Georgetown Guatemalans tend to be young Maya-descended immigrants from the rural hamlets of San Marcos where there is very little infrastructure (roads, schools, hospitals, electricity, and potable water). In Guatemala, many practiced subsistence farming, supplemented by migrant labor to the large coastal plantations and domestic work in the cities. Guatemalans from other regions, such as Santa Rosa, Quetzaltenango and Huehuetenango have also gravitated to Georgetown.

In Selbyville one finds Mexicans, and Hondurans who are mostly from an area outside the capital city Tegucigalpa.[5] The Twin Cedars Apartments in Roxana house mostly Mexicans from Veracruz and Salvadoran families, who, like many Guatemalans and Mexicans, are also from rural areas. Salvadorans have also settled in Lewes and Milton. Mexicans predominate in Milford, Lincoln and Bridgeville. Dominicans have settled in Seaford along with Mexicans and some Guatemalans.[6]

---

[5] Honduran residents report that over half the people from their community are now living and working in the United States. They cite generalized corruption and high crime rates as their reason for emigrating.

[6] Information from Maria Mendoza, recruiter for the Del Tech ESL program, summer 2000.

Differences within the Hispanic Community

One of the common misconceptions about immigrant communities is that immigrants, because they are from developing countries, are poor, and that they come to North America to improve their economic status. Yet to emigrate requires economic resources or investments. The trip itself as well as fees for "coyotes"[7] can be substantial. Therefore, those with some economic and cultural capital are much more likely to emigrate from home than those who live in grinding poverty.[8] The Hispanic population in Delaware, while containing substantial numbers of rural peasants from Mexico and Central America, also contains many middle-class town and city dwellers. Generally, urban born immigrants demonstrate higher levels of schooling than their rural compatriots. Some are professionally trained. While middle-class urbanites tend to experience a decrease in social standing by immigrating–from office to factory worker, for example–this decrease is often only temporary. Immigrants who were middle class in their countries of origin are generally more adaptive than rural-originating immigrants. They recognize the importance of learning English, learn more easily in a formal school setting, and are more likely to be promoted at work or to identify alternative work opportunities outside the field and factory.[9] Working class and peasant immigrants on the other hand have fewer transferable skills in the new environment, tend to remain in ethnic enclaves, and are more likely to make lateral shifts in employment–from one factory to another, or from factory to field to construction. This picture is complicated by the fact that many immigrants retain strong ties with their home communities, often sending substantial portions of their earnings back to family

---

[7] Coyote is the slang term for individuals who help smuggle illegal immigrants across the border in exchange for money or other compensation.

[8] See Portes and Rumbaut, *Immigrant America: A Portrait*, 1990.

[9] In his study of historical immigration, John Bodnar asserts that class standing in the country of origin was one of the strongest predictors for success in the new country among 18th and early 19th century immigrants.

members there. In this way, working class immigrants can experience a rise in social status in their country of origin, even if they remain at the bottom of the economic ladder here. Motivation to work, then, even if promotions are not likely, remains strong, due to real financial and status gains in the home country. Over the past 25 years immigrant "remittances" to Mexico, Central America and the Caribbean have become a substantial part of those countries' economies. In 1997 remittances to Mexico alone approached five billion dollars. In the most extreme case, remittances constituted one quarter of Nicaragua's Gross Domestic Product.[10]

By far the greatest attraction to Sussex County has been the availability of low skill jobs in the poultry processing plants. The plants have grown astronomically in the past few years—necessitating a large workforce.[11] As little as fifteen years ago the only poultry plant in Georgetown was a small, family-owned business, Swift and Company. When Perdue arrived, they took over that facility and began to diversify the operation. As the demand for more and more processed forms of chicken has grown, so too has the need for labor to cut and package the chicken. Poultry conglomerates quickly outstripped the local labor supply.

Portes and Rumbaut point out that historically, migration patterns have been established through direct recruitment of workers by agents in the host country.[12] Border recruitment of workers is nothing new in Delaware. As far back as the early 1980s, King Cole Canning Company in Milton operated a recruitment office on the Texas border with Mexico.[13] That's how the Ruiz and Lopez (this volume) families found their way here.

---

[10] Please see the report by Inter-American Dialogue and The Tomás Rivera Institute: *The Developmental Role of Remittances in U.S. Latino Communities and in Latin American Countries,* June 2000.

[11] For a very extensive history of the rise of the poultry industry on the peninsula, see William Henry Williams, *Delmarva's chicken industry: 75 years of progress* (Georgetown, DE: Delmarva Poultry Industry, 1998).

[12] *Immigrant America: A Portrait, 1990.*

[13] King Cole closed its Milton cannary in 1998.

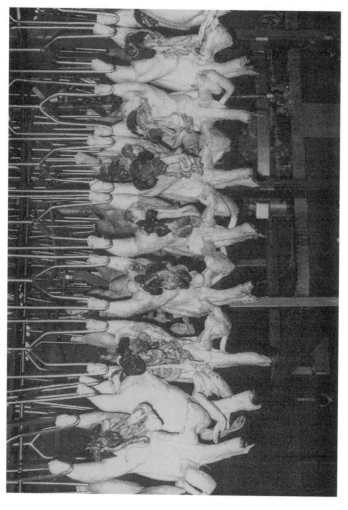

Mountaire Chicken Processing Plant, Sussex County
(Courtesy of the Picture Delaware Collaborative
and the Delaware Art Museum
Photo by Teia Johnson)

By 1993, workers report that Perdue's labor shortage was so great that the company offered cash bonuses to anyone who could bring in a new pair of hands (see Capriel, this volume). The few immigrants who had found their way to the area spread the word through their information networks that jobs were available in Delaware, thus activating an immigrant stream.

Hispanics had gained a reputation for being excellent workers–prompt, obedient, and rapid.[14] They willingly accepted jobs that other groups avoided, due to the low relative wage, unhealthy working conditions, and the high risk of worker injury.[15] Recognizing Hispanics as a desirable worker pool, the poultry plants themselves were the first to adapt to the Hispanic, non-English speaking worker. They began providing training in Spanish and offered basic English language classes in the plants. In addition, they identified adept Hispanic workers and promoted them to leadership and even supervisory positions.[16] Some Hispanics see working in the poultry plants as a stepping stone to some other opportunity. However, others expect to remain in the low skilled workforce–perhaps drifting from one plant to another or from factory to construction to field work as they become disillusioned or bored by their current jobs.

A substantial portion of the community continues to remain highly mobile, circulating from one rural area of the country to another in search of better opportunities or simply a change. Yet, Hispanics, particularly Hispanic families, are settling down in the area. In the past three years, Hispanic immigrants have begun to buy homes and put down roots. Often the greatest change in

---

[14] A border Mexican asserted that the Hispanic community recognizes a scale of "good" workers that almost exactly reverses a groups' rights and privileges. Thus, folk opinion would rank Guatemalans as the hardest workers, followed by other Central Americans and Mexicans from the interior. Next on the scale are border Mexicans, Chicanos, Puerto Ricans, Blacks, and finally Whites.

[15] For more on injury, see the 1998 publication of the Public Justice Alliance, *The Disposable Workforce*. Also, see the 28 Nov 1999 special report of the *Washington Post*, "On Chicken's Front Line."

[16] This information provided by community worker, Allison Burris.

perspective occurs when children of immigrants begin to attend school. Recognizing that children, many of whom are U.S. citizens anyway, will have greater educational, health, and work opportunities in the United States, parents begin to consider making their stay here permanent.

The large influx of Spanish-speaking workers has created a need for bilingual workers, not only in the poultry plants, but also in social services, government, the professions, small business, education, and religion. A number of these workers came to the area through the military and, having retired from the Dover Air Force Base, moved to providing direct service to the new community. For instance, State Police Officer Edwin Justiniano, a former serviceman, has been instrumental in alleviating tensions between Hispanic immigrants and the police.[17] Nancy Soriano, recruiter for the Summer Migrant Education Program, also retired from the military to start a new career. Having grown up in a Tejana-to-Michigan migrant family, however, she sees her work with migrants, now defined as both field and factory workers, as coming full circle. Margarita Gonzalez (this volume), an entrepreneur and volunteer community worker came to the area as a military wife. In addition, a substantial number of Hispanic professionals have moved into the community as part of that other recent influx of Washington and Baltimore urbanites to Delaware's shore communities. Many of these professional Hispanics perform a crucial mediating role, simultaneously representing the community to the larger English-speaking population and providing the human face for larger institutions to the new community.

Immigration Status

A second common misconception is that all Hispanic immigrants are illegal. While a substantial, if immeasurable,

---

[17] As early as 1993, State Troopers have actively tried to improve relations with the immigrant community through visible involvement with community programs, outreach and education.

proportion of immigrants use fraudulent documents or work under the table, most immigrants are authorized to live and work in the United States. Under U.S. Law, it is possible both to apply for residency from abroad and to enter the country without permission to reside and subsequently "adjust" one's legal status. A brief look at the complicated world of immigration legislation will help to clarify these issues.

The United States has always been a nation fueled by immigrant labor. However, immigration has not remained constant over time, but rather has occurred in waves. The last great wave peaked at about 1910 when the foreign born in the country reached 14 percent of the total population. At that time massive numbers of Southern and Eastern Europeans were arriving each year through New York City. In 2000 the foreign-born represented 10.4%, clear evidence of a second great immigration wave. Settlement patterns had also changed with California becoming the largest recipient of immigrants. Moreover, a new pattern of immigration to rural areas and small towns developed, as immigrants fled crime-ridden urban areas and followed industry out of the major metropolitan centers.

Throughout the first half of the 20th century strong restrictions barred nonwhite immigration from Asia and Africa. In keeping with larger social transformation, the Immigration and Nationality Act of 1965 sought to eliminate preferential acceptance of immigrants based on race or country of origin and established a uniform system, retaining a distinction only between the manner of processing émigrés from the Eastern and Western Hemispheres. The law also created a means by which those who had arrived here on a non-resident VISA, a student or tourist, for example, might subsequently apply for residency.

At the same time that the Immigration and Naturalization Act was opening up immigration to people who were not from Europe, the Bracero, or Mexican guestworker program was terminated. From 1942 to 1964 the Bracero program had allowed Mexican nationals to stay in the United States for limited terms in order to work mainly in agriculture.[18] Critics of the program cited exploitation of guestworkers. Others complained that the availability of guestworkers kept wages for citizen farmworkers low and functioned as a disincentive to mechanization in agriculture. Yet when the Bracero program ended, the number of undocumented workers in the United States, particularly from Mexico, began to rise.[19] Between 1966 and 1993 17.4 million immigrants were admitted legally to the United States, while 25 million, most of whom were Mexican, were apprehended for illegal entry. By 1993, however, Mexicans made up only 30% of the undocumented population; 50%, coming from 160 different countries, simply overstayed their visas.

In 1978, Congress further modified the 1965 Act to create a uniform, worldwide system. However, illegal immigration remained a problem. Recognizing the need for immigrant labor, particularly in agriculture, Congress passed the Immigration Reform and Control Act (IFCA) also known as Amnesty in 1986. This Act allowed undocumented workers who had entered the country before 1982 or who worked in agriculture to apply for permanent residence. Applicants under the amnesty were required to take 40 hours of English language and civics classes. A great number of Mexican immigrants and some Guatemalans living in Sussex County have legalized their status through IRCA. (See, for example, Chavez, Lopez and Mendoza, this volume.) Across the country three million undocumented persons applied for amnesty. By the fall of 1993, 88% had been granted permanent resident status.

Recognizing that the promise of jobs provides a powerful magnet for illegal immigration, IRCA also increased sanctions against employers who knowingly hired undocumented workers.

---

[18] For interesting studies of the positive effects on Mexicans and Mexican communities of the Bracero program, see Herrera-Sobek, 1979 and Grimes, 1998.

[19] One might argue that a migration pattern had been established in the preceding 20 years that was difficult to break.

Yet these sanctions were difficult to enforce, creating a situation in which employers might use the threat of INS enforcement to prevent unionization and get rid of troublesome workers. While IRCA assisted millions in legalizing their status, it did nothing to appreciably stem the tide of illegal immigration. In the absence of enforceable employer sanctions, the intensification of INS policing activities on the U.S.-Mexican border, while it raised the economic and human cost of border-crossing, failed to appreciably limit illegal immigration.

The 1996 Illegal Immigration and Immigrant Responsibility Act (IIRIRA), as its title suggests, made the process of applying for adjustment of status more restrictive. In yet another effort to limit illegal immigration, the legislation increased border control efforts, streamlined deportation procedures, called for more employer sanctions, and denied illegal immigrants most social benefits. None of these initiatives has succeeded in its goals, while a negative effect of the Act has been to further criminalize the undocumented immigrant and endanger the civil rights of documented immigrants.[20]

The Special Circumstances of Refugees

At the same time Congress was attempting to regularize immigration policy, it was trying to develop a coherent refugee policy as well. Prior to the 1980s, refugee status was granted in an *ad hoc* way as part of the country's foreign relations policies and generally applied to those fleeing enemy governments. The Refugee Act of 1980 allowed 50,000 people to enter annually, as well as providing an opportunity for 5,000 people already within the country to apply for political asylum. A refugee was defined in this Act as a person who is unable to return to his or her homeland "because of persecution or a well-founded fear of persecution."

---

[20] For a general overview and assessment of recent immigration policy, see Marc Rosenblum, U. S. Immigration Policy: Unilateral and Cooperative Responses to Undocumented Immigration, a paper presented at the International Studies Association and available at http://www.columbia.edu/dlc/ciao/isa/rom01

Yet during the Cold War, political considerations prevented this test from being applied uniformly to all refugee populations. Cubans fleeing Castro's regime and Nicaraguans fleeing a 1979 socialist revolution in their countries were virtually guaranteed asylum, whereas Guatemalans and Salvadorans fleeing torture and massacres perpetrated by their countries' right wing military dictatorships were routinely denied asylum.

In the 1980s the Central American region as a whole was engulfed in civil war, which was augmented by government corruption and mounting external debt. In El Salvador, a recalcitrant military dictatorship refused to democratize, forcing some of the opposition into armed guerrilla warfare. In March 1980 Archbishop Oscar Romero, a critic of the military and a supporter of the previous civilian coalition government, was murdered by elements on the right. His death was followed in October by the murder of six members of the opposition political party, the Democratic Revolutionary Front. In November, three North American nuns and a religious worker were raped and killed by government security forces and, in December, the head of the agrarian reform program and two U.S. advisers were assassinated. As the military government sought to eliminate all opposition, terror spread through the capital and across the countryside. Yet, when the Salvadoran guerrilla movement launched an offensive in early 1981, the United States resumed its aid, including military equipment, to the government. Salvadoran students, union members, peasants–anyone who might be viewed as oppositional– became a target for torture and assassination. Meanwhile, in the United States religious communities formed the Sanctuary Movements whose aim was to smuggle Salvadoran refugees into the country and offer them safe haven.

In Guatemala civil war was endemic. A move toward social democracy initiated by President Arbenz in the 1940s had been toppled by a U.S.-backed coup in 1954. Guerrilla activity in the 1960s provoked the United States again to intervene by training the Guatemalan military in counter insurgency methods. By 1966 "death squads" were operating in the countryside and the term "disappeared" was coined for their victims. By 1979, thousands of ordinary people had already been killed by a series of military dictatorships. From 1978-82 General Lucas Garcia sharply increased the levels of repression, targeting especially catechists and other rural community leaders. He was followed in 1982-83 by General Rios Montt, who initiated the scorched earth approach, in which rural communities, presumed to be supporting the guerrillas, were wiped out in order to destroy the opposition's popular base. From 1981-1983 between 100,000 and 150,000 civilians were murdered, hundreds of villages were destroyed and over one million people were displaced by the violence.

A particular focus for the repression were the Maya Indians who represent at least half the population of Guatemala and occupy the lowest rung on the socio-economic ladder. Centuries-long prejudice and repression of the Maya culminated in what some have called outright genocide in the late 1970s and early 1980s. To sharpen the tragedy even more, poorly educated rural Mayans were recruited into the army, sometimes forcibly, and taught to torture and kill Mayans from unrelated communities. Many communities found themselves caught between the military and the guerrilla forces. If they helped one side, which they were obligated to do, the other side would exact retributions. To escape this nightmare thousands fled across the border to Chiapas in Mexico, an area also largely inhabited by Maya communities.[21] Some Guatemalan refugees arrived in the United States as early as 1980. While most Guatemalans living in Sussex County were children at the height of the repression, many nevertheless witnessed the torture and assassination of older community members.[22]

---

[21] This is the area where the Zapatista guerrilla movement became active in the mid-1990s, led by the enigmatic and media-savvy Comandante Marcos.

[22] A summary of Guatemala Memory of Silence: The Report of the Commission for Historical Clarification: Conclusions and Recommendations is available on the web at http://hrdata.aaas.org/ceh/report/english/toc.html. This report, based on interviews of thousands of victims, places responsibility for most of the violence on Guatemalan government forces.

Church advocates, activists, and immigration lawyers, aware of the gross human rights abuses being perpetrated in El Salvador and Guatemala, and of the miniscule number of refugees who were being granted asylum, brought a class action discrimination suit against the INS. To settle the suit the INS granted temporary protective status for these refugees in 1990, a compromise which gave them permission to work in the United States, but failed to provide a blanket amnesty. This change in government policy, however, prompted some Guatemalans who had spent years in Mexico trying to regularize their status to venture North and apply for political asylum here.[23]

The 1996 IIRIRA Act was followed in 1997 by the Nicaraguan Adjustment and Central American Relief Act, which was designed to minimize the negative effect for refugee groups that increased restrictions on immigration posed. However, the 1997 Act enshrined in legislation the preferential treatment of Nicaraguans and Cubans, by offering them adjustment to permanent resident status if they could establish continuous residence in the United States since December 1, 1995. Meanwhile, the Act allowed Guatemalans and Salvadorans to apply for Suspension of Deportation and Cancellation of Removal, but did not offer them adjustment to permanent residency status as a group. Instead, these refugees would be required to go before a judge and prove "persecution or a well-founded fear of persecution."[24] In 1998, Guatemalans requested parity with Nicaraguans under the terms of the 1997 Act, which they finally received in May of 1999. Under the Equal Justice for Immigrants Act, Salvadorans and Guatemalans who arrived in the United States before October 1990 are eligible for permanent residency.

In addition to these changes in the treatment of refugees, a Temporary Stay of Deportation was offered to undocumented immigrants from four Central American Countries: Nicaragua, El Salvador, Honduras and Guatemala in recognition of the

---

[23] See Juan Perez and Esteban Perez, this volume.
[24] See the account of Sister Ascension Benegas (this volume) on the difficulties of proving persecution in court.

devastation caused by Hurricane Mitch in 1998. Meanwhile, hopeful immigrants from Mexico, Central America and the Caribbean continue to arrive in Sussex County, following the path that neighbors and family members have beaten before them.

Women's Immigration

One final misconception about immigrants relates specifically to women's immigration patterns. The assumption that women are more tied to family than men and therefore do not migrate as individuals but as wives or daughters does not hold true for all communities. Surprisingly, women have constituted the majority of all immigrants to the United States in the twentieth century. Working women, some of whom are single mothers, have as much need to migrate in search of jobs as men do. In the Georgetown Guatemalan community women routinely report having arrived not to reunite with husbands, but to find work. (See the stories of Yanitza Delgado and Carmen Garcia, this volume.) Therefore, the growing birthrate in the mid-1990s must be viewed not simply as a consequence of family reunification, but also as the result of new family formations on the part of young, single immigrants.

Of course, women immigrants rely on networks of family and friends just as their male counterparts do. An individual's decision to come to Sussex County will be based partly on knowing someone who lives in the community already. Once a migrant stream is established, social networks take over to insure a steady flow. While most immigrants are young and send financial support back to their parents, a few are older and sending support to their children. Considerations about which members of a family immigrate appear to be related to personality and interest rather than being dictated by one's family position.

Challenges in Sussex County

The rapid influx of large numbers of immigrants has presented a number of challenges to Sussex County communities. First and foremost has been the issue of housing. Since the poultry plants, which are the largest employers of immigrant workers, do not provide labor camps or other housing, immigrants have had to solve the problem of where to live on their own. The housing stock in many of the older towns is limited and deteriorating, while workers' housing needs continue to grow. Overcrowding has further taxed the housing that is available, and some landlords have failed to keep their properties in good repair. The resulting deterioration has become the number one concern for immigrants, immigrant advocates and non-immigrant residents. So far, the only official response to the problem has been to enforce housing codes. Without increasing the supply of affordable housing units, however, the overcrowding and deterioration of properties seems likely to continue.

The inability of immigrants to communicate effectively in English has been frustrating for both native residents and immigrants. Moreover, communication difficulties lay immigrants open to exploitation not only from landlords, but also from other unscrupulous businessmen, who feel justified in cheating immigrants because they don't speak English. Immigrants have become the targets for robberies as well, since they are known to carry large amounts of cash and, until recently, they have been unwilling to report crimes. This issue has been addressed at least in Georgetown by increasing patrols where robberies have occurred and by hiring a bilingual victim services officer on the local Police Force. In spite of these problems, many immigrants remark that they choose to live in Sussex County precisely because there is less crime than in other, more urban, communities.

Finally, undocumented immigrants face a host of problems. The undocumented may share or purchase valid or counterfeit proof of identity in order to work. However, shared and multiple identities wreak havoc in the criminal justice system. One person may become liable for the criminal record of another person. Being stopped for a minor traffic violation may result in the more serious charge of criminal impersonation. And as adolescents use papers belonging to an older friend or relative, child labor laws are circumvented.[25] On a more general level, the fear of detention and deportation makes undocumented workers less willing to speak out and defend themselves against exploitation and abuse. Cautious and sometimes fearful of outsiders, the undocumented immigrant relies on informal networks within his community to meet his needs.

The presence of large numbers of undocumented immigrants should be a concern for citizens and legal residents of Sussex County. This circumstance creates a two-tiered system in our democracy: those included in and protected by the democracy and those left unprotected. Historically, our nation's response to groups excluded from full citizenship has been to extend rights to larger and larger groups, enfolding them in the blanket of democracy in order to strengthen the rights of all. But resistance to the extension of rights has also historically been strong. Today, the challenge that the undocumented present to our democracy has resulted in two opposing stances. On the one hand, anti-immigration activists call for greater and greater militarization of the border and criminalization of both employers and undocumented workers. Such efforts have constituted a huge cost to taxpayers, with very few positive results. On the other hand, legal immigrants, immigrant advocates, industries that rely on immigrant workers, and unions that represent them are united in resisting these kinds of sanctions. Recognizing the historical importance to the United States of immigrants and the increasing globalization of markets, these sectors urge cooperation as opposed to conflict and normalization of worker status as opposed to criminalization as the best solution. While establishing a common market and permitting the free flow of peoples across our borders

---

[25] Information gathered by author at interview with State Trooper Edwin Justiniano, 8/17/00.

would entail a complex process of planning and coordination among host and receiver nations, it provides a solution in keeping with our country's ideals of equal justice and democracy.

A Word About Method

These narratives were collected and tape recorded over a period of several months in 1999 and 2000 by the author, who visited the narrators in their homes, businesses or at public sites in the community. In some cases, the interview occurred during the first substantial meeting between narrator and interviewer. Thus, these narratives should be viewed as preliminary statements of life experience–what one would say about oneself to a stranger. They represent an initial conversation, but should not be read as the final or defining narrative for the individuals who so generously offered time out of their busy lives to share something of themselves for the record.[26] Moreover, the reader should keep in mind that many potential narrators, when invited to tell their stories, refused to participate in the project, preferring to keep their life experiences private. So, these narratives should not be extrapolated to stand for the whole community.

Upwards of 50 life stories were collected, transcribed and edited for possible inclusion in the volume. Interviewer questions, though edited out of the final transcripts to improve readability, are implicit, I think, in the final texts. Generally, the interviews were conducted as open-ended conversations, with the narrators determining the shape and progression of narrative themes. Narrative sections have sometimes been reorganized for clarity of presentation. Of course, the translation from Spanish to English has also introduced some changes in the manner of expression. Repetitions of words and "filler" words, common features of oral discourse, have been deleted. Throughout, however, I have tried to remain faithful to the narrator's voice.

---

[26] Many Hispanic immigrants, particularly Guatemalan immigrants, have experienced great personal trauma. Yet understandably, this aspect of their life experience is rarely shared with members outside the community.

Several factors resulted in the selection of certain narrators over others. First, I was interested in identifying those members of the community who were likely to remain in Sussex County. I visited individuals who had purchased homes, begun their own businesses, attended English or GED classes, or resided in the community for a number of years. Second, I was interested in working with people who were in some way involved in establishing or strengthening the community. Therefore, I contacted self-identified community organizers, religious leaders, and social service workers. Since I was an outsider to the community, I relied on recommendations from those people working most directly with the community. Since I am female and over forty, I tended to have greater rapport with older community members and women, both minorities within the population as a whole. The final selection of narratives was made with an eye toward revealing the variety of voices that make up this community as well as the eloquence and power of individual stories. The narratives are divided into four sections: Community Organizers One and Two, Workers, and Entrepreneurs. The accompanying CD contains a selection of excerpts from the Spanish language interviews.

Note on Style: In the initial chapter on Community Organizers, the Rev. Jim Lewis has concurred with those paraphrased sections not in quotation marks as his own words. In the subsequent narratives, after my introductory remarks, the words used are the exact words of the speaker.

First Grader Johnny Alvarado April 2000
(Courtesy of Allison Burris)

COMMUNITY ORGANIZERS

Midfielder Dribbles Past Defense
(Courtesy of R. Flores)

Community Organizers

In the last five years Georgetown has become the center of organized efforts to serve the Sussex County Hispanic population generally. Georgetown now is home to *La Casita*, a small Hispanic outreach office, *La Esperanza*, a multiservice community center, *La Red*, a bilingual clinic for the underinsured, three bilingual child care centers, several Hispanic churches of various denominations, an annual Hispanic Festival, Del Tech's for-credit and non-credit English as a Second Language (ESL) program, and the Indian River School District's summer migrant education program. Several factors contributed to the concentration of outreach and services in Georgetown. It is centrally located in Sussex County and, as the County Seat, it houses government services, such as the courts, the Department of Motor Vehicles, the Department of Health and Social Services and the Department of Labor. Equally important, however, has been the arrival of several extraordinary individuals—volunteers, religious workers, and service professionals who have come together to quickly and productively build infrastructure for a group that would otherwise lack access to services.

Community organizers often speak *for* the community while being marked as separate from the community, usually by class standing or by their elective involvement in community life. Therefore, they are generally regarded as cultural intermediaries. Yet their work helps to transform a population aggregate into a functioning community that can identify and act on its collective interests. The life stories of these community members are as compelling as those of ordinary immigrants who exercise less social power. In this chapter I will trace the paths of some of the most influential of these organizers, people whose work has contributed significantly to raising the quality of life among Hispanic residents.

While numerous individuals in a variety of capacities have assisted the Hispanic community in powerful ways, I will focus on five influential figures who came together sometime in 1996 to form *La Esperanza*, now the central institution for the Hispanic immigrant community: Gonzalo Martinez, the Reverend Jim Lewis, and the Carmelite Sisters of Charity: Rosa Alvarez, Ascension Banegas, and Maria Mairlot. Each has a particular focus and style, but all embrace their community work as a mission that links social service with social justice issues. Each has a fascinating life story, and each eloquently describes both the joys and challenges of working in and with the community. These individuals have in turn inspired others to emulate them, and so the group of Sussex County community builders grows with each year. As their stories intertwine, the recent history of community building in Georgetown, Delaware, unfolds.[27]

Gonzalo Martinez

Gonzalo Martinez, a native of Chile, grew up in a privileged, urban environment. He describes his family as being well known. His father was Mayor of Providencia, a municipality of Santiago, and relatively well off. His maternal grandmother, Elivira Rodríguez Escamilla, daughter of a wealthy Guatemalan family, married his grandfather while he was serving as Chilean ambassador to Guatemala. When he was 21, Gonzalo visited family who had remained in Guatemala, and he continues to be in touch with them today. Still, a great gulf exists between the Guatemalan upper classes and the majority indigenous population. While he did have some contact with Guatemala then, in his early years, Gonzalo's social conscience remained undeveloped. He recalls, "My father was also totally Don Quixote, and because of that he lost much of his money helping people. And I [said], "I will work for myself. I will never help anybody!"

Gonzalo became an attorney and worked for awhile as a bureaucrat in Chile. Then he found himself in Washington, D.C. working for the Inter-American Development Bank. He was

---

[27] In this section, life stories have been paraphrased extensively in the interest of space. However, each narrator has read and approved all changes.

assigned to Central America, where he visited community projects and distributed funding. As a result, he became more aware of social justice issues:

"Once I started working with the bank, I had a lot of social projects. When the civil war was going on in El Salvador, I went there. All the bombardments, I was there. And because I was working with the poor of the member countries, I had to do a lot of work, and I had to solve real social and economic problems. I got to know low-income people of Costa Rica, El Salvador, Guatemala, in Jamaica, also in Guyana. So I started to be involved with—a lot of projects had to do with agrarian reform, with education. So I started getting involved with social justice issues."

Even so, Gonzalo recalls, working for the Bank did not allow for sustained interaction with individual communities. Instead, he was the one who flew in and stayed for a couple of weeks observing the projects, always a visitor.

When he retired from the bank in 1989, Gonzalo moved permanently to his weekend home in Lewes and began remodeling the house. His first interest was the arts, and he soon became involved with the Rehoboth Art League, providing Hispanic representation on the board. While thus involved, he noticed a newspaper article about a Sussex County Arts Council project to build a *zócalo* or Mexican plaza for the Hispanic Community in Georgetown. He remembers,

"And that was my first time I heard of the existence of the Latino community. Because when I travel, I never stop in Georgetown. Frankly I did not know where Delaware was, know where Lewes was. I bought [the house] because it was a beautiful place. It was very convenient for Washington, D.C., but I didn't know anything. After I started my work, I discovered the canal, I discovered Wilmington, I discovered where I was."

Thus, like many other shore residents, Gonzalo's personal map did not include Delaware itself and was much more oriented to the Washington area.

Pedro Ospina with Project Organizer Dana Long at the *Zócalo* in Georgetown

(courtesy of Dana Long)

The *zócalo* project took place in 1994, directed by Dana Long of the Sussex County Arts Council and Pedro Ospina, a Colombian artist from New York. Ospina urged Gonzalo to try to help the community, which in his view was totally abandoned. Gonzalo straightaway got in touch with Father Giuliano, who was then at St. Michael's Catholic Church. Tony Asión, a Delaware State Trooper of Cuban descent was also working in the area, and he helped Gonzalo get his bearings by introducing him to the people in the poultry industry. Not much later, Asión was promoted to Sergeant and stationed elsewhere, so Gonzalo began to take over Asión's organizing role.

Meanwhile, a group of professional Hispanics in Dover formed a fledgling volunteer organization called Latino Empowerment Association of Delmarva (LEAD). They had raised some money to fund a community center in Milford, but Gonzalo and Asión took them down to Georgetown and showed them why it would be a better location. The group agreed, and Gonzalo became the volunteer executive director of the proposed center. In March, 1995 *La Casita*, a one room, all-purpose outreach center in Kimmeytown (a neighborhood in downtown Gergetown where many hispanic workers have settled) opened for business. The center provided a space from which several already-functioning volunteer activities could operate. Sister Ascension, a Spanish Carmelite nun, had arrived the year before from New York to help community members with immigration matters. She used *La Casita's* space for her appointments. Volunteers provided English classes, and the locale generally functioned as a place to access translation services for the surrounding Spanish speaking community. Gonzalo quickly realized, however, that he did not want to be an executive director. So, in November of 1995, Sister Margaret, a former American missionary to Bolivia who had been invited to the area by a friend, was hired to do that job. Gonzalo was now free to concentrate his energies on his own organization, *El Centro Cultural*.

El Centro Cultural is dedicated to fostering arts and heritage among the immigrant population. In 1995, it sponsored the first *Festival Hispano* in September, which has become an annual event.[28] If he had known what organizing a festival entailed, Gonzalo swears he never would have started. The first festival, held at the Wesleyan Methodist Church was both a great success and a disaster for its chief organizer:

"I wrote to two hundred people, and I don't think I got more than $4,000, $5,000. And on top of that I decided to make *tamales*. I got a woman making the *tamales*, and we made it at the church. And the church smelled *tamales* for two weeks, and they called me, and I had to take the *tamales* away. It wasn't easy.

"But we did the festival. It was a huge success. We almost died of suffocation, because I planned [for] two hundred people. We were like one thousand inside of the [church]. The day before the church forced me to take the *tamales* out. And then we brought them back in. It was a circus. The bathrooms. I was in charge of the bathrooms, because it was forbidden to use the bathrooms inside, and I have to put an out-of-order sign, and everybody was pushing to use—so, between the *tamales* and the bathrooms I never saw the festival."

After the first year, the festival was moved to the grounds of St. Michael's Church and, over the following four years, it grew tremendously.

Gonzalo hopes through his cultural work to encourage the community to retain their special traditions, arts, language and identity. The festival gives local groups an opportunity to perform their traditions, and it also brings more accomplished groups in from the nearby urban centers. While the Hispanic community has responded enthusiastically to the festival, attendance by English-speaking residents has remained small. Gonzalo feels the festival has been tolerated rather than embraced by some of the members of the Georgetown community. This feeling contributed to the decision to move the festival in 2001 to nearby Milisboro, where

---

[28] *El Centro Cultural* has also helped organize *Posadas*, Mexican Christmas plays, at local churches.

Tamales, Tamales!
(Courtesy of Katherine Borland)

better facilities can be provided, when a calendar conflict at St. Michael's Church prevented the festival from continuing there.

El Centro's festival planning committee now includes Diana Roche, a non-Spanish speaker who is nevertheless a strong ally of the Hispanic community. An urban immigrant to Sussex County like Gonzalo, Diana first became involved through her love of soccer. She remains the volunteer secretary-treasurer for the soccer league, which was one of the first organized groups that emerged from the community itself. She is joined by Rocio Flores, the editor of the Spanish language newspaper, *Hoy en Delaware*, and Maria Mendoza, coordinator for the Del Tech non-credit English as a Second Language (ESL) program (see her story this volume). Together this team works to promote Hispanic Arts and culture through the festival, school programming and scholarships, and other arts activities throughout the year.

Although Gonzalo's first draw to the Hispanic community and his enduring passion is the arts, he was not through institution building with *El Centro Cultural*. On November 11, 1996, Gonzalo collaborated with Jim Lewis, Sister Rosa Alvarez, Sister Maria, and Sister Ascension, to open *La Esperanza*, a larger community center located on Race Street. The new community center was initially funded through a grant from an Episcopal Foundation with which Jim Lewis had strong ties. A member of Jim's discipleship group at a local Episcopal church bought the building and rented it to the fledgling organization. *La Esperanza* provided assistance with immigration and English classes, but it also provided connections with federal assistance programs, services for victims of domestic violence, pre- and post-natal care, and leadership development.

Sister Margaret remained at *La Casita*, even though it was experiencing serious financial difficulties. *LEAD* members were enthusiastic volunteers, but they were not prepared to do the kind of sustained fundraising that an organization, no matter how small, needs to survive. In December of 1997, *La Casita* was scheduled to close its doors, when Georgetown's then-Mayor Steve Pepper bailed it out by locating an anonymous donor. In a *News Journal*

Youngsters Performing at the Festival
(*Courtesy of Rocio Flores*)

article Mayor Pepper noted that while *La Esperanza* was now providing equivalent services to the Hispanic community, Sister Margaret had been working more closely with local government, and thus, *La Casita* remained a valuable resource.[29]

In the spring of 1997, a few months after *La Esperanza* opened for business, Gonzalo helped found *Primeros Pasos* in the Georgetown Police Station. It was the first Spanish-language day care to serve working mothers. The day care was important for Gonzalo not only because it responded to an immediate community need, but also because it insured that Guatemalan children would receive adequate stimulation and preparation for school success later. In 1998, he helped establish a second child care center for infants, *Primeros Pasitos*, in the Georgetown Apartments.

In 2001 after several years of work, Gonzalo has launched a fourth community institution in collaboration once again with the Rev. Jim Lewis. *La Red*, a program of *La Esperanza*, is a medical clinic for the uninsured and underinsured, the first of its kind in Sussex County. *La Red* not only provides direct service, but the organization has developed a network of doctors and medical practitioners who speak Spanish and are willing to work with the immigrant community and other at-risk groups in Sussex County. The clinic, which received a federal grant of more than $500,000 and a grant from the Episcopal Diocese of Delaware of $147,000, represents the largest financial responsibility yet for the *La Esperanza* board. Gonzalo's next project is to provide a similar network of services for legal problems.[30] Then, he says, the

---

[29] 12/4/97, "Mystery donor saves Hispanic center," (Kent and Sussex edition). By the summer of 2000, *La Casita* had elected to become a program of First State Community Action, the largest social service provider in the area, due to its inability to remain financially viable as an independent center.

[30] This project has already begun with the collaboration of the Baltimore based Public Justice Center (PJC) and the Delmarva Poultry Justice Alliance, an organization spearheaded by the Rev. Jim Lewis. Currently, Ricardo Flores, a young lawyer from the PJC, is based at the Local 27 Food and Commercial Workers Union offices. "He is deposing chicken catchers who have launched a

community will have a complete array of programs to meet their most pressing needs.

Gonzalo makes a strong distinction between the kind of institution building he does and the direct service that his colleagues the Carmelite Sisters do. He says he is like the man who brings water to the workers in the field, or again, "I'm salt–or bringing the salt to the cook–the woman who's doing the cooking. I'm not doing the cooking." The Sisters identify the need, and he tries to find support for them to do their work, largely through fundraising and networking. He confides:

"Maybe one of my talents has been the fact that I have been able to create organizations with different people. Some of them are in the same organizations; some are not. Then that has allowed me to be able to work with different talents, so the board of *Primeros Pasos* is quite different from the board of *La Esperanza*. And the board of *La Esperanza* is different from the board of *El Centro Cultural*. And that I think has allowed me to work with more people. And instead of having one huge organization with one board, and I think that has been the problem—I see that in areas—that only one organization tries to embrace everything.

"There are always going to be people with different mentalities and different ways of doing things. So I prefer smaller groups, as long as they can work together and people can get along. I think that has been a good approach.

"And there are other organizations that I don't belong to. For example, *La Casita*, I'm not a member of *La Casita* anymore. And *La Casita* is still doing good work. Now it's specializing in after-school education. I think it's very important. There are so many needs. It's like a black hole so if anybody wants to do something, even if I'm not part of it, I'm delighted. First of all I don't have the time to be part of everything, and second, I shouldn't be. I think the nice thing is to have people doing things and, when you are gone, nobody even notices that you are gone."

---

class action suit against Perdue for having willfully and negligently cheated them of wages."

Not only is Gonzalo good at identifying people who can work together, he also has access to another important group in Delaware: state officials. He has served as a representative on the Governor's Council for Hispanic Affairs as well as for the Delaware Division of the Arts. He has had some success as well luring professional Hispanics, who also reside on the shore but have very little contact with Hispanic workers, into his volunteer activities[31].

One important advantage he identifies with working in Delaware is its small size. For instance, anyone can go and speak personally with the Governor or Congressman. Yet there have been problems with building infrastructure in Sussex County, as Gonzalo explains:

"The other problem is at first, I didn't know the existence of the canal, and that Wilmington had all the political and economic power. So that to me has been difficult to deal with, and I had to learn–it's taken six or seven years and I think I'm learning now. The other one is I'm a very impatient person. And things move slow. And at the beginning I really was–I think I stepped on the toes of too many people, because I was asking, I was pushing.

"I still have the tendency to be a little bit impatient, when I see people with intelligence, power, and all that take so long to understand the issues and act accordingly."

The clash between some of the newer non-native Sussex Countians who see the great needs and injustices suffered by immigrant Hispanics and the slower response of representatives from the "native" rural area contributes to the dynamics of cultural change in Sussex County. Gonzalo has learned that direct confrontation in these circumstances is ultimately less productive than a gentler, more accommodating approach. He sympathizes with local government leaders when they express impatience or exasperation with Hispanics who continue to disregard local laws and customs. Yet, Gonzalo cautions that, as community

---

[31] See, for example, an article about Gonzalo and those he has pressed into service: "Delaware's Hispanic Peace Corps," in *National Journal,* 8/14/99:2357-58.

Governor Ruth Ann Minner
and former Gov. Thomas Carper, now a U. S. Senator, flank Sister Rosa Alvarez
(courtesy of Allison Burris)

representatives, these local politicians ought to demonstrate greater than average patience, because their jobs require it of them.

The experience of becoming a community organizer and watching the organizations he helped found flourish has transformed Gonzalo in profound ways. He says:

"[At Inter-American Development Bank I was working with communities] but I was the one giving the money, the bank lends six billion dollars a year. Now I am the one with my hands out begging. I am the one writing the grants and going to other people to convince them that my projects are worth being financed. But I never worked with the community. I was never on the other side. I was on the bank's side.

"Now my family doesn't recognize me when I go to Chile. When I tell the stories that I have—, I have a radio program[32] or I do this or I do that. They see a totally different person than they have been accustomed to see, because they–they see in a way Don Quixote, my father."

Jim Lewis

Gonzalo, then, has played an important role as a fundraiser and an institution builder in Georgetown. His concern is focused on providing services to Hispanic immigrants as well as encouraging them to retain their Hispanic identity and values. A second institution builder who has been instrumental in getting organizations off the ground has a somewhat different focus and a different personal style. The Reverend Jim Lewis came to Sussex County with a strong background in social justice issues and a particular understanding of the poultry industry. For the last six years, he has been a thorn in the side of local leaders who would like to maintain the *status quo*. If Gonzalo has learned to accommodate, Jim thrives on conflict. For him, conflict and tension is the essence of social justice work. An Episcopal Priest,

---

[32] Several years ago, Gonzalo collaborated with the Rafael Orlando Dosman, the announcer at *Radio La Exitosa* in Milford to deliver a series of call-in programs on legal matters of interest to immigrants.

Jim has challenged religious congregations to practice the gospel in the real world. His concern is not only to provide necessary infrastructure for marginalized communities, but also to develop a structural analysis of the causes of social inequality and suffering.

While Jim has been viewed by his detractors as an outside agitator, he traces his roots to the peninsula:

"I grew up in Baltimore, Maryland, but actually my father was from over here, Accomac. So I've got some history over here, but I really didn't grow up over here. I grew up in Baltimore. My own background, I guess it would be fair to say, I grew up in a working class neighborhood. My father had a fourth grade education; my mother had a high school education. Nobody in the family ever went to college, so I came out of a Baltimore neighborhood, and that was important to my growing up."

Jim attributes his religious vocation to a bout with rheumatic fever when he was nine. His forced inactivity and daily visits from an Episcopal priest taught this normally active and athletic youth to reflect. When he recovered, he was sent to an Episcopal school. After graduating, he studied philosophy at Washington University, by which time he was considering ordination. Then he joined the US Marines, where he served from 1958 to 1961. He recalls:

"We were just beginning in Vietnam, Laos. I was stationed over in that region. I really got my eyes opened to what we were doing overseas. That was pivotal to me too in my growth. I began to see more about Yankee imperialism (laughs). Trying to figure out what we were doing over there. What was I doing over there?"

When he returned, Jim attended Virginia Seminary in Alexandria for three years. His first job was at St. Anne's in Annapolis, where he was serving a number of distinctive constituents simultaneously. While some were in school, others were going to war. In addition, Jim began work in the Black community right outside the segregated church. From there, he became a pastor of a church in rural Martinsburg, West Virginia, for seven years, after which he moved to downtown Charleston, West Virginia, the capital city, where he became rector of a large church. Throughout this period, Rev. Lewis was looking for ways to open the church to the community. He explains:

"My understanding of the parish church was that the doors should be open. People should be coming in and out. And we oughta' be dealing with whatever God gives [us] that day on our plate. And if you really do that, you're gonna really find out about your neighborhood and really open up. We did that. Every church that I served, the doors of the church were open all day. People came in."

Opening the church to the community brings not only understanding but conflict, as Jim quickly discovered:

"When I went to Charleston, West Virginia, I really got involved with major controversy, national kind of controversy. I was there four weeks and the schools blew up. People were shot. The schoolbooks were taken out. A Fundamentalist/Right Wing political wedding came together to throw [out] a set of Language Arts books that were multicultural and multiethnic. And in those days I didn't realize what it was when it broke loose, but I knew it was dangerous... We had every Right Wing lunatic come in. It was when busing had been done in Kentucky and Boston, the riots.

"It was a tough time and to make a long, long, long story short, I got involved with that struggle in that church and it resulted in a tremendous amount of conflict. My life was threatened. The Klan came in. I had people arrested for trying to kill me, threatening to kill me. And I got up to my ears in it, and the church got up to its ears, and I got introduced to the community in a quick way. And it was wonderful, because–in a terrible way– because St. John's Church became a community center. We then opened it up to poor people on the streets. We began feeding people, housing people, opening up a community drop-in center, taking cases all the way up to the Supreme Court around jailing drunks. It just was wild work.

"My church today feeds four hundred people off the street every day! Every day, Sunday included. Two meals a day. It has an outreach center that you wouldn't believe. So we were involved in that. In the 1970s that was radical work for the Episcopal

Church. Got involved with the Gay community. Did two gay blessings while I was there, and all hell broke loose. These were the people coming in to the church because it was wide open. Got involved–that was my first trip into Central America. I went to El Salvador and to Nicaragua and to Honduras. That was the early '80s. I went there right after the sisters and the lay workers were raped and killed in El Salvador."[33]

Lewis's interest in the Central American conflict emerged as just one in a constellation of justice issues with which his church was involved. In fact, he began to draw parallels between what was happening in Central America at the time, his earlier experiences in the Vietnam conflict, and the exploitation of Appalachian communities where he was then located. He took four trips to Central America over the next ten years and gradually became an international figure. Jim explains this movement as a natural process of growth.

"It was just a movement out. Always connected to parish base, I had my people involved in this work. I was trying to connect what was going on locally with what was going on globally. I knew that if it came time to fight a war in Honduras, they would come get local kids, and they would be called upon to kill people in Vietnam. I was dealing with pastoral problems. Local people having come back screwed up from the war in Vietnam. So when they were trying to tell me that, you know, you should do the pastoral problems, that is, help somebody with drug addiction or [who is] sick or their marriage, I always wanted to know well, why the marriage was messed up and why they had the drug addiction and how it's connected to war and poverty and all the structural stuff."

At the same time he was going global, Jim remained vigilant in his own community:

---

[33] December 1980. These assassinations for which government security forces were responsible, were symptomatic of the increasing violence sweeping through the country at that time. Even so, the U.S. continued to provide military aid to El Salvador to counter a guerrilla offensive early in 1981.

"Buffalo Creek, West Virginia took place while I was there, and that was the flooding of a creek area by a Pittstown Coal company dam that broke and killed over one hundred people in the flood. The governor wanted to call it an Act of God. I thought that was sacrilegious and blasphemous. It wasn't an Act of God. It was an act of a lousy coal dam."

Jim's work in West Virginia also made him aware of the tremendous power of harnessing the media. He was invited to speak on Phil Donahue and Maury Povich, and became, as he says, media savvy.

After eight years of invigorating frontline work, he went to another congregation in Ann Arbor, where he worked with a more economically and educationally privileged congregation forming a coalition for the homeless, but he missed the energy of West Virginia. Then the Bishop in Raleigh, North Carolina, invited him specifically to do the organizing work that was his passion. During the next seven years he continued to challenge his people both on the international and home fronts. He explains:

"I went to Iraq, October before the war. Brought hostages back. Tried to organize people in the diocese against going to war, successfully... Normally I always have a foot in charity, more like two feet, but also in the justice issues and how to deal with those, the hardest ones of all. And I got away with that. I got away with that for seven years in North Carolina. I did a lot of wild work with migrant workers, and that's how I got introduced to poultry."

Jim describes his analysis of poultry industry abuses as a process of discovery, the social justice issues emerging out of work rooted in charity:

"Yes, what I knew was, where I discovered it was, we ran a Migrant Center in Harnet Johnson in Sampson County near Siler City in that area of North Carolina. And we did a lot of outreach to migrant workers. It was pretty much charitable work. Some Head Start work. But then I began to see that they were staying around to do poultry. So we got some money and started a little clinic for women and all [those] whose hands were messed up.[34]   And I began to see what was going on. Then I began to meet the farmers who were producing the chicken and the catchers and everybody who was connected to it. I began to see how defective the product was and how disastrous the industry was. So we began to address it... All kinds of stuff and got in a lot of trouble and got that diocese in a lot of trouble doing that. It was hard work."

In North Carolina, Jim got Episcopal Foundation money that allowed him to do more radical work than would have normally been supported by a diocesan council. However, after seven years, a new Bishop was unwilling to take the same risks as the one who had hired Jim. At the same time, Jim's wife, an oncology nurse, had been diagnosed with cancer. So he took a year off and dedicated himself to home and family.

The next year, 1994, Jim was invited to Delaware by Bishop Cabell Tennis to assess what was going on in the peninsula south of the canal, and propose a plan for Episcopal action. He spent a year looking around:

"I wandered around, and where I needed to I put on my collar, and I went from the Bishop's office. And where I didn't need to, I just wandered around and took notes and drank coffee and talked to people and knocked on doors, etc. I really like to do that. Explore. I was all over this county. I wrote the report, gave it to the council and worked with the Bishop, got foundation funding from the same people I got it from in North Carolina to begin this program. Got the diocese to buy into it, and then it was finished.

"The Bishop offered me the job. I was reluctant because I thought there ought to be someone who was Latino. Somebody who spoke Spanish for sure! I looked it over, and I looked it over, and I thought, no, I think the first phase of this [is] building some infrastructure.   There was no infrastructure here in terms of

---

[34] Line workers in the poultry industry experience high rates of carpel tunnel syndrome. See the publication of the Public Justice Center, "The Disposable Workforce: A Worker's Perspective," 1999, Baltimore, MD; "On Chicken's Front Line," *Washington Post* 11/28/99:A1ff.

meeting problems. I mean this state didn't have it. This area didn't have it. I can come in there and I can do that and I can begin to build some infrastructure to deal with problems for people who live on the fringe. It was defined not strictly as poultry. It was defined as Prison, Gay community, Black community, Latino community. Anybody who was on the fringe, invisible, or who is not acceptable for some reason…

"I did three years of this work, and in the first three years we were able to begin *La Esperanza*. We were heavily involved–I was heavily involved in that. We were able to start discipleship group work here in three churches. One church took and began to move towards prison and has now developed its Way Home program.[35] It's powerful.

"The third thing that we undertook is the Delmarva Poultry Justice Alliance. That's huge, growing. It is the watchdog organization here on the poultry industry. And that by the way now has spawned and spread into a national work. I'm half crazy with what we've got. I've gotten back six zillion times what I thought I'd ever get from this work. We've been able to get a lot of attention in the media. Which means more contacts with people all over the country. It means more organizing. We're real lean. I don't have a secretary. I have an executive director now of the Poultry Justice Alliance."[36]

Once infrastructure building began, Lewis recalls, the coming together of people generated rapid growth:

---

[35] This program ministers to prisoners, ex-offenders from Sussex County Correctional institution helping them transition back into civil society after having served their sentences.

[36] The Delmarva Poultry Justice Alliance opened an office in Pocomoke City, MD in early 2000. The executive director is Carol Morison, who became involved in the organization as a grower who found herself a victim of the poultry companies' vertical integration. For a good discussion of vertical integration, see Miller, Horowitz, Martin and Kee, "Immigrants in the Delmarva poultry industry: The Changing Face of Georgetown, DE and environs and a note on migrants in Delmarva agriculture: the case of Delaware." Paper presented at The Changing Face of Delmarva Conference, University of Delaware, 9/11-13/97.

Groundbreaking at the new *La Esperanza*

From left: Sister Ascension Banegas, Allison Burris, Sister Maria Mairlot, Olegario Capriel, Alan K. Warfel (Warfel Construction), Sister Francesca Mota, Sister Rosa Alvarez, Gonzalo Martinez, Maria Picazo, Ofelia Crowic and Jim Lewis.

(Courtesy of Allison Burris)

"...When I first pulled into town there was nothing here and when I came back, as I was coming back in, and when I finally took the job in 1995, *La Casita* was there, and that's how I met Gonzalo. Piece out of the newspaper and we talked on the phone, and I said, ' I've been in and out of here and I've never met you.' He said, 'Well, I've met you, and I'm fairly new to this,' and so I met Gonzalo and had an instant communication..."

When Jim became aware that another community center was needed, he called a meeting of all the interested parties: Gonzalo, the Carmelite Sisters, police, local government. Using part of his budget, and with the full support of the Episcopal diocese, he provided the financial wherewithal to get a new, larger community center started:

"*La Esperanza* started out as a project of the Episcopal Church. It was umbrella'd for a year and a half. All the books were kept at the diocese. All the money was collected there. Every grant we got went through the diocese. They took not one penny from it. I never got paid for it, so there wasn't any money in it for the diocese. There weren't any converts in it for the diocese. It's been a true outreach program in the best sense of the word, evangelization and bringing good news to people in that sense of the word."

Jim remembers that the Catholic diocese was initially suspicious of the work being done at *La Esperanza*. The Sisters, on loan from their order, had been basically functioning on their own without support from the hierarchy or even much help from the local Catholic church, which has been hampered somewhat by leadership turnover during the decade. That has changed as the work being done at *La Esperanza* has been recognized throughout the state.[37] In the early days Jim functioned as a sort of fill-in

---

[37] By 1998, the Catholic Diocese had realized it needed to do more direct outreach to Hispanics living south of New Castle County. They held an *Encuentro* (a gathering of the faithful) in 1998, followed by a second smaller gathering for Hispanic youth in 1999. The Carmelite Sister Francesca was hired by the diocese to provide coverage for the entire peninsula, while outreach worker Ignacio Franco conducted a survey of Catholic Hispanics on Delmarva

executive director until Maria Picazo was hired to do that job in 1999:

"She's inherited a real bag of worms because now we get money from a number of programs. We got Juan[38] working on the street. We've just taken off. I put it this way. All the organizations that I'm working with are big dogs with small organizational legs. The Justice Alliance is really that way. We are doing enormous work with very small institutional legs.

"In the course of time here, we've spawned a lot of other stuff. The way this thing works is like some kind of nuclear explosion. Figuring out where it all started. You never can. I know that when Gonzalo got together with the sisters and myself and we all sort of got together, there was a lot of fertilization going on. I met with a group of people over here at the church and began to go to prison. Stuff starts happening. Passion and energy starts moving. A lot of stuff has gotten spawned."

This sort of chain reaction can be seen in the work that is going on throughout the area, as volunteers and service workers become inspired by the example that folks like Jim, Gonzalo and the Carmelite Sisters provide.

Jim was also involved in programs reaching out to other communities in the rural areas, a teen pregnancy program in the Black community, for instance. All the projects with all the diverse communities, he emphasizes, are guided by a common vision of empowering people to take control of their lives. Despite the diverse directions of his work, Jim has become most identified with one project, the Delmarva Poultry Justice Alliance. Currently, the DPJA is helping chicken catchers bring class action

---

that identified both social and religious needs. The Franciscan Brothers based at St. Paul's Cathedral in Wilmington, particularly Brother Chris, have been centrally involved in reaching out to the Spanish speaking community with an engaged, less formal, more joyful style. The Catholic Church is also actively incorporating some immigrant folk religious practices into the Spanish-language worship in a gesture of welcome to the new arrivals.

[38] Juan Perez, outreach worker based at *La Esperanza* for Children and Families First. See his story in this volume.

lawsuits against Tyson and Perdue for "cheating them out of wages." The catchers, largely African American men, are those workers who actually pack the live chickens in crates to be sent from the poultry farms to the factory for processing. Until recently catchers were hired as independent contractors, and therefore received no benefits or overtime pay, even though, by other standards, they were full-time employees of the companies.

These same catchers have recently made labor history by being the first group of workers to unionize at Perdue. Two groups of catchers in Georgetown and Salisbury voted to unionize in July of 2000. The catchers in the plant at Accomac, Virginia, voted against unionizing but, in March 2001, after a judge found Perdue guilty of intimidating workers, the Accomac group voted to unionize.[39]

With regard to those working in the plants themselves, the DPJA has pushed the US Labor Department to investigate whether standard industry practices result in underpaying employees.[40] Jim has also pressed the Department of Labor to disseminate videotapes in Spanish of workers' rights, so that immigrant workers can learn what our government expects of an employer. For Jim, though, the workers' plight must be connected with other industry excesses. He explains:

"My ministry has been a ministry of conflict. I get up in the morning and if I don't get conflict or some unhappy call, some trouble through the day, it's not been a good day. I woke this morning to pictures in the news—we have thousands of dead birds pitched alongside the riverbed and I was ecstatic. They finally

---

[39] A fourth group of catchers in Milford was unsuccessful at challenging the company, because several members of this largely Latino team lacked proper documentation. When the company realized they might vote to unionize, they reexamined the documents and fired the undocumented workers.

[40] At issue are practices such as charging employees for necessary uniforms and safety wear, and not paying them for time spent putting on and taking off this gear. In January 2001, the Department of Labor concurs with local advocates that widespread wage and hour violations exist in poultry plants. Weiser, Carl, "Poultry Industry bosses meet U. S. Labor Secretary," *Coast Press* 25 April 2001.

caught them! Tyson. We're going after them. I woke up last week to a phone call from–and they talked to me like this! A farmer said, 'I got good news for you Jim.' I said, 'give it to me.' He said, 'Johns Hopkins has determined that the spray that the company has made me use was responsible for my health problems.' Which means now there are a number of other people out there with the same thing. I said, 'that's great Tom.' 'Good news man!' I got a lawyer involved, and I'm going to go after them. Most clergy–a lot of them, not most of them–like to wake up in the morning and keep it calm and keep it cool, and let's not rock it. I've learned that after 35 years of doing this work, it's fun and it's right. It challenges the *status quo*."

One of the first events that brought Jim in contact with the Hispanic sector of poultry workers was the 1996 wildcat strike at the Mountaire plant in Selbyville. He remembers:

"Local 27 of the United Food and Commercial Workers Union was small here, out of touch with its Latino membership. We had a strike when I first came here four years ago. In a union plant. Oh that blew things wide open. I housed the workers from the plant in the church in Selbyville overnight, about 150 of them. Everybody was mad at me. The best thing that ever happened. The best thing that ever happened! The union got a wake up call. They now established themselves here, and they are trying. They are really working at it. The plants are all nervous, and the church has had to wake up too. The changing population and they can't avoid them, so let's embrace them. In the long run, it was a good conflict.

"...Everybody wanted to blame me for the strike and I thought that was really interesting. They said, yeah, this guy came in and caused a strike.

"Oh really? A white guy who can't speak Spanish. Got 150 workers to walk out on the job. Oh really? Risk going back, getting sent back to their countries, lose their jobs. What are you saying? Saying that Latino workers can't organize themselves. Are you saying they are not smart enough? Saying that they don't know enough? Saying they're not gutsy enough? Racism. How about I say that publicly? They stopped blaming me (laughs). They didn't want to be accused of being racist."[41]

Jim remains very clear about the role he plays in making things happen. He may provide support, but the affected individuals are the ones who make it possible to mount any lasting offensive against injustice. He argues:

"It's individuals that make the difference. It's one chicken catcher who came to our last meeting and told what it's like to catch a chicken and someone from the Public Justice Center there listening and some Union people hearing it for the first time. They didn't know what it was. They just do the plant. I'm hooking these people up. Then surfacing two or three more catchers and then finally having 150 of them and taking it to court and winning! And now taking it to Tyson. It started with one guy.

"What discourages me is when people say, 'Oh this is just too big for me to tackle.' It's usually middle or upper class people who say that. 'It's just too much for us.' Well really, it's too much for us. The power of individuals coming together and being driven by a spirit, passion is really what makes social change."

Jim also suffers no illusions that he will be able to do away with all injustice. He sees social justice work as a continuing process in which each generation contributes its energies to solve the great problems of our society.

One aspect of building infrastructure that concerns Jim, however, is the tendency of structures to perpetuate themselves. As the Sussex County activists move into the next stage of organizational development, he cautions:

"I think once you bite this apple that we're biting out of, expanding like we're doing, you immediately have to raise the question at least once a day, 'are we becoming something that's the enemy?' I work at a prison, and prisons were thought to be the solutions to the problems, and now they are the problem. Puerto

---

[41] In February, 2001 Mountaire workers voted on whether to retain their union, a move that worker advocates argue was instigated by management. Jim Lewis was arrested for causing a disturbance at the plant. Ultimately, workers themselves voted 581-216 in favor of union representation.

Rican Community taught me in Chicago when I was there visiting. They took me down the street and showed me where the Puerto Rican Community is being destroyed and the agencies that were dealing with them. You'd go by an agency they would say 'Poverty Pimp'. That's what they call them.

"Becoming a poverty pimp is what any of us can become with our grants and our money, and we become fat. We serve people, and we don't even do a halfway decent job of that. Do we ever help people find their own power to come together and change things so that we would even go out of business, God forbid?

"As programs become larger and federal grants become more intricate and demanding, it becomes harder and harder to actually do the work the organization was set up to do. The mission statement for *La Esperanza* asserts that the organization will promote leadership and organization within the community it serves:

"Now we have to put a grid on ourselves and see whether we're really doing that. At this point I must tell you frankly, I don't think we're doing that. And it disappoints me. And it will judge us. We will become a social service agency only. And I— that was not my intention when we got started and I hope we are able to keep our focus. I know Maria Picazo understands that focus and that mission. She's a good executive director. She's learning the job. She understands that. I mean if we're going to work with women who are battered, we have to help them stand on their own feet and take [charge of] their own lives. If we're going to carry pregnant women to all the programs we do—taking pregnant women to the hospitals and the doctors, seemingly we have to develop a network of women out there in the Latino community who are able to help, to help do that too. We have to be careful of dependency..."

For Jim, social justice work involves more than providing services and developing leadership within the base community. It also involves challenging all community members to see beyond their narrow interests and experiences and identify how they are

49

implicated in the oppression of others. This is particularly an issue between the Black and Hispanic communities. Jim reminds us:

"...The Black community has been the minority community here for a long time, and taken it on the chin for a long time, and wound up in the jails and prisons for a long time, and died younger for a long time. And now they see a Latino population coming in to be held up to them as 'see, this is how people really work. Hey, these people really work! Not like you lazy shiftless people.' Well that's not right. Black people have been providing chicken for this nation for a long time, been raising our children, they've been building our country. And now the Latino population. So you can understand the resentments.

"The other thing that goes on here—it's a hard thing, but [the] Black community has had to struggle for any kind of political power here, and they haven't got much. And so they don't have much leverage anywhere. So, my job, my hope is to bridge this Latino-Black thing. Plants love that split. They just love it. They wouldn't say that but—and get a Black catcher and a Latino worker together, and get the white farmer together. That's what the Alliance's goal is. We try and work at that. Working hard at that. It's hard work.

"We're trying to show the community that from the time a chicken is hatched to the time it's put in your mouth, that it's a belt line, assembly line—all the people are connected to one another, all dependent on one another, and none of them ever see one another hardly. Farmers never get to see what goes on in the plant. Plant people don't know what the chicken catcher does. But we're trying to say, 'Hey look at the whole factory line.' And it's really—people being hurt all along the way..."

If the distinct groups involved in and affected by the poultry industry can collaborate across their differences, Jim is confident that they will be able to find the power to take control of their lives.

One other important front for social justice is the question of legalizing the status of immigrant workers. As long as the workers fear detection by the INS, they will lack the security to organize for their own well being. So part of Jim's work is to push for Amnesty for immigrant workers. Ironically, this is one area on which the DPJA and the Poultry industry agree, as Jim explains:

"They want it because they wouldn't have INS people running around all the time and they'd have a steady workforce, and that'd be good. We want it because once they've got a steady workforce, they are free to organize."

While some fear that the poultry industry would just pick up stakes and move if the cost of labor rose, Jim sees the industry as rooted in the area. It's a good location as far as transportation is concerned, and the companies have developed a network of farmers, growers and processing plants–a considerable investment of resources:

"Perdue threatened. Perdue said two years ago, 'if you stick us with this environmental pfiesteria thing,' Jim Perdue said this, 'we'll probably have to move.' Trying to scare us off. Two years later he's now created a plant in Laurel to pelletize that manure so that it can be moved to phosphorus and nitrogen poor areas—sell it. So we've come a long way in two years just on that. There's still enormous environmental problems around here, but from saying 'I might have to move' to saying 'okay let's create a plant here, take care of that manure', it is more real."[42]

Jim is still haunted, however, by the long view. What happens over time to a community that is controlled by an industry as powerful as poultry? And what happens to worker protections when the workforce being recruited is desperate to work?

"The plant interprets it that, you see, American workers are lazy and they don't want to work. I interpret it differently, because I don't think American workers are lazy. They fed me. They clothed me. They housed me. They put coal in my furnace. And I have dealt with what's left afterwards—homeless shelters in Charleston, West Virginia. I dealt with homeless black lung miners, who put coal in my furnace in Maryland as a kid. And

---

[42] Poultry's Price: Goodman, Peters. The Cost to the Bay, *Washington Post* 1 August 1999:1Aff

they were not lazy. They died because they worked so hard. If you saw them on the streets you'd call them bums. But they weren't bums. So I'm suspicious about the analysis about lazy American workers. I don't believe it.

"What I know is that we've worked long and hard against great obstacles in this country to develop safety procedures and a decent workplace and a minimum wage, for what it's worth. I mean we've worked hard in this country for days off and for what it takes to be fair and just and nice to people without sexual harassment or any of the rest of it. We've worked hard, and we're continuing to work hard. And I know it can be washed out in a moment by desperate workers who come here because they have to work and they will do anything to work. And even use their own psychology—the companies will use their own cultural backgrounds and ways of thinking and being—there's a certain macho nature for a number of Black men I know who actually kill the birds in the process plants. This is what men do.

"And I think that probably in the Latino population that we work real hard and there's a certain esteem in that. Well, wait till they work five or six or seven eight years with those hands. They'll see that they're a disposable workforce, because if those hands don't work, they're gone. And we set in place a lot of standards and we need more standards and enforcement, and this population coming in is willing to do just about anything to send money home and to live here. So we can't stand for that.

"And what is it doing to treat people like this? What it is doing to the product and the people who eat it and the social contract with one another is totally being ignored. What is it doing to the spirit and soul of people? To the fish, the earth, and what is it doing? All those things are spiritual issues and that's why the church has to be involved with it. Even when the church doesn't know it should be involved in it. Because the church sometimes thinks it should be involved in prayer and heaven and all that. And I do think the church should be involved in prayer and heaven and hell. But I can introduce people to as much hell as they want to take, and to heaven as well. And it's right here."

Rosa Alvarez, Ascension Banegas, and Maria Mairlot

The Carmelite Sisters of Charity are the community organizers who most provide direct assistance to the immigrant community. Sister Rosa Alvarez, who has received substantial local press, is sometimes called the grandmother of the community. She estimates that she has been present at 95% of the births that have occurred in the last six years. Initially dedicating herself to providing translation and transportation assistance, Sister Rosa quickly identified a specific set of urgent needs among the women of Georgetown—help with pregnancy and childbirth, safe and stimulating child care, and protection from domestic abuse. The many young women she has touched express unfailing gratitude for her skill, guidance and warm friendship.

Sister Ascension Banegas has been engaged in the equally important work of assisting with immigration matters. Through her work, she knows intimately the life circumstances of most Hispanic residents of Georgetown. In order to allow the other two to volunteer their services, Sister Maria Mairlot has taken on the job of earning an income at a variety of things. She worked as a nurse with Delmarva Rural Ministries, and then part-time for St. Michael's Church, where she provides religious and musical instruction. She has also been heavily involved in housing issues. Sister Francesca Mota is the fourth member of the team. She arrived in 1998, hired by the diocese to help develop a diocesan plan for Hispanic Catholics on the peninsula. Together, these religious workers struggle to promote social justice while at the same time ministering to those in greatest need.[43]

The order to which the Sisters belong was not always so radical in its vision. Sister Rosa remembers that when she was a young girl in Spain, the nuns were cloistered and she kept a vow of silence for five years. Members of the order had been martyred

---

[43] While Sister Francesca is accomplishing important work at the regional level, she arrived after much of the local initial institution-building was already underway. For that reason, I focus here on the stories of Sisters Rosa, Ascension and Maria.

during the Spanish Civil War in the 1930s[44], and Sister Rosa remembers them being strongly pro-Franco as a consequence.[45] As a young nun, she says, she had very little idea of the reality of people's lives outside the walls of the convent and parochial schools where she taught. The vision of the founder of their order, Joaquina de Vedruna, had been eminently social. The order was dedicated to serving the poor and to educating women in particular, when it was established in 1826. The communities that developed to further this vision founded hospitals and schools throughout the north of Spain.

Yet by the mid-20th century the order had strayed somewhat from its initial vision. The Sisters were still providing educational instruction, but their students did not necessarily represent the poorest, most needy sectors of society. They had schools in England that provided an opportunity for Spanish young women to learn English, and missions in Japan, where Japanese students learned Spanish. In California, they ran several parochial schools in segregated neighborhoods where neither Blacks nor Hispanics were permitted to live.

Sister Rosa had a difficult childhood. She was born in Asturias, a region in the North of Spain. Her father lost what little the family had during the civil war, and her mother died when she was only five. Her brothers and sisters were split between two sets of grandparents and, at age 13, Rosa was taken to the Carmelite Sisters of Charity School in a nearby town. Since she had no money, she worked for her education from age 13 on. But she enjoyed life at the convent and elected to join the order at age 22. After teaching for five years in Galicia, she was sent to England

---

[44] For an interesting account of atrocities committed against religious figures during the Civil War, see Bruce Lincoln's essay "Revolutionary Exhumations in Spain," in his collection, *Discourse and the Construction of Society* (New York: Oxford Univ. Pr., 1989): 103-127.

[45] The Catholic Church in Spain was allied with the Franco dictatorship which lasted into the 1970s and sought to promote a quiescent acceptance of the *status quo* among working people.

Six Carmelite Sisters. From left: Carmen Benegas, Ascension Benegas, Amaya Duralde, Maria Mairlot, Mary Masden and Rosa Alverez. *(Courtesy of Allison Burris)*

for language studies to prepare her to teach in California. She worked in California for several years directing primary school.

Sister Ascension, on the other hand, describes having fallen into the order by a series of coincidences. She grew up in Melilla, Morocco, an area under Spanish control. The daughter of a military man who was not particularly religious, she remembers that when she was studying in university, entering a religious order was the farthest thing from her mind. However, she was drawn in by her participation in a catholic action group and, having received a call from God, she succumbed.

She'd planned to enter a Benedictine order in Oviedo but, sometime earlier, her older sister had traveled to Madrid to continue her university studies, and had ended up rather serendipitously living with the Carmelite Sisters of Charity. This sister decided to join the convent, but became ill. While she was recovering, a second sister, having heard about the order, decided to join, and she was quickly followed by a third sister. So, when Ascension experienced doubts about the training she would receive with the Benedictines, she turned her attention to an order where she already knew three sisters. She laughingly relates that her father has now accepted his daughters' religious vocation, saying "my son-in-law four times over cannot condemn me." After five years teaching in Andalucia, Sister Ascension was sent as a missionary to Japan, where she worked for 12 years teaching Spanish in a university there.

However, in the 1960s and 1970s a series of dramatic changes, both within the church and in the world, transformed the focus of the Sisters' work. Rosa explains:

"Every six years we have a general chapter. Normally it's in Spain, because that's where the majority of people are. And so, well, that comes from the beginning of the 1960s when the Vatican Council, John the 23rd, may God bless him, made a strong change in the Catholic Church. And one of the things he said, he said, 'We have to open the windows so that the air can come in. That is what is happening in the world. We are isolated.' And in that he encouraged the religious orders to go out and see the reality and how we could help more—and in that Council they gave some very clear guidelines about social justice. And so all the religious congregations in the world, not only ours, well, we had to make an evaluation. How did the congregation begin, what happened during all those years, and what is it that we want to do? So, [we tried] to return to the sources from which we started and from there apply it to the reality that we saw."

In addition to a radical shift in the perceived role of religious workers, practical concerns with the changing face of the congregations emerged, especially on the East Coast of the United States. Ascension remembers:

"Meanwhile it was the time right after Vatican II, and they had made those Vatican II reforms. The immigration to the United States, here on the East Coast of the United States, brought many Puerto Ricans and Dominicans. So the bishops were very worried, because those who were coming were all Catholic. And they didn't have anyone in the churches who could speak Spanish. So those people would go to the Protestant Churches that welcomed them. And they were asking all the Spanish-speaking religious congregations, those that had Spanish speaking nuns, if they could send volunteers here. So I thought, 'well, what am I doing here teaching Spanish at the university? I'd better go there. So I came here. I came in 1977."

Rosa remembers that the reaction of the Sisters was mixed. Some embraced the new change and the new work. For others the transition was slower and more difficult. However, the order as a whole is now committed to the idea that the church should make a preferential option for the poorest, the neediest, and the most marginalized members of society. It has broken up into small communities and is gradually ridding itself of property in the belief that the sisters should be mobile, ready to respond to needs as they arise and free to leave locales where needs no longer exist. Moreover, there is a strong push for all members to engage in missionary work–particularly in the areas of the world experiencing natural or man-made catastrophes.

When in the 1970s the members of the order elected to focus their work on the East Coast, they chose two areas, Washington, D.C. and New York City. Both Rosa and Sister Maria Mairlot worked in Washington; Sister Ascension found herself in New York:

"When I came here, I was in New York, in Brooklyn, in one of the worst neighborhoods, Bedford Stuyvesant. When you said to a taxi driver, 'Could you please take me to Bedford Stuyvesant?' he said, 'Ah, I won't go there.' It was a neighborhood to fear. You could hear shots constantly, at the corner of my house. There was always shooting all the time. It was an awful neighborhood. Even so, nothing bad ever happened to us. Everybody respected us. Everybody loved us. I was there for ten years, as if I were in my own house, working with Hispanic people, with Puerto Rican and Dominican immigrants. At the same time I was teaching the priests Spanish, because they didn't know Spanish. And the priests got to know Spanish quite well, and they could work with the people.

"After ten years, I went to another neighborhood where we opened another house. It was Williamsburg and, if the first place was bad, this was worse."

Among other things Sister Ascension worked as an immigration advisor, helping people to file forms correctly:

"Well, it was part of the commitment I had, no? To help the immigrant who was arriving. That was what the bishops asked us to do, to help the Hispanic immigrants who were arriving and who had no assistance. Well, then, my help was total. My help wasn't just, look they should continue to pray in Spanish or have their masses in Spanish. No, the person has many things going on. So it was holistic help for the person, starting with what he needs. And within all that keeping their faith will also come, but who's going to keep their faith if they don't have anyone to help them and they lose hope? Or they go with the Protestant sects to see what they'll tell them there. That it's God's will that he should always be poor, no? But that is not true. So we will have to squeeze the brains of the people too, telling them, 'No, you have some rights and you have to defend those rights. If you live here and work here, you also have to have your papers in order to be legal.' And that's what we are fighting for here too."

At that time with that population, most of the work involved family reunification appeals. In other words, an immigrant had become legal and was now attempting to bring wife, children, parents or other relatives to his new home.

Meanwhile, Sister Rosa was being radicalized in the ferment of Central American politics abroad and homelessness in Washington, D.C. She and Sister Maria lived for a time in a Black neighborhood and worked at D.C. General, the *de facto* hospital for the poor, Rosa as chaplain and Maria as a nurse. Rosa remembers:

"When I came to Washington, D.C., there were already some Sisters in Washington who were very involved in all the things that were going on and with other religious people from other congregations that were also [there] and so, I began to go to listen to find out what was happening. For example, Hélder Câmara from Brazil[46] came to Georgetown University. I went to other conferences. Other personalities like that came from Latin America as well. And so my eyes were opened more and more, and I became more and more and more committed.

"That is, the congregation began, and it gave us the opportunity, but some were faster, others were slower, and others really slow. But in that sense, they are all really wonderful Sisters, and very giving, but some were more radical in the compromise for justice and I'm really [claps] there. When I was in Washington I was in a lot of demonstrations. I performed civil disobedience several times, and I was arrested in Washington in the Rotunda, in the State Department. Civil disobedience but not violence. I'm against all violence. But yes, I committed myself very much and I feel that way, I feel that I must."

---

[46] A Bishop heavily involved in the Latin American liberation theology movement of the 1970s and 1980s. For more about liberation theology, see Gustavo Gutierrez *A Theology of Liberation* (Maryknoll, NY: Orbis, 1973)

Sisters Maria and Rosa in Washington demonstration.
(Courtesy of Allison Burris)

Sister Rosa subsequently visited El Salvador and gained first-hand experience of the effects of the war. She traveled to a Guatemalan refugee camp and was able to share with refugees, which she remembers as a profound experience. While the Sisters were learning about Central America, they were also seeing homelessness grow in Washington. In 1980 they decided to open a homeless women's shelter in a building donated by the diocese, Saint Mary's Convent in Chinatown, where Sister Rosa worked for fourteen years.

Sister Maria was also working in homeless shelters, having begun as a volunteer at a Lutheran women's shelter when she first arrived in Washington. At that time, she says, the group worked more with the Black population. As do the other sisters, Sister Maria describes her experiences as steps toward a greater understanding of humanity and the religious mission:

"I used to go in the evenings, because then I became the coordinator of the evening volunteers for the shelter. And that time was so enriching for me, because I got to know a lot of the families—women. Many of them [were] very, very crazy but so interesting, their lives. There are many well-educated women and, like, we became friends. I knew many of them. They were crazy in one way, but there was some point where you could get to them and be able to communicate on a different level, and that was wonderful. I still remember there in my heart some of the women that I met to the point that it was, sometimes on my day off–Washington is beautiful–and on my days off I wanted to go out and maybe enjoy a little bit of the beauties of Washington [laughs] not just the life that I knew like in the homeless and the craziness. It was impossible for me because anywhere I went, I found the homeless women.

"The nice thing I remember–one woman told me, Black woman, who one day was running around the street, and it was around lunch time and I said, 'Chloe, did you have–have [you] eaten?' 'Oh, let's go and have lunch,' and we went. There was a Sears in the neighborhood there, so we went and had some lunch together. A year later, or two years later, one day I met her on the street again, and she asked me, 'Sister, have you had lunch?' "

And I said, 'No, I haven't yet.'

'I invite you,' she said.

And I said, 'Chloe, you're invited.'

'No, no. You invited me once, and I want to invite you.'

"So we went back to Sears and we had lunch together. It was that kind of relationship. That woman for everybody was crazy, crazy, crazy, and we could relate! That was an experience that I will never forget, working with those people."

When the Sisters opened their own shelter, the experience changed somewhat. Now Sister Maria was coordinator of the volunteers. She has many vivid memories of the people who volunteered in the shelter, whom she got to know well. Many were quite wealthy, powerful people. It was there that she met Frank and Pat Duchesne, two volunteers who would later be instrumental in bringing the Sisters to Sussex County, Delaware.

Sister Maria stayed in Washington ten years and then moved to Silver Springs, Maryland, where the Hispanic population was concentrated. There she was working in the health field again for the Spanish Catholic medical center. Sister Rosa was still at the shelter. The Duchesnes had meanwhile moved to Bethany Beach, Delaware. And Pat Duchesne became aware of the plight of Hispanic immigrants inland. Recognizing that the community needed Spanish speaking advocates, she contacted her old friends from the shelter. The reaction was at first cool, as Sister Maria explains:

"And [Pat] (laughs softly) was always looking out for the Hispanics for some reason. She came to *Casa* San Francisco in Milton,[47] and their parish started helping out. And she said, 'You

---

[47] Originally a mission that served the migrant population who were attracted to Milton by the King Cole Cannery. It was very actively involved in outreach to Hispanics in the 1980s, when Amnesty required applicants for residency to take 40 hours of English and Citizenship classes. By the 1990s *Casa* San Francisco had become a Catholic Charities program and had shifted its emphasis to meeting immediate needs of the Milton poor (which, with the closing of the

have a lot of Hispanics there, and there is nobody to help them because nobody speaks Spanish.' So that was one time.

"And we said, 'Oh yeah?'

"Nothing. She saw us again.

"You have a lot of Hispanics. You really should come and see because there are a lot of Hispanics; they have nobody to help them. We cannot help them.

"So it was like a drop of water only [laughs]. So finally, it made a difference."

There were other reasons for the move as well. As the Washington shelter transmuted from a mission to a social service agency, the Sisters found themselves less and less able to function effectively. Sister Maria again explains:

"Several things happened. First of all when those two agencies were started, the shelter didn't ask any fee or any money [from] the women, but they were requesting a lot of money [from] the government, government agencies, that I thought [was] just out of this world. That was incredible. And a lot of regulations, a lot of things that we didn't agree. Our way of working was ministry.

"So finally Pat [Duchesne] talked to Pilar, that was our regional superior at that time, and she said, 'Well, let's go and see.' Because she was so persistent. So Rosa and Ascension came for one year just to come and see what was the need. And when they came here they really saw the great need; they were not great numbers, but the few people that were here, say, maybe two or three hundred people[48]; they [had] no help at all."

A young Guatemalan priest was working in the area at the time and had a program called, *El Camino*, The Road. He would

---

cannery no longer included large numbers of Hispanics) and crisis needs for Sussex County. According to Marion Bau, *Casa* San Francisco's former director, the organization is currently embattled, because the population it serves does not fit into the picture of what Milton wishes to become—an inland version of Lewes, Delaware–a summer and weekend holiday community for Washington and Baltimore urbanites.

[48] This estimate is probably low for 1994. However, 1993 and 1994 mark the beginning of the great Hispanic influx into the area and specifically to Georgetown.

transport people to the hospitals and clinics, mostly pregnant women, and translate for them. When the Sisters arrived, he was more than happy to hand over these responsibilities to them.

Sister Rosa then began to provide transportation and translation services, particularly for pregnant women. She found that Nanticoke Hospital in Seaford was most receptive to her efforts and, therefore, she began to work exclusively with them. After seven years, she can now claim to have been present at the birth of almost every Hispanic child from Georgetown. Many of the mothers, in fact, tell their children to address Sister Rosa as grandmother. When I spoke to her in April 2001, she had 50 pregnant or recently delivered women that she was actively working with.[49]

As she became intimate with the young women she was serving, Sister Rosa began to identify other needs in the community. Safe, stimulating and affordable child care was a top priority, as working mothers sometimes had no other recourse than to leave their infants with a neighbor who might have them sitting strapped in their car seats all day. Moreover, the children were not being exposed to the English language or prepared in any way for the tasks they would be expected to master in school. Having identified the need, she set Gonzalo Martinez the task of finding the resources to create a child care center specifically directed toward serving Hispanic immigrant mothers.[50]

Sister Rosa has a particular vision and method for providing needed services to the community. She explains:

"First, I think one of the things that we need is to get very close to the person. And work with them as equals. Accepting them, loving them, and I tell them, 'I'm part of you. We are all a family,' and so, they share a lot with me. And they tell me their problems. So they have a lot of trust."

---

[49] 124 Hispanic children were born in 2000 in Georgetown proper and the surrounding trailer parks.

[50] *Primeros Pasos*, established in April 1997 was the result, and it was followed by *Primeros Pasitos* for younger children in 1998.

Sister Rosa with Patricia Cervantes with baby Michelle
at her Baptism on Easter 1998
(Courtesy of Allison Burris)

Building this trust requires not only giving the community complete access to one's self (indeed, Sister Rosa admits that community members call her at all hours), but also being able to confront the difficulties that community members then reveal. For example, Sister Rosa quickly discovered that domestic violence was a regularly occurring, accepted practice in the community. She immediately began work to provide a shelter for battered women (established 1997) and to bring affected women together in self-help groups to talk about their common problems and support one another in finding solutions.[51]

Although *La Casita* had provided a centralized space for outreach work to the Hispanic community when it opened in 1995, the Sisters were delighted to participate in Rev. Lewis's 1996 meeting at which the idea for the *La Esperanza* community center was born. Sister Rosa echoes Sister Maria's distinction between the mission model of social action and that more prevalent in government or government funded services.

"The mission of *La Esperanza*, and we are quite clear about this, is a coming together with the people. And to respond to the most urgent and most pressing needs of the community. To treat everyone with great respect, dignity, and as equals. Because we aren't different. We are equal."

While Sister Rosa was attending to these crucial needs of a young community, Sister Ascension was helping immigrants in their efforts to legalize their status. She describes how her direct experience with community members altered her view of how to proceed in her work.

"And when first I came here, when [immigrants] talked to me about political asylum, I asked 'But, young man, what are you going to do? Do you have any political case?' But when I realized that it was the only means to get a work permit, I asked 'Have you

---

[51] The battered women's shelter was first administered by People's Place in Milford with *Esperanza* board member, Alicia Sosman, providing the direct service. Subsequently, responsibility for the shelter shifted to *La Esperanza*, and the direct service is provided by staff members Ruby Kepley and director, Maria Picazo.

From left: Alicia Sosman with Sister Rosa and Gonzalo Martinez
(Courtesy of Allison Burris)

filed for political asylum? Well, let's do it.' Sure, because it was the only means to get the work permit and, look, there are still some cases that immigration hasn't even touched yet. And they're getting their work permits every year, every year."

Thus, expediency and a firm understanding that immigration laws were unfair led Sister Ascension to her present practice. She describes her relationship with representatives from the INS offices, however, as cordial if not completely trusting.

"It is true that even in immigration you can find good people and, when I call asking for an orientation, they give it to me. Although at the beginning they told me, 'send us the person.' And I told them, 'The last thing that I am going to do is to send the person to you. You tell me what I am supposed to do, because if I send him to you, and he doesn't know how to explain himself, you will put him in jail. No.' So they laughed at me, and now they don't do that.

"Now they respect me a lot. They respect me, and we are good friends now. They help me, and they know that I help them too. Otherwise, they would have a great line there, coming with paperwork that we can do here. Then finally, I send them directly to the offices, not to immigration."[52]

Nevertheless, working with political asylum cases is much more soul-wrenching than her previous immigration work. Of a bank of file cabinets full of asylum applications, Sister Ascension points to a thin folder of those who have won their cases. The process involves a continual struggle against the Courts with appeals and letters and arguments and counter arguments because, unlike family reunification, the petitioner must prove his case. Sister Ascension explains:

"It's desperate. I have seen people who have very tough cases. And even a young man who had a very good case. I told

---

[52] The INS opened a regional office in Dover in 1997. On the one hand, this office has made it easier for residency and asylum applicants who had previously had to travel as far as Baltimore or Philadelphia to pursue their petitions. On the other hand, it has increased the INS enforcement presence in Delaware.

him 'Go there with confidence. If you present your case well, you'll see how they are going to give it to you.' And he came back completely disillusioned, and he said, 'I am leaving!' And I asked, 'Why, what happened? What did they say about your proof?'

"They need proof. And one of the proofs he had was that he had been tortured. They had left him beside a road, thinking he was dead. After having beaten him, having hit him all over, and even having shot him. And before daybreak the young man regained consciousness, and by crawling he got to a nearby house. And then, after he recovered a bit, he came here, to the United States, once again on the road. So sure, he had marks all over his body. Yes, the boy had been shot, but he was lucky that the shot instead of affecting his heart or any more critical part, it went in his arm. And it just went in through one side and out through the other. But that part of the arm–since it hadn't healed well, there was a like a callous. He had an ugly mark there, discolored and calloused. And then he had, well, scars on his body from where they'd kicked him, and all that. And he said that sometimes it was as if he had amnesia. And then he'd come back. So, that was from the blows to the head he'd gotten.

"So, he told all that to the judge. And the judge said, 'Well, if you want me to believe all that, bring me pictures of them torturing you.' And the young man said, 'Are you pulling my leg? I think this guy thinks I am stupid or a liar, because where I am going to find on a road at night, when I was being tortured, a cameraman to come and take pictures?'

"And he said 'Well, that's the only way I'm going to believe you.' He showed him his scars, and he said, 'Ooh, you could have gotten that from fighting with somebody.' So, disappointed, the young man went back to his country. Or he went to Mexico, I think, because I think he was afraid of returning to his country. He was in Mexico. Things like that, discrimination.

"On the other hand, another, who said, 'no, well when I was young, the guerrilla pressured me to join them, but I didn't want to join the guerrilla, so I came here.' And they gave him political asylum. So, what's happening? This is like the Lotto;

you get the number, whether it's good or bad. What kind of discrimination is this? Later, when you see the number of the statistics of how many were approved this or that year, when you get to the Guatemalans it is always very small. That is a fight a little bit like David and Goliath, but we don't have David's slingshot. I wish I had David's slingshot and the aim that he had to strike Goliath. But we will have to resign ourselves, calm down, and keep on, until we can see where we are headed.

"And now we are struggling to get amnesty. Because, why do they offer to Nicaraguans and Cubans the possibility of permanent residence if they entered the country before 1995, and they don't offer that to Salvadorans and Guatemalans? They are told that the most they can do is to order a suspension of deportation. But they have to be within very difficult parameters. They get suspension of deportation, which means that if immigration decides to say, 'No. Since there's peace now in Guatemala and in El Salvador, and nothing's happening now, now it's a calm sea, well now you can go back to your homes, peacefully. You can go voluntarily to your homes.' After they have been here ten, eleven, twelve years, after having made a family here, worked here, paying taxes and social security, and they're not going to see any of those benefits. And when they retire, no one is going to count the years that they worked here to give them their retirement. No one. So the country which is already rich, is enriching itself without any benefit to them."

Sister Ascension points out the complexities of the immigration system. While on the one hand, judges are required to distinguish between legitimate and fabricated claims of torture, political repression, or other grounds, on the other, they require a particular perspective on recent Central American history which may also be a self-serving construct on the part of the U.S. government. In other words, petitioners must learn what is believable in an immigration court but, by doing that, they may transform the "truth" of their experience. Telling the truth under these conditions becomes a complicated proposition.[53]

Even more absurd, citizens from different Central American countries are viewed differently when it comes to immigration privileges. Guatemalans must prove individual harm, whereas Nicaraguans are understood to have been harmed collectively. And finally, bureaucratic complexity has led to situations like that involving the temporary protections provided to immigrants from countries that had been devastated by Hurricane Mitch in 1998. This legislation provided a way for those in the United States to remain here and renew their work permits temporarily in view of the chaos and destruction wreaked by the natural disaster in Honduras, Nicaragua, Guatemala and El Salvador. However, the application forms were not issued for a year, leaving potential applicants without any way to file correctly or receive work permits.

Sister Ascension continues to provide direct assistance to individuals, but she also views advocating for a change in immigration law as a very important part of her work. She and the other Carmelite sisters attended the Washington protest in January 1998, to call for equal treatment of Guatemalans in immigration accords. They also attended a Washington demonstration calling for the United States to close the School of the Americas in June of 1999.

Sister Maria arrived in Georgetown sometime in 1995. By the time she got here, Sister Rosa and Sister Ascension were immersed in their work.

This made Sister Maria's community work a bit more complicated than the work of the other two Sisters. Since the order was not being supported by the Catholic diocese or any other

---

[53] For a parallel discussion of the El Salvadoran cases, see William Westerman, 1998. Central American refugee testimonies and performed life histories in the Sanctuary Movement, in *The Oral History Reader* eds. Perks & Thomson. 224-234. A full length study by Susan Bibler Coutin is entitled *Legalizing Moves. Salvadoran Immigrants' Struggle for U. S. Residency* 2000 (Ann Arbor: The University of Michigan).

group, someone had to have a paying job. Sister Maria began working at a home nursing service, but soon found that she would not be interacting with Hispanics in this capacity. She then moved to Delmarva Rural Ministries,[54] and worked in the Match Van, providing direct medical service to rural low-income communities throughout Sussex and Kent counties. She also began a series of Spanish language pre-natal classes, which she taught at the Wesleyan Methodist Church that borders Kimmeytown. When Delmarva Rural Ministries began to experience financial difficulties, she decided to leave and look for something more locally situated:

"I was still working at Delmarva Rural Ministries when Father Greco said that he really needed someone to work, because so many Hispanics–because we had one Mass on Sundays and that was all. And they needed, they need other care. And many wanted to baptize a child and they needed something, somebody there." And so I started working at Saint Michael's Catholic Church in Georgetown. So I was working part-time at Delmarva Rural Ministries and part-time in the church.

"And now everything is mingled to me. Everything is church to me. I am working with the same people, and I am still working part-time for the church, but now I can say that I work full time. But I do a lot of transportation and translation and making appointments for people, but this to me is church work also. It's working [to meet] the needs of the people."

More recently, Sister Maria has specialized in housing issues, another serious problem for the Georgetown immigrant community. She is a member of the Interfaith Mission of Sussex County, which hopes to build new affordable housing in Georgetown to meet the growing need and alleviate overcrowding

---

[54] A private, non-profit organization, DRM was founded in 1972 to meet the needs of farm workers and other low-income rural populations.

in substandard buildings.[55]   But she has also helped a number of residents purchase their own homes.[56]

She explains that she just fell into this line of work. After assisting one family to purchase a home, word of mouth got around that she was the person to talk to, although Sister Margaret of *La Casita* is also helping individuals purchase houses.   Sister Maria describes her system of providing assistance as one of scouring the field to find, first, a realtor willing to work honestly with Hispanic clients, and second, a bank willing to provide mortgage assistance. She relies on these contacts to then usher the potential buyer through the process, confident that they will be dealt with in a fair and dignified manner. Most recently, she's been asked to assist with the purchase of cars as well, and she is following the same system–identifying reputable dealers who wish to attract Hispanic business and then recommending them to the potential buyers.

With regard to their plans for the future, Sister Maria emphasizes that the order has reformed itself to become "lean and mean," able to shift with shifting needs and priorities.   The one thing they do not wish to do is to insure their own place in the community by creating dependency.   At the same time Sister Maria observes,

"For myself I will stay as long as the need is here, and the need is not going away, because there are lot of newcomers. People are coming every day.   A lot of newcomers, and the

---

[55] A great deal of newspaper coverage has been devoted to the housing problem in Georgetown, and among Hispanics in Sussex County generally.   Some "Native" residents complain that degradation of the downtown area is due to Hispanic lifestyle differences and landlord negligence.   Advocates for the Hispanics argue that the problem stems from a lack of available housing, which forces families and individuals to double up in the space that is available. In the spring of 2001 Housing advocates and the Georgetown city government have held a series of meetings to try to overcome fixed positions on housing and find common ground.   See, for example, Chris Guy, "Melting Pot heats up," 11 March 2001. http://www.sunspot.net/news/local/bal-md.hispanic 11 Mar 01. story.

[56] See Fernando Natareno, this volume.

newcomers, they are in better conditions than before. The reason is because they have others that can help them now."

The Carmelite Sisters have not only provided direct service and helped build infrastructure, they have also been the inspiration and model for other volunteers and community service providers. Alicia Sosman, for example, the first domestic violence outreach worker for the Georgetown Guatemalan community and a member of *La Esperanza's* board, is a Uruguayan who, like Gonzalo Martinez, came to the United States to work for the Inter-American Development Bank in Washington. There she met and married her husband and eventually moved to the family's vacation home in Lewes, Delaware. She believes the trust that *La Esperanza* enjoys with the community to be a direct result of the work of Sisters Rosa, Ascension and Maria. Alicia remembers that she tried to follow Sister Rosa's example as much as possible in working with families affected by domestic violence:

"You have to have an open mind. You cannot say, for example, with my experience with domestic violence, I was told, 'This is what you can do, and this is what you can't do.' But thanks to the open mind of the program director who told me: 'you do what you think you have to do the way you think you have to do it. Don't tell me about it.' The program grew. We also at times had to help the abusers because in my mind, in my heart, the men were victims also…

"Now we have to have people in *La Esperanza* who will work with an open mind and respect. Everybody is welcome in *La Esperanza*."

The great challenge for *La Esperanza* as it grows, according to Alicia, is to retain the flexibility to work with whoever comes through their door, in whatever way they can.

A majority of the volunteers and social service providers working with the Sussex County Hispanic community are former immigrants themselves. One exception to this general picture is Allison Burris, one of the youngest members of the board of *La Esperanza*. Allison grew up in Milford, Delaware, the daughter of a prominent political family. Having lived in Mexico for a year in

1996 and 1997, she speaks fluent Spanish. Allison became involved with the Hispanic community in Georgetown when she began to work as an assistant to Sister Rosa at *Primeros Pasos* Child Care Center. As Allison got to know the families of children in the center, she quickly made friends and fell headlong into community outreach work. She began attending Sunday mass at St. Michael's Catholic Church with the community. And she frequently offers her services to families in need of transportation and interpretation.

Allison and her brother even visited Tacaná, the area of Guatemala from which many Georgetown residents have come, and they were able to see first hand what having a relative working in the United States meant for the people back home—a new house in town, perhaps a car or business. Equally important, she notes, workers are helping other family members go to school:

"I know a lot of people are here but, like they say, my two younger sisters are studying. I'm sending money home so that they can study. I only went to third grade, but my nieces and nephews are still there, or they left two kids at home, and they have two kids here, but they're sending money so that their kids are studying. And I think it's very different than [sic] when they went, they didn't go to first or second or third grade."

Allison is now an ESL instructor at Del Tech. She gives free English classes at *La Esperanza* as well. She reports that her enrollment has quadrupled recently, far more demand than she or the center can possibly meet. She takes this as a sign that community members are finally grasping the importance of learning English. Others would say that it is the teacher herself that attracts such interest, since she has proven herself to be a trustworthy advocate for Hispanics. Allison's role models, however, continue to be the Carmelite Sisters, who share their lives with the community. She remembers watching Sister Rosa, for example one morning at church:

"She went around the whole church and just–you didn't even notice it. You almost don't even feel it. But just by observing her, you can see her–and everybody kind of waiting to talk to her, or waiting for her to say hi to them. A lot of times when people plan activities like conferences or workshops, and we want to have some participation—'How do we get to the people? How do we get the word to the people?' Well, if you tell Sister Rosa, she is the people. I mean she can get to the people. She has the contact with the people. And they all do. All the sisters do...

"Everybody that's working in Georgetown, it's because Sister Ascension helped them fill out their work permit. I mean, you're talking thousands of people that have work papers. Nobody knows how to do that on their own, or no other organization in the whole county really does that. She has people come from Kent County, people that come from Maryland, people that come up from Virginia almost. Some people that move away–they go to North Carolina. They can't find a *La Esperanza* in North Carolina, and they make a Saturday trip up, so she can renew their papers, because they used to live here."

La Esperanza, the people who built it, and the people who have come to work there are indeed very special. The organization has created infrastructure, vision and hope for the immigrants who will continue to arrive as long as the demand for their labor continues. While Gonzalo Martinez, Jim Lewis, and Sisters Rosa Alvarez, Ascension Banegas, and Maria Mairlot express different personal styles and emphases, they are united in a common commitment to advance social justice in Sussex County and the world.

WORKERS

These individuals are from the following areas in Guatemala:

Olegario Capriel .... Tierra Blanca, San Bartolo
Chavez Family .... Gueguetenango
Yanitza Delgado .... Tacaná
Carmen Garcia .... Juliapa, Santa Rosa
Fernando Natereno .... San Marcos
Esteban Perez .... Tacaná
Juan Perez .... Tacaná
Zenon Perez .... Tacaná
Ticha Roblero .... Juitan, Huetzeltenango

Esteban Perez

Esteban, born the eldest in his family in 1945, is now one of the elders of the Georgetown Guatemalan community.[55] He lives in the *Red* Apartments with a number of younger men from Tacaná, where I interviewed him in May 1999.[56] His wife and family are in Tapachulas, Mexico, across the border from Tacana. They fled political persecution in 1981. Education is extremely important to Esteban, and he has managed to send all of his children to University by working in poultry plants, Vlasic, and most recently, construction. Because his wife and children are in Mexico, Esteban vows he will not stay in Delaware. He returns periodically to Mexico but has continued to come back to Georgetown to work. While Esteban and his family became refugees of the 1980 violence in Guatemala, he has been denied political asylum in the United States.

Esteban was a traveling photographer in his native land, taking people's portraits at fairs and school events. Upon emigrating to Mexico, he joined a photographers union and worked as a professional photographer there for many years. When he first came to the United States, Esteban worked in the Florida fields. There he was recruited by a relative to work in the Delaware poultry plants. Esteban continues to practice photography in Georgetown, and even participated in the *Collage of Cultures* exhibit, sponsored by Phyllis Levitt of the Dover Art League. His exhibition photographs showed candid shots of Hispanic poultry workers inside the plant. Unfortunately, Esteban relates, there is too much competition to make a living as a photographer.

Besides, Esteban's heart and soul remain with his family in Tapachulas and his community in Tacaná. A member of OGAM,[57] Esteban was particularly interested in having that

---

[55] He is perhaps the most politically outspoken of Guatemalan immigrants.

[56] I have also incorporated some excerpts from an earlier interview Esteban granted with Jessica Payne for the Delaware Folklife Program in 1995.

[57] The Guatemalan Mutual Aid Society, a community organization founded in 1998 in Georgetown, Delaware.

organization assist in community development projects in the rural hamlets of the Tacaná area. Many of the stories Esteban tells about his life and community reflect the strong prejudice against indigenous people that exists in Guatemala and Mexico.

Early Life

I'm the son of a farmer, totally, completely rural. My parents were also rural farmers, my grandparents and many more remote [ancestors. We had] very little land. We began to work that way, we began to work the land without technology, without knowledge, nothing that a good working farmer has. They were workers, but rustic. And my first years of school, my parents took me to school. We weren't familiar with a pencil, composition books like those used today; instead, they bought us an erasable blackboard, that—and material for writing, but it wasn't permanent. It was a stick but in the form of a pencil, and one wrote with chalk on that, lesson after lesson, letters. We finished that, we have to erase it, and begin learning over again. So that there was no archive of any kind, there wasn't homework. There wasn't any of that.

Fortunately, I lived close to a school. Fortunately. But the others, brother farmers, live up to three or four miles away from the school. They have to send their children, wake them up early, and the children have to walk, having already eaten breakfast and there is no kind of assistance. It didn't exist at that time. And they returned hungry again. They didn't get home until two or three in the afternoon. Everything on foot, everything walking, most of the children barefoot, totally and completely barefoot.

In my town, some of the teachers were from other municipalities, perhaps from the same region. And there were few municipal teachers. They were the so–called *Ladinos*, but my town is Tacana. In Tacana the teachers didn't work very well. They didn't teach the rural farmers. They didn't arrive until Tuesday, and they went back on Thursday. And we didn't advance. They worked very poorly with us. For that reason, no,

Father and Daughter in Tacaná wearing indigenous dress. Most
residents of the area no longer dress in this fashion.
(Courtesy of Esteban Perez)

no, no–that is, there weren't certified teachers in the whole country. Now, by finishing the sixth grade, a person who finished the sixth grade could give classes. So, we couldn't advance because the teachers weren't very advanced either...

The dialects are now disappearing. I speak a dialect. I dare say about 80%. And during the years that I was in Tapachulas [Mexico], I didn't speak it, only with my wife. With my children no. I don't know what the idea was to not teach them. And since I've come here to the United States, I've met other people who speak the dialect of my town, and it made me very happy, because I have someone to share my dialect with. I have someone to joke with in my dialect. And we laugh a lot, because my dialect is very pretty. We can like exchange jokes. Some are simple jokes, some are sex jokes, whatever joke. And we amuse ourselves in our dialect...

Only my father knew how to read and write. My mother, no. My mother didn't know, but she also struggled a lot with all my brothers. I don't know how she did it but she struggled a lot to buy a notebook now for my other brothers. I'm the only one who used that chalkboard, I was the only one. And the others, they used notebooks.

[My father] went to school. And he was the only one of 12 brothers and sisters. He was the last, and he was the only son of my grandparents who knew how to read and write. So, my father also made a lot of effort on his part. He gave each of us two years of school, to the oldest two or three, and for the rest, he sent them up to sixth grade. Then, he could do no more. And so, he always inculcated the idea that one had to study. And to read, read whatever. We never had books. Whatever thing, when we visited the towns, we would see a paper, a newspaper thrown away, whatever it was to read. We never had the luxury of having books.

This comes from an inheritance of my father. We always talked of a famous Democratic party, which is now the DC in Guatemala. He, I don't know by what means, got a pamphlet, and one day, I opened his old truck, and I found that pamphlet about Democracy. It was then that the idea lit in me as well, of a

Democratic Party. And I read the statutes, I read the internal rules of a party, when I was very young. And from that time the idea remained...

My grandfather was a leader.[58] And he tried to get rid of some of those bad customs that existed because of the *ladinos*. He who was elected as a *prioste* had to spend a lot of money—he had to give out food, music, a party, to celebrate a Saint. For example, the Saint—St. John, St. Peter, St. Lucas, or the Patronal Fair, the Virgen of Tránsito. A rural farmer was elected for these fiestas—and he had to make a lot of wheat bread.

To make the bread. To give it out for the day of the Holy Cross, to the townspeople, who are called the *ladinos*. When they were making the bread, just as it had come out of the oven, my grandfather took a piece of bread—and he didn't even take it from the basket. Instead, it was because one fell. When they were pulling the bread out, one fell on the ground, and it rolled on the ground. And he went after it a little way away, according to my father's story—he cleaned it off, and he smelled it, and he tore it apart to taste that piece of bread.

And a famous *ladino*, called Filimon Roblero, comes up. He told him, "Disgraceful Indian! You brought very little flour." And he went and he refused the bread. Because he said that the bread wasn't going to be enough for all the people. My grandfather didn't like that. He was very angry. His sons were with him, his sons–in–law and his daughters. And they brought the animals to carry the flour. So, he ordered them (coughs) he ordered his sons and sons-in-law to bring the animals and take all the bread back to his house! To his rural hamlet.

"Because, here the *Ladino* is not going to order me around. It's my work and my product! And there's no reason to give him even one piece of bread. And if they want it, let them work!"

And he went back angry. And in that case, since they were great muckety-mucks, Necon Perez and that Filimon Roblero and

---

[58] The following anecdote is excerpted from an earlier interview conducted by Jessica Payne for the Delaware Folklife Program in 1995.

other families, there was the Espinosa family, the deLeons, and they get together, and they grab my grandfather and they put him in jail. And from that time, he began to be a leader and to say to all the population that they shouldn't make that kind of fiesta again. My grandfather was imprisoned for a number of hours. And the other people got together and they went to get him out. But he was in the jail for a number of hours.

Because they were unjust fiestas. And the rural farmer had to sacrifice a lot and go into debt. The rural farmer, he didn't want to make a fiesta, it was the *ladinos*—they named people, that's all. They named people—"He's going to do the fiesta, he's going to bring the bread, on the day of Holy Cross." They were opportunists, they were muckety-mucks. And in that way, they got rid of, they lost those customs. But I was able to still see that. I still was able to see and live that fiesta.

Well. That's at the municipal level. Now, the fiestas of the community in a rural hamlet, where they celebrate, for example, the Fiesta of St. John, St. Peter, also the Cross, or Esquipulas. They use the same system—they name a First *Prioste*, a Second, a Third *Prioste*, the Fireworks provider, a commission, the commission for decorations, the commission for food, the commission—but the custom is to call them *Priostes*. The word, festival commission is something strange, something modern, but the word itself is *Prioste* in the dialect.

The Army

When I was 19 years old, I went into the army. And what we wanted was to buy a pair of shoes... I joined the army in September, 1965. And during those years one heard the revolutionaries in the east of Guatemala. So, well, it's something that, we didn't know anything about that. They just told us that the country had to be defended because communism is coming close, and we, since the whole army is made up of untutored people, people who haven't been to school and even today, even today there are people who don't have even one day of school. So, it's an army that, no—they prepare them savagely...

At that time the revolution wasn't very strong yet. The revolution, what they call the guerrilla, whose authentic name is revolution, it was only in the east of Guatemala, in Peten, Zacapa; it didn't exist in the west...

And within the army there was someone there as well who talked to us about the revolution. I remember the name, I remember the surname, the hour, perhaps the hour–the date and month I don't remember. I only remember that we were in a pasture when he told us that the revolution is in favor of the poor man. The revolution is in favor of the proletarian. I didn't know what proletarian was. And that the revolution is an agrarian reform. We as soldiers who are inside a jail are against our own brothers who are fighting.

So, I couldn't understand anything at that time, because at the same time, it threatened me. Esteban, we've got a machine gun here and we can even kill you if you say anything to anyone. So, years later, when the revolution broke out in the whole country, then I could understand that that person was an infiltrator in the army. And, well, I never saw him again, we never saw each other, but for me, well, it was as if he injected—the revolution is in all the people, it's not against the people. And through life experience–over the years one learns many things.

The churches were affecting us a lot. The churches, more than anything the evangelical churches, although my father was Catholic, but it affected us a lot that the pastors–even now I don't know if they were pastors or not–said, "don't join the unions, don't join the farmer's union, because we are children of God and we have a big and beautiful crown up there in heaven, and you will tarnish and corrupt it. We are fine the way we are, even though we are barefoot, even though we are undernourished." So, they used religion like a weapon, so that the people wouldn't wake up. So, well, the majority of the older people were in favor of it, but they couldn't speak, because it was totally prohibited, and even worse to read a book that was about the revolution, no. One would be burned with one's entire family. There, from an elderly person to a just-born baby, the army could burn those people if they found a book about revolution. So, well, it's something that even though they wanted to talk, to express themselves, there wasn't liberty. That didn't happen only with my parents but with many people.

I left the army two years later, and I was in the house, without work–agricultural work, but you don't earn anything that way, and well, the moment came when I married.

A Photography Career

Three years after marrying I had an accident and I ended up with a badly hurt foot. So–but I was thinking, how am I going to work, how am I going to take care of my family? And I remember an old lady arrived and said that I was a useless man because of the accident that I'd had. And it was truly a shame that with such a beautiful wife, she was going to be left like that. Instead of making me angry, that helped me to raise my morale. And fortunately, I was listening, me and my wife. And the next day, I said that I wasn't sick anymore. And my wife, my mother, my mother-in-law said to me, why wasn't I lying down? I told them that from that moment on I wasn't sick anymore. Although I felt pain. The next day I told my wife to go to the house, that I have some pamphlets about photography courses. And look for something to sell to help me. "You have to sell a chicken or something to pay for the first course."

At that time, it was very cheap. It was four or five *quetzals* for the course, for the lesson, what you had to pay monthly. And I signed up for the course in photography. And I made the promise to my wife that my first two girls, Floridalma and Gloria Isabel, one two years old and one perhaps less than a year. It was then that I promised my wife that we were going to even eat better, dress better and give my daughters a profession, because I always hoped to have, even before I was married, to have girls. I adored girls. And I managed to have three girls, and afterwards, my three boys arrived. I'm the father of six children. And what I proposed for myself, and I promised my wife, was our children had to advance. And thanks also to my wife's contributions, who has helped me a lot. She has been a good mother—she has played the part not only of mother but father, perhaps as grandmother, a good director as well. And I am thankful because my wife has been alone with my children.

And years later we made a promise all together, that we were going to fight poverty–everyone against everything. We had to get one out first, and that's how it was when my oldest daughter finally became certified as a beauty stylist. Two years later, three years later Gloria Isabel graduated engineering. And in these days, we're in the month of May, 1999, my daughter Yiseña is also going to graduate as a graduate of business administration. So, but this comes from a very long effort, since a long time ago...

The first camera that I obtained in the town in a—well you couldn't call it a store, because it only had shelves, the stands, but without things. But in one of those I saw a camera, a very old camera and—and I asked how much it was. And we came to an agreement, and I admired him so much–the person who sold it was called Luis Lopez who also died at the hands of the army. He was assassinated. Luis Lopez sells me the little camera and he smiled because, he was very happy, because I told him that I was reading some pamphlets about photography, and he was so surprised that a rural farmer like me—"you're going to go very far"—he helped me by counseling me and giving me encouragement. "Go forward, continue and you're going to get good results." That was the first camera that I got.

But I discovered that it wasn't a professional camera. I wanted a professional camera. It was a camera with fixed visor, there wasn't anything to move, it was totally amateur. And it used 120 film. And at that time, that same week, there was a person who—a couple that was getting married. And I took him aside and I said, "I'm going to take photographs." It was a surprise. As much for many people who accompanied them as for me as well.

To develop the photos, and I was still sick from the accident, we went to the city of Quetzaltenango, me and my wife.

Son, Jorges Luis models traditional dress
(Courtesy of Esteban Perez)

I remember that we were sitting in a park, waiting for the doctor's appointment, but me always with the pamphlet in my hand, reading, reading, rereading, and looking at the camera. But what it said in the pamphlet about the camera, I didn't see, because this camera was automatic, completely ordinary. But it gave me very good photos. And my wife was carrying a girl who is now Isabel, the engineer. She played in the grass. I took photos from behind, from in front, just as she was. Then, in that moment, we even stopped eating–looking for something to eat–buying fruit or something—in order to look for a laboratory or an agent who could develop the photos for us, there in Quetzaltenango. And I found it. And he told me to come back the next day to pick them up. And I went full of emotion and looked at my first pictures.

So, I convinced my wife, "Look, this can make us a lot of money. I'm going to be a photographer and all my children are going to live off photography. And I promise you that from here on out, I'm not sick. We're going to get a checkup, take vitamins and I'm not sick. Ah, but this, yes. I'm not going to work in the plantations, I'm not going to work as a rustic, I'm not going to work in the fields, but I'm going to be a photographer. That is an easy life. And in that way, I'm going to earn money every day. And so, I can manage our expenses better..."

I abandoned my town of Tacaná, and I went to Chiapas. There, yes there it was very cheap. I worked in black and white. And it cost, at that time, five pesos for a photo. Five pesetas, which was, it was pretty cheap. But the thing is, for me, I would take ten photos, and at five, that's 50 pesos. And for a rural farmer to earn 50 pesos, he has to go a whole week to earn it. And well, I could earn that in one day. And that's how I got into it.

And then color came, the color photos, that also, there wasn't even in Tapachulas, it's a city in Chiapas, the state of Chiapas, and even in those years, one didn't see color. So, when I first saw color, "I'm going to work in this," and I consulted with another person, and looking at my magazines, that color is the same sensibility as black and white, ah good, so there's no difference. So, at that time, we had to develop, we had to send the negatives to Tuxtlan in Chiapas, a state that was eight hours drive, eight hours. The work came back eight or ten days later. It was a lot of work. And nevertheless, years later some labs came to Tapachulas and we began to work more formally, I became more professional, and my children were advancing until, then in '91, I came here. And even here I continue working with photography...

In my town I was the first photographer, one might say in history. I was the first photographer. Photographers arrived but with the camera—a mountain of a camera. In the past–one of those cameras where they put the box, and they put their hand in a sleeve, like the the sleeve of a jacket. And that's a dark room. Years later, I could understand that that box is a dark room where they manage fixer and developer and paper and all, and even their little tank of water. So, it's a laboratory, that little black box is a dark room. And they came only in the August festivals, so when I was a child, they would give me 25 cents at that time, or even 50 or 75 cents, because I faithfully took care of my mother's cows. I would go cut their straw, where? Who knows, but the cow had to eat before I left, they say, to promenade, but barefoot, barefoot with an old hat.

But my father loved me a lot, because I was the oldest son. He bought me a jacket, a grey suit jacket—I remember it very well. Well, I put it on with pleasure, because there I was the most distinguished in the community and barefoot. With a jacket but barefoot. And so, like that, what I did was, I didn't buy a sweet or peanuts, nothing like that. What I wanted was to take photos. And invite my friends, we would stand there, "ay here look, look watch what they're doing..." They came from other municipalities. They knew what day there would be a festival and then they came. And there were also very good artists painting as well. On a cloth that was two and a half meters, by two or two high, square, and they stood them up by means of—it's a work of art.[59] And, well, there they made a Virgin of Guadalupe, big, a temple of Esquipulas, for

---

[59] Esteban refers to painted curtains used as backdrops for portrait photographers at fairs.

90

Virgin of Guadalupe Festival in Georgetown, Delaware
(Courtesy of Rocio Flores)

example. And so there the people stood in front of that work, that drawing, no it's a work, that's the name for it, no? And there they took our photos...

And so some of the photographers would chase me away from their booths. "Eh eh eh boy, get out of here!" What I wanted was to see. Why did they put it in the water, why did they put their hand in? So, since I was 10 or 12 years old, the idea came to me that I would, I was going to be even better than them. And unfortunately, perhaps I didn't achieve that, because I continue working. I didn't become independent through my profession. Right? But I promised that I had to be a photographer some day. Ever since I was a boy, I dreamed of living by means of a camera.

"But why them? Who are they that I can't be, if not better than them. I can be a photographer too!" And I got the opportunity, and thanks to the camera—I say thanks to the camera because, sometimes when we gathered, my fellow photographers, perhaps in a café or in a bar drinking a beer—I tell them, "boys, take care of the profession. It's very good."

I say to them, "I have even kissed the camera. One must love the camera like a woman. The woman you make her happy and the camera, and the woman brings you food."

And sometimes they have even asked me, "eh Esteban, when are you going to kiss your camera?"

"When I want to. When my wife wants a kiss, I give it to her. It's the same with the camera. Why? Because I earn money there. And you, why don't you kiss it? Why don't you kiss it?" to the one who was kidding me and all that...

Community Organizing in Tacana

After I left the army, I began to look around me, that there were a lot of needs to work with the community. We needed a school, we needed potable water, we need light, we need, well a lot of things. So, we saw the need to organize ourselves to petition for a school from the government and they gave us a school with two rooms. It was the first community at the municipal level that had a school made out of materials, of concrete, and with a floor, and with windows even. That for us was a great advance. And, but at that time as well, I formed part of the directive to petition for potable water. And I was the 5th vocal. The President was Don Inocente Diaz, Secretary, Octavio Artolon, Pedro was Treasurer, Erminio was 4th vocal and I was 5th. But it was easier for me to go to the capital of Guatemala, so neither the president nor the secretary went. I as the 5th vocal took that—I did that work, the role of the president. We succeeded in benefiting 171 families with the piped water.

That was from external aid, from the government no. It was an external aid and we were left owing money and now I'm informed that it's all paid for. Before me, there were other people who also had that desire for piped water. But they, it's that they collected funds, perhaps there were bad intentions. I remember, there was a man, Don Ternudo, a certain Anthony, and "we're going to collect," we collected a quota of 25 cents at that time. It was one day of work so that we could make a job for the potable water. But they did it on their own. It wasn't organized. So, I spoke with a person who is named Isaias Escalante and he also lives in Tapachulas. "Do you know, we need to help the community." He was a social promoter. He had taken a course in the University Andina there in Guatemala. So they had been trained how to organize, how to form a committee. So, he said, "You know what, can you get the community to meet?" I said, "Yes," and through the auxiliary mayor, we invited the whole community. And they came, and we made a committee. And we wrote a petition, and that's when we began the process through a now more formal committee. But anyway, there were people who gave us direction.

[Before] it was very lamentable. And in some places it's still like that. Even now, it continues. Many families continue with that problem even today. There are wells or springs. The mothers, the homemakers, are in charge of going to get the water. And some live 500 meters away, 400 meters, successively, like that. It depends on the place you live. The woman generally would go to

Perez family in Tacaná models traditional dress
(note sizes of jugs)
(Courtesy of Esteban Perez)

get water. She used a vessel that we call a *cantaro*, in other words it's a *tinah*, of clay and on her head. But we, when we were little, they made us go and fetch water. And so, we the boys, and my younger brothers, carried the jug with an *ikabal*. And as we grew up, the jug that we had to carry also got bigger, because now we could bear more. And that's how it was, according to your age, that was your contribution.

And years later the plastic one came. And the gallons and the receptacles of 20 liters. Well good, now I'm going to bring 20 liters of water. I go running. And in that way, it's a great suffering. And so, that was one of the ideas, because I fetched a lot of water. I fetched a lot with the jug on my head. And then, years later, with two pails in this way with a rod, here, like this, two buckets hanging here and the man placed here. In that way, and the two buckets there, and we went forward to bring the liquid to the house.

I was so tired, and my wife also suffered a lot and when we were there we helped, but when not, we were in the fields, we dedicated ourselves to working in the fields. With her child, wrapped on her back and the jug of water on her head. She was very hardy, a good woman. Good legs, she walks a lot, but that isn't to say that it was very healthy, no. It was lamentable. It was that this was imposed on us. So, that was the idea that I got–that there should be a change where we lived. We ought to have a better school, we ought to have piped water. And lamentably, there were houses that were very isolated that we wanted to bring the water to, but we couldn't. That's not a town. They are communities of private lands and we couldn't get the water to the farthest corners.

The community put up the sand, the stones. We brought them, and the institution put up the pipes and the labor. And we were left paying it off. And inaugurating that water. In the inauguration of the water, a project was left that nobody finished. We also wanted a mini-irrigation pipe, for gardens and that, but no one followed up with it. And in that time the persecution of the leaders began, when those so-called military people came into power, and whatever rural farmer was a leader in his community, they sent them out to destroy us! Especially Efrain Rios Montt and Lucas, they were the great generals who massacred the people without any fear of anything.[60] I say it openly, you can't hide that, because the people know it. So, many of my companions were assassinated. That was the reason why, when I saw myself as a leader, I was pursued in my town.

Flight to Mexico

And precisely, in this month of May it will be 18 years since many people in the population fled. And many people also died in my town of Tacana. I was remembering a lot. May is very important–that we're living 18 years, those who survived outside the country, and those who also died. And I wanted to mention as well my comrades who died unjustly, we didn't owe absolutely anything to the army, nor to the revolution, because we weren't even incorporated in the revolution. We weren't revolutionaries. We were just leaders of the community.

[In Tacana] there were people who distinguished themselves within the revolution and there were people who distinguished themselves within the army. In my town there are many army officers. And perhaps their relatives are barefoot, or perhaps their ancestors are rural farmers. But even so they get in the army, and they are strongly trained but not for a good career. But to be an officer of the army and be a rural farmer—perhaps the rural farmer isn't at fault, but there they brutalize them, they make them into animals. And it's the same thing, being part of the poor population, and going to assassinate your poor people. This happened. It didn't just happen in my town, it happened in the other towns...

On the first of May a paramilitary pointed me out and turned me over to the police, mistakenly, erroneously on his part. And for my part I am grateful that he committed this error of

---

[60] Lucas 1978-1982, Rios Montt 1982-83.

pointing me out because, fortunately, I saw when—in a mirror, because I was always taking photos, I had been taking photos. I saw when he pointed me out in the mirror. And since we knew positively that people who are pointed out are already corpses, I had to leave immediately. I left May 4th. After the first two or three days I was there secretly. My family prepared themselves. They didn't take anything but some clothes, and everything was left in the house. Everything was left there, completely. And I entered Mexico May 5th, 1981. And then I began to survive in Mexico. But I didn't have anything with me...

There were already a lot of people, it's just that they didn't go into the city. They stayed on the plantations, like that. So, I didn't go down to the plantations because of my work. As a photographer, I could establish myself in the city. In that way I went to the city. Then I began to inform myself where other people from my same town were. I visited them, I brought them, for example, things to eat, and fruit no, because there's always fruit in the countryside. I brought, for example, the tomatoes, things like that. I visited a lot of people to animate them, to raise their morale, and that we should be calm, have patience, not return. Because the army was going to keep going.

And in that way, a lot of people stayed in Mexico. There were a good number who went and looked for refuge. They went to the refugee camps, to the churches, requesting protection. And a lot of people went and they set themselves down where they could, in the plantations, in the cities, in the little towns, and they mixed with the people from there. And some of them stayed permanently. And in my case, I didn't return, I didn't decide to go back to my town to my country with those repressive laws. It wouldn't be good to go. And so, I stayed in Mexico...

In Mexico, they celebrate the day of the heroic children in the Battle of Puebla with the French. And they won that battle against the French, because France wants to invade Mexico, and they lost. So, well, they have a party, on the 5th of May, and parades and programs. And I crossed the border where there weren't roads, where there was no photographer. In spite of my fleeing, in spite of having my children, there were five of them, 3 girls and 2 boys—I started taking photos, like any other photographer. I crossed, and I worked. And I stayed one day more within the territory of Guatemala, but in a place very far away. And on the 6th of May I entered Mexico formally. And I got to Tapachulas. I have relatives... We met May 9th, and they helped us look for a house.

A very cheap rent, but without a floor, a door all banged up–we were all living very badly. The 10th of May I went to a school called Flores Magon. Ricardo Flores Magon. There I worked and I took about 200 pictures. That helped me a lot to support my family. And that's how I got to buy my first chair, a table, and successively until then I was able to furnish—I carried two or three cameras. I sold two or three cameras. I was left with one to buy a bed, to buy a number of things. I succeeded in surviving, and now, the most difficult step for me was school for the children.

And there was a recently founded neighborhood there in Tapachulas, quite separate from the town, from the city. So, I was very active there. I joined in to collaborate with the teachers. I remember the professor was called Director Alfonso Loarca, Alfonso, yes, Alfonso Loarca. And he liked my contributions, my help, and so then he named me a member of the parents committee, but I turned it down because I was a complete foreigner. And I said that no, I didn't have the time, but I asked how I could help, when I was present, but I'm not part of the officers. And they accepted me like that. I was an activist, and they accepted my children without a birth certificate. And I got those later on. And that's where they ended up.

And when they were going to finish fifth, sixth grade, then was when I really pushed. But the director couldn't dismiss them, because I was an activist, I collaborated a lot with the school. I saw myself obliged to find a way to register my children. And I succeeded by means of money and friends, I succeeded in registering my children as Mexicans, not as children of Guatemalans, but as children of people of Mexico. And that's how they stayed, and they continued in secondary school, and they've all made it to the university.

And I'm very thankful for the democracy that one experiences in Mexico. There's more liberty. A little more liberty. Well, anyway, they've had their great heroes, their revolutions. And everything that one lives in Mexico is liberty. It's not a work of God nor a work of the Devil; it's the work of the great revolutionaries who mixed their blood in the clay and the dust, and [I give] thanks to the great revolutionary men, and for that liberty that they also gave to all the Guatemalans, and not just the Guatemalans but also for all of Central America.

Photographer in Mexico

Years later, the number of photographers began to grow a lot. And now there wasn't any little town, there wasn't any community, as small as it might be, where there weren't one or two photographers. So, then it wasn't lucrative to go around with a camera. And after that, the commentary among the old photographers—we said, "now it's embarrassing to go around with a camera, because now we're all going to die of hunger!" So, I remember a phrase of one old photographer, who now is dead for sure. "Now," he says, "even the dogs have a camera!" [He was] angry that, well, now he didn't have work due to his age. And I didn't believe at any time that that same thing was going to happen to me, what is happening to me today. Right now, a lot of people have cameras, and they dedicate themselves to work, so now they've taken away my work. I remember a lot about that old man, Carlos he was called, the photographer. He said, "Now even the dogs have cameras."

So due to that, I saw the need and the end of abandoning, of leaving, the work of photography and going out and looking for new horizons. And I had bought a little house with a humble roof by taking photos, and most of the work is at the end of the school year. The primary, secondary, and I even got into, not just the secondary schools but even in the universities where there was work. And because then I was part of an organization of photographers...

We had some small advantages. We were organized to present ourselves at an event or a church, and if there were two or three photographers, we had to find out who the work belonged to in an organized way. There were three different organizations. If you had a contract you had to present a previous agreement that you had been contracted. And if you show the contract, and you call the bride or the groom and you say, "who signed this contract?"

"Ah, it's me, I've contracted him." Perfect, now we don't interrupt his work. Perhaps it's a wedding with few relatives, 10, 15, 20 people. And five or six photographers are going to work? Who are you going to sell all those photos to? And so, that's an example of the benefits of a photographer's union.

We had brotherhood with the other unions. And even, I was delegated the photographer of a municipality that is called Tuxtlan Chico. And I was delegated to coordinate the other photographers, and they had to report to me at whatever event. And if I wasn't present, well, they still worked. They had to have respect. If not, then to throw the famous *volado* to raffle the work. A coin toss to see who gets the job. No one is contracted, we all want to work, but it's better to raffle it and see who gets it...

We improved the photographers' union. They felt very good when a month later I read an act, Act number one, such and such and so, is an Act. I had learned that in my community. And then a few months before, perhaps a year earlier on an occasion, with those old officers that I spoke of before, they named me like a moderator. They called them the moderator. He's the one you ask permission to speak, and who controls it and all, no? And unfortunately, I was the last one to arrive. And always the times, in the previous sessions, I always sat at the very back. So no one would see me. I greeted people and I entered and I sat down with my paper in my hand. That was all. I expressed an opinion once in awhile. One day I got there a little late and there weren't any seats in the back. There was a space close to the table, and there was a

Wilbert Perez models traditional *compasino* dress and tools.
(Courtesy of Esteban Perez)

place and I went to sit there. And I was sitting there. And the assembly commences.

And perhaps because of my physique, or I don't know, they always said that I was from the country, a country man, but I wasn't from Guatemala. Always from Chiapas or from the edges of the wilds there. And a joke, a smile, a jest was never lacking. Why don't you go up better all the way to the table for the debates, and they let out a cackle, laughing. And I remember the general secretary, Rafael Damian, said, "Yes, comrade Esteban, that's how you will learn. Yes."

And I said on the inside, "If they only knew, sons of the M. I come more experienced than you do." And that was when for the first time I participated in the officer's table, as a debate moderator. It's spontaneous, only the assembly, not as a member of the officers. A brother-cousin named Nectali and another named Gonzalo—Nectali just died two months ago—and Gonzalo is alive, but he's also as old as I am. They were worried and they thought that I was going to commit a lot of errors there, not filling the role. And it was the contrary, because I put many things in their place, and I presented myself, perhaps not with great talent, but I said, "here things are going to be like this—I'm going to be the moderator, and you are going to ask permission to speak and so and so," everything went. And finally, a photographer–whose last name is Culebro–so he, I don't know, he can resolve personal issues with the general secretary and he stands up and I said, "and where are you going comrade?"

"I have an issue with Rafael Damien."

"If it's particular issues or private issues, that's why there's the agenda item, a point exists that says, general issues. Leave it in general issues, or resolve your private matters in a coffee shop."

And that was when an applause from all my comrades interrupted me. They said, "let's see, grab your ranch hat, grab your sheepherder's staff, we're going to see if it's like we all think, mango. Esteban is more experienced than all of those who are sitting at the table!"

And the applause began, and the congratulations began and fortunately, the table was placed close to the door and all who were leaving came to congratulate me and not the other members of the board of directors. It was the first time that I let myself be known there in the company of the other photographers...

The Decision to Come North

The time came when the very teachers in the schools now had their cameras. And the time came when the teachers didn't let the photographers come in. So, that's why there was a union of photographers, because the teachers were fined. Why? Because they had a salary and we are temporary, and so the union fought that. And they protected us. And they weren't taking away people's liberty to buy a camera and work with it, but they also had to respect the rules of all the unions. And they can't work unless they belong to a union of photographers. Even though they work in that school. And that's how the photography work grew so much, and even the teachers were taking photos. So, I saw myself obliged to abandon my country. And also, well I never had formal papers in Mexico. I was always afraid of immigration. Always with the fear of immigration. And I couldn't go to Guatemala for even one minute, with the fear of persecution, there in my town. They killed various relatives of mine, various leader-friends of mine, leader comrades, so what am I going to do in Guatemala? And in Mexico, I don't live peacefully because I personally don't have documents. My children do, but I don't.

Well I already owed a lot of money to other people. So, I couldn't pay it. And now there wasn't much liberty with regard to my work. So, since I heard some denunciations, that they were going to denounce someone, why was I going to wait any longer? I did what I had done in my town, I got together my stuff and from Mexico to here [claps hands]. And my children, well, once they didn't see me, then they left them alone.

I had already traveled in Mexico, to Mexico City, that wasn't a problem anymore. And it was ironic that some others accompanied us to the border of Nogales, at Alta Sonora. And then at Alta Sonora we looked for someone to take us across and that was it. That was it.

I was in Colorado for a few days. I was a few days in Atlanta, Georgia. In Georgia, the town was called Brinbeach. And from Brinbeach I went to Florida. And in Florida I worked for eight months, very sad, very desperate, because I had never abandoned my family. I had never, never abandoned my children. They had always been there for the good and the bad times, persecutions and all. And I always planted in them that they should study, and I also taught them to work. They went to work in a carpentry workshop. My three boys are carpenters. And my girls sold in the streets. They sold swallows, supervised and controlled by their mother. We never abandoned each other.

Today [my daughter] is going to finish her university. She also sold in the streets a lot. She helped, we helped each other, all together. My wife also contributed a lot, and we always inculcated in them that they should study. And I couldn't send all my children together, because the expense was too much. I had to send them two at a time... I would take them to the top of some buildings and say, "look at those who work here. They consume *Maseca* the same as everyone. So, why don't you grow wings," and like that. I always injected good things in them.

Now the youngest, he's the last boy, I feel sad about him, because he was hardly around me. So, for that reason perhaps—he isn't finished, but he's a little slow in his studies. He's 17 years old and he's just finishing his first year of high school. And I don't agree with him. He's got no energy. He didn't want to continue studying. If not, he would have finished high school by the age of 18. I even gave him a vacation to Mexico City. Then he realized, he saw the highways, the buildings, the bridges, the agriculture. Let's see, "who does these things? They're people who've been to the university. So, why don't you do the same?" So, that's how, when he came back from his vacation that I gave him, he came back very contented and now, now he's finished his first year of high school. In that way.

Work in the United States

[In Florida] I worked for a company that cuts grass. Then I worked in the tomato harvests. Picking tomatoes, I picked cucumbers, I picked eggplant but I never got ahead in the harvests, when I did that work. Instead, I always had my camera, I was always taking photos of the tomato harvest—how the people ran, how the people carried the pails, and how the people threw the buckets in the air to put them in the truck. And, so, I lived more off the photos than off the tomato harvest.

I sold them. Yes exactly, to the same people. And I sold them in this way... One marker meant one pail. So, the photo, in order to make it equal to two dollars, one had to make six markers. So, six markers for a photo. I want three photos, well, give me 18 markers, 18 markers. And then I reported it now in my work, as if I had picked the tomatoes. In that way, I got to 80 or 100, even a 100 and something. But picking itself, I wasn't doing that. [The managers] were amused by me because well—And later they bought my work which wasn't any old work, but well-exposed photos, centered, with the right colors. And unfortunately, I lost the negatives when I came here. It's a shame.

I came here because a relative came and was looking for people, and they looked for me and they brought me. So, that was the 8th of June, the 5th of June I came here. The 8th of June, 1992, I began to work in Allen's poultry plant. And I didn't like it at all, the work of the poultry plant. Because I worked three months on the line, and then they raised me to the work of the box room, where the boxes are assembled, all that's related to boxes. And that's where I was for about three years in that job. I quit because it also is very tiring. They take advantage, they exploit you, they yell at you, and there was no union. The union existed but they didn't know anything about what was going on with the workers.

And until several years later, when they had the first strike is when there were changes...[61]

So, and a message for the big businessmen, I don't have any reason to greet them.[62] Because, they have manipulated us, and to say it well, they've paid us, but years ago, when there were two or three poor Americans in a line, four! Now there's only one Hispano, because he does more work than an American. Now, the American lower class doesn't like the Hispanic. And it would benefit them to forgive us, because they aren't at fault either. Instead—I'm going to repeat what I said before—but it was the United Fruit Company that overthrew our government, and that's why we came here to take the bread and the work away from the poor Americans.

And if that hadn't happened, we would be cultivating the great lands that the big people possess, the Big American, German, even Chinese, Spanish landowners. More than anything it's the Spaniards who have the great farms in Guatemala. So, if the government were a little more intelligent in avoiding war, and avoiding hunger, and avoiding polemics, well, "Here you've got four farms, why don't they take away two and sell two to the peasants?" But no, they did the opposite! He gets to be a representative and he wants another two or three farms. And the rural farmers, well, they can get out. Let them go to America. There the American businessmen want them. No, well. My greatest message to the poor Americans is that they go on forgiving us. They aren't at fault and the Hispanics aren't at fault. The ones at fault are the ones who overthrew our government.

---

[61] April 1996, Mountaire workers in Selbyville held a wildcat strike. See Maria Martinez, this volume.

[62] The final two paragraphs are taken from an interview in 1995 with Jessica Payne for the Delaware Folklife Program.

Fernando Natareno

Fernando Natareno and his wife are the first Guatemalans to buy a house in Georgetown. They live on Cedar Street in Kimmeytown. Fernando works in a local poultry processing plant, where he is in charge of fixing the machinery. His wife, who is diabetic, cannot work outside the home. She prepares food on request and provides child care for many of the single mothers who live in the community. In this interview, Fernando describes his earlier life in Guatemala, but focuses on some of the problems for Hispanics here in the United States. The Natarenos originally emigrated to California in 1985, where they have relatives who have lived there since the early 1970s. They were fleeing the civil war in Guatemala, but were also eager to take advantage of the more advanced fertility treatments available in the United States. They are now the proud parents of two healthy children, a boy and girl. After receiving their residency under the general amnesty of 1986, the family moved to Georgetown in 1994.

Although they come from San Marcos as do many of the Guatemalans in Georgetown, they are different from their neighbors in a number of ways. First, they lived on the coast, where Fernando explains, schools were more accessible. Second, they are more mature than the majority of newcomers. Fernando was born in 1957 and has been married to his wife for 22 years. As adult members of the community, they try to counsel their younger peers. Fernando is particularly concerned with the number of single mothers in the community. He also identifies public drinking, or drinking and driving as a serious problem. However, Fernando reminds us that this is a problem in society at large. If Americans have been injured and even killed by Hispanic drivers, Hispanics have been killed by American drivers as well.[63] Here, then, are excerpts from Fernando's interview:

---

[63]In 1993 a Georgetown cheerleader was struck and killed by an inebriated Guatemalan immigrant, which increased tensions between native and immigrant residents.

107

Early Life

Yes, I still remember well how I used to go to school. We had to leave the house clean. There, people are used to sweeping, milking the cows, feeding the pigs–we call them *coches* in Guatemala–and the chickens. And from there we would go to school. We'd come home from school and have a glass of water, and we'd go into the hills to tie up the animals, we'd go to tie up the ones in the hills. We'd come back and prepare the corn to give them—in the morning, really early in the morning—[to feed] the animals, right? I remember a lot about my childhood there...

Oh, the school was really nice with me, I really liked school, but what I didn't—my parents wanted me to study to be a teacher, but I didn't want to be a teacher, because I saw my cousins who already had graduated in teaching. They didn't have jobs. They were at home doing the same things I was doing.

So, I told my father, "if you don't let me go into the army, I'm not going to continue studying." I wanted to study to be an army officer, and my father wouldn't let me go. So, I said, "Well, don't let me go for teaching or for anything. I'll just stop here."

[I wanted to go into the army] because I like it. I still like it. To do military service, and from there we could move to the police, working there in Guatemala. I went into the ar—three and a half years. And from there, I became a guard for a big ranch. I was working there seven years as a guard for the ranch, and well, for "x" motive, I requested to leave. Problems with the guerillas, problems that my family couldn't live happily in the town, because by then [they] had something against us, and so for that reason, I came here, right? It pained me to come here to the United States, the motive being they could have killed me, my wife or something, someone from my family. That did happen that they killed one of my uncles, whose sons were in the army. Because you are in the army, they kill your parents...

The Crossing

Well, we came in—from Guatemala to Mexico. We left with our passports and visas, right. But there in Mexico there used to be a lot of corruption; there still is today. They would look at you, "You. Where are you from?" We said, "From Guatemala. Here's the passport." "Okay. You want to keep going, 5,000 pesos each."

And that's how we came, that's how we came with 5,000, 5,000. They stopped us four times. And it was four times we paid 5,000 each. That's 20,000 pesos at that time–it's… We, um, we spent like $3,000 to get to cross Mexico by land. About $3,000. There in Mexico, they made us all get out. I got to Tijuana with 1,000 Mexican pesos. And thank God one of my cousins was in Los Angeles there. Being in Tijuana, I called her. She said, "Don't worry, some money will come to you there before you know it." And that's how it was. She sent money to Tijuana and when we saw the little dollars, we said, "Now we are in the United States."

But until then we didn't know what it was going to cost to cross the line, because, well, we went over the hills. In the hills they grabbed us—once immigration caught us and they had us, they had me in jail for two hours, and they returned us to Tijuana. The next day at dawn we tried again and they caught us again. The third time we did do it. But we walked a night and a day. That's what we walked in order to cross over the hills. One suffered, yes, but thank God, I give thanks…

Columbians came, Nicaraguans came. There were Hondurans, Guatemalans, and Mexicans, eighteen of us came. I was carrying a gallon of water on my back. It was here by my side, since they told us, "Take enough water because on the way— we're going to walk a night and a day." That's how it was. Where it started to get light, we went into a forest to rest a bit. And at two in the afternoon, well, the Coyote said, "Up, up, up, because we're going to keep walking like this." Then we went into a—well there they call them freeway—under a freeway. We walked, walked, walked, walked, kilometer by kilometer.

When we arrived at San Isidro, they put us in a house. There in that house, they fed us. We ate avocado and tortilla and chiles. But I'm not a big chile eater. They just gave us avocado and tortilla to eat and to pass the time, until at night a bus came for us. And that's how it happened, at night. The next day at 6:00 in the morning, I was in Los Angeles.

Coming to Delaware

Well, my motive was that one of my cousins was here, and she told me that she earned good money, that the city was very nice, and that you didn't see the things you saw in California. I requested vacation time in the Toyota Dealer and I came first. And yes, thank God, I liked it. And I told my wife and my son, I told them to wait for me, that yes, the little place was nice. Here there weren't drugs—there are drugs. There are drugs wherever I've gone, right? But here there's more familiarity. Here you don't see bullets, you don't hear scandalous goings on, too many scandals, like in a big city. Right? I've seen that in Philadelphia, in Philadelphia [there are] a lot of problems. In Baltimore, the same. But it's a really big city, right? The city is really big. In contrast here, the city is tiny—no, no you don't see many problems with drugs. And that's what I liked. That there weren't any drugs, there wasn't that vandalism–two or three [incidents]—but we're not aware of that....

No, what's nice about this place is that one doesn't suffer with one's work. Here, one can leave, one can go to another place—there's work all over here. But with good papers. If one doesn't have good papers, one does suffer. A lot of people are suffering here right now, because they don't have papers. And I don't know how they are organizing things over there, but yes, it makes me sad that a lot of people—I've helped a lot of people.

[When we first came], we were wetbacks. There in California, thank God, and I do thank the Lord, that he—I suffered one year without papers. Then when the amnesties came, it was '85-'87-'87-'86 I think it was. So, we put our papers in there. I suffered one year only not having papers. In '86—like mid-'86 I already had a paper from immigration so that I could work anywhere. In '87 I already had my residency. Two years after we came in, we had our residency…

Oh yes, every month we send money to him, to my father. I went two years ago. Just two years ago we went in June, and I went to see how the situation was there. And I saw that it was good. So, I told him, if he wanted to, I would get one or two cows or—so that he wouldn't work any more in agriculture and he wouldn't dedicate himself—only take care of the animals, and "Yes," he said, "That's good." Thank God, right now he's doing all right. Now the animals have gotten big, and they are better off. And we send them every month—not a lot, right, but yes, $150 a month so that they can help themselves, for food, right. So, well, that's monthly, monthly…

Becoming a Homeowner

Well, the story of the house is long. I give God thanks also to my God for bringing us here. And the Sisters at the Catholic Church arrived. And so, there, since we would go to the church, they introduced themselves to us and we to them. Before, there weren't many Hispanics here. There were some, but not like now, right? Like six years back, there weren't so many.

And so we were living in a rental, and unfortunately, we had problems with the owner of the house where we were renting. And I said to myself, that—we told him, right, to come and fix a refrigerator. And he said no, that that wasn't something he did. So we told him—well, then we left, we said, right. "No, then, but how are you going to leave and you have to pay for the refrigerator?" We, "No because it broke, and whose responsibility is that?" So it happened that we even went to court, and well, and unfortunately, at that time when we were in court the weather got cold, and a pipe broke, and it filled the house with water. So he came. We called the police and then the firemen and [explained] that the man didn't fix the house well and that. They came, they made a report and all. Then when we got to court, we showed the judge that.... He said, "No." It was a lie we were telling. And then later, he brought us an icebox, but a little icebox.

My children were still small, right. He said, "To store your things." The milk is going to spoil. The meat spoiled; the milk spoiled. Everything that goes in the "fridge" spoiled. We told the judge. So he came. The judge said, "How much did they lose?" Approximately, we—if you'll understand me here—we spend $80 a week. Now in fifteen days, we are four people now, let's say, in the family, and now that's like 150 dollars every fifteen days now for food, right? So, we made the total for 15 days, now $150. So the owner of the house made a big fuss. That, that was a lot of money. That we didn't spend all that.

But then we came, "Here are the receipts. Here are the receipts. Are you going to say it's not true? Here are the receipts." Well, in sum, we won the case, because in the first place, we told the judge that he brought us that icebox, but it was just a freezer to freeze. "How are you going to put milk there for the baby?" "Does he want us to give the boy the ice cube to suck? Or does he want us to give him ice there, or the frozen gallon?

The judge just shook his head and he said, "alright."

So our—we had gotten lawyers—and they came, and they cited him, but he didn't realize. And they gave a $5,000 fine to the owner of the house, yes. Three months not paying rent, and the $5,000 he had to pay, the owner of the house...

So then he came and called the police on us to throw us out, if we didn't leave. So we came out, and by then we had a judge's order, and I told the police, "We aren't going." And unfortunately, the police who arrived speaks Spanish.

And we told him, "You're going to throw us out by force?"
"Yes," he said, "If you don't understand, we're going to get you out by force."
"Are you sure?" I say. "Are you sure?"

"Yes," he said, "This is how I evict people," and he made as if he was going to put the handcuffs on me.

"Are you sure," I say. "Do you want us to win our case against you as well?" When I mentioned whether he wanted us to win the case, then he said, "What, if you have a court order, let's see it." I had an order from the judge.

"Oh my God," he said. And he said, "Forgive me, forgive me. I haven't said anything. I haven't said anything."

"Remember," I said, "I'll even go to court for you as well," I said.

"No," he said, "forgive me, no, I wanted to pat your back," he said.

I said, "One moment. I'm not your horse, for you to be patting my back," I said. "Because in our country, we only pat the back of the animals." I said, because that's how you calm them when you're going to mount the horses. "Not me," I said. I told the policeman that. And the police turned around...

And so I came and told the Sister, I said, yes, I went to *La Casita*. I say, "Look, please," I said, "It happens that they're throwing me out of my rental," I say. "Where—and I need right away, if you don't have some rental that I can rent for myself, for my wife, and for my girl."

"What happened?"

"Look, problems." I showed her the paper from the court.

"It's going to be hard for you right now, but you know what?" she said, "Yes, here are some houses that are for sale. How much money do you have?" "Well, I have about $5,000," I say...

So, I spoke with the owner of the rental. "Give me three months more," I say. "I'll pay you in advance."

"No," he said. "You can't pay the rent for it," he said. "You don't have to go until you've completed the three months. I don't have any problem with you, it's the other young man." The other young man [living there] didn't have anything to do with it. He changed...He changed his mind, because of that problem that

Sister Maria Mairlot in Georgetown. August 2000
(Courtesy of Katherine Borland)

they had taken his $2,000, plus the lawyers, plus the court fees.

So, "Do you know what I'm doing? I'm going to buy a house," I say.

"No," he said, "You're not going to buy a house," he said.

"I'm in the process. If the bank gives me a loan," I say, "I'm going to buy the house."

Okay. A month later, they send me a letter. I just have to sign at the bank. Good. The next month, two letters. I had to go with a witness saying that I was asking for a loan from the bank for the money. Okay. After two months they told me, "Look for someone to come and change the cable, and the insurance to examine the house, in what state it's in." And thank God the house was left like this. Painted, painted like this...

And so, the person came from the insurance. He said, "This house is good."

"So, I want a note to take to the bank." So, I give him[64] Ms. Carol's card and asked the insurance agent to call, that he had seen the house, that he was going to give us the insurance. And then we went to the bank. "Okay, your loan will be here in a few days, $30,000 for you to pay for the house."

So, I'm paying this back to the bank. The bank gave me, they call them mortgages, right. Okay. So, I'm paying the bank. And I thank God, and the Sister, and to God, I thank God a lot because he gave us his strength. And her, Sister Maria, helped us buy the house and God first, in a few years I will have paid back...

The rent for the house is $200 a month, but I'm giving $300 more. I'm paying, paying more, paying more. The faster we pay it back, the better. That way I don't pay a lot of interest. In the four years that I've been here, I've paid $8,000 just in interest. And the house is, it will be paid in 30 years.

---

[64] The real estate agent working with Mr. Natareno.

Unidentified child in Guatemalan dress taken in
Georgetown, Delaware April 15, 2001
(Courtesy of Esteban Perez)

Ticha Roblero (pseudonym)

Guatemalan Ticha Roblero is 49. I met her at the battered women's shelter in the spring of 1999. She came to Delaware six years ago, because she was afraid that her estranged husband's enemies might harm her. Her husband of 25 years had already emigrated to Georgetown in 1990 or 1991. Ticha speaks both Mam and Spanish. She's originally from Juitan, in the department of Huetzaltenango.

Ticha impressed me as being reserved, and humble in her demeanor towards strangers. Although there was a large social and experiential gap between interviewer and speaking subject, Ticha was quite frank about her life experiences. She speaks as a woman who has endured great indignities but who now sees the possibility of living independently with dignity in the United States.

Rural Life

I was born Nov. 3, 1949 in Juitan, Huetzaltenango. And my life before—I planted the *milpa* [cornfield], I planted *milpa*. I worked in the mountains, that's how I worked. Yes, my own land, yes...

When I was 15, 16 years old I left from there. I left to work. I worked in Huetzaltenango.

I didn't go to school [when I was young]. I don't know how to read, I don't know anything, anything. [Because I had to] to work and because my father was a very poor person, very poor, they didn't have money, they didn't send us to study. So, I don't know how to read, I don't know how to write anything...

There my clothing was a *corte*, we called it typical *corte*, typical *huipil*. That's how we dressed, indigenous...

Our house was very poor, it was a house of what they called *pajon* [straw], very small houses, we lived in there. My life was poor, a very small house we lived in. We are four. The others, my brothers and sister, who knows what they did. My

117

brothers stayed there. They're there somewhere. Yes, since people have land to plant corn, plant things like that, the houses are a little distant from one another, in the mountain, yes.

There one has to work. One has to make food. In that time one ground the corn on the ground, a couple of stones to grind with, to make tortillas, then to work, and from there to fetch water, since the well, there aren't any like there are here, there aren't wells. One has to get water from far away in jugs on the head, and from there one has to go and get wood from the mountain, go and fetch wood. It's not like here, well, with the stove. From there one had to go and pasture the calves and the sheep in the mountain.

That's the work and one works to plant the *milpa* so that there's something to eat all the time. There, there's no time to go visiting, or—only when there's a party at Christmas, and then one has to go and pass the time a little in the town. But that's two days only, three days, and from there, to work, to work, nothing more. That's how one spends all day. Working, making things, yes…

[My husband] was from a town, what's it called? Momostenango, Dept. of Totonicapan. Another town… I was working in Cela, I was working, and he was in the army and we met there. And two years, then we married. There when you get to know someone, then you have to go to the house to ask permission, to give their daughter to him. No, there's no other way, so he had to ask for my hand and all. And then the people— you're going to marry—and you go to get her, and then you take her with you.

I had one [child]. Um hum. I had one. My husband went to work in the police, he worked that way, and I was working in houses [in the capital]. Working in houses… Then [came] all the others. I have four, yes. Right now [the oldest] is 24 and the other one is 23 I think, 23 or 22, the other one is 21 and the other one is 19. I have four…

I cleaned, I swept, to dust, make food, iron, like that. That's housework. To sweep. To do inside chores. To wash and iron. Yes, thank God, [my employers] treated me well. They liked me a lot. They helped me. Because of them, too, I came here, because they helped me, they had my money, my life savings. They gave it to me...

Marital Problems

Oh yes. The problem was from the time we were married. For one year we were calm. From there, he—well he had, he had another woman. He was going out with other women and me in the house with my children, always struggling, working. And he, was always going around with other women, and I was with my children, working in houses...

He hit me. He hit me. He didn't give me anything, not even for the expenses. Nothing for the children. He was in the street one hundred percent, always. And I with my children. My children were studying, they needed to eat—if you earned a little money, and then, he told me, no. No, they didn't get their good education. Only one got—one didn't study, the other one got to ninth grade. Now, the twenty year old got her seven grade—there wasn't any money, because he didn't help me. For all that. To give to them so that they could have more education, and money so that my children could go and study. He didn't give me anything. Yes.

Reasons for Emigrating

[My husband] came because the guerilla were looking for him, since he'd been in the zone. He had been in the police. Who knows what problem, they were looking for him, so he came here.

I stayed working in houses. I was always working in houses. But since that, afterwards I came because they would ask where my husband was. I didn't say where he was. I said I didn't know where he was.

Then, "You know very well where he is, and you have to say where he is."

I told them, no. "I don't know, I don't know anything about him. I don't know anything about him."

"Yes, you know very well," they say.

Then, I was—I was worried, scared. So, I got my visa, nothing more, because I came legally. I came here. I came to look for life.

[I was afraid] that they were going to do something to me, because I was alone then. Since they were asking about him. I told them that I didn't know where he was. Then, they told me that I did know where he was. What happened was I didn't want to tell them. I told them I didn't know anything about where he was. So, with that worry, well, them asking about him, where he was, then I became more frightened.

Life in Delaware

Well, I felt sad, desperate. I thought and I prayed [about what I had] lost. Since we didn't have a house. We didn't have a house and where I grew up, no one lives there now. Well then, I came, because in Guatemala we don't have a house. Well I felt strange coming here. It's different.

Here I don't know. I don't know anyone here. Only my husband. I don't have anyone I know here.

My children came before. They came before. I was left by myself there. They were working. One was in Los Angeles. And then when I came here, he came here. Yes. They weren't together. Each one was working.

The problems with [my husband] continued. He hit me. He didn't give me anything for the rent, for lunch, for—no, he didn't help me out with anything. So, I went and asked if they would give me permission to work with my visa, since I had a visa. So, they let me. And so the permission came to me, so, well, to work. To pay for the rent, for my lunch, and to help my daughter and well, my grandchildren. Yes. Yes. Working. He didn't give me anything, not to pay my rent, my lunch, nothing.

And that was when my daughter came last time, she came, and she had a little baby, and she helped out with the food and clothing, when she had the baby. The little sister came. That's

View of Race Street, Georgetown, Delaware
On this street, *La Esperanza* is located.
(Courtesy of Katherine Borland)

how I met Sister Maria. So, that time I had problems in those days, my husband threw me twice in the bathroom. So, I called on a Saturday, I called the Sister Maria, [to ask] what I could do.

Because now I can't take the many things that he has done to me, and since I took my [car back] the problems arose because of that. I took my car, and he called the police, [and told them] that I bought a car, but I didn't have a license, he said. But I can have it, because I don't drive it, it's only my son-in-law that drives it. That's what he didn't like. He sent the police, that I didn't have a license, that they should take away my car. That he wants the keys. That's fine, and then they took the keys from me and gave them to him. But I didn't drive it!

I'm studying to get my license, I'm studying a book, but I don't know how to read, I don't know anything. With my children, I asked them to do me the favor of teaching me, what means all the—how one drives. So, I went to try, but no, I wasn't able to get a license. So for that reason he sent the police to me, so I called the Sister Maria, and said, what could I do, he sent the police after me, just to get my car.

I have to take my grandchildren to the doctor, they are sick, but I didn't drive it, it was my son-in-law. And so she told me, it was a Saturday, wait, she said, "on Monday we'll talk [about] what we can do," she said. And that's how I met her. Since I don't go out, I go from work to home, from home to work. I only go for lunch. And we go to the store when we need to buy something. I didn't go out, I didn't know anyone. I don't know people. I only pay the rent…

Yes. Now, since he sent the police, we went to court. So I went there telling why he was doing that to me. They gave it to me, because I don't drive it, but yes I have someone who drives it for me.

"No, but," he says, "You hit me," he says. I didn't hit him. He said that I hit him. But I, that day, he put me in the bathroom and he hit me, he kicked me in the bathroom, but there wasn't a frypan there. He said that I hit him with a frypan. But I didn't hit him. I only wanted to defend myself, I grabbed him like that, and I made a scratch here. And he told the police that I hit him with a frypan. There wasn't anything in the bathroom.

And so, I went and then I said, "I didn't." And so, that's where Sister Maria entered. And so, they took me out of there to here so that he wouldn't continue to hit me. They moved me here [to the shelter]. On Monday it will be eight [days].

No, I don't want to go there. I'm tired of it. Since Guatemala he's been doing this. And so, now I don't want to anymore. I'm looking for a house to live in with my grandchildren and my daughter. I'm going to look for another house. I need a house that they can entertain themselves in, big. That's what I'm thinking. Now I'm not thinking that I can put up with so many things that he's done. So now that's what I'm thinking. I'm going to look for a house to live only with my daughter. Uh huh.

Because why do I want to go back? It will go back to the same thing. And he doesn't help me in anything. I pay all the things. And I work. For what? Only for him to hit me and tell me. He wasn't good for anything. No.

[My children speak] only in Spanish, since—it's that we didn't speak that way because my husband speaks in another language called Quiche, and I speak Mam, so we can't speak. He doesn't understand me, and I don't understand him. So, my children grew up speaking Spanish. No one knows how to speak Mam. Yes...

My grandparents, my parents, my mother didn't speak Spanish. My father spoke a little. But my mother didn't know Spanish. I didn't know either. So, when I went to work in houses, I learned Spanish, because I didn't know Spanish either. Working, speaking a little in houses is how I learned Spanish. Yes.

All by myself. I just heard what they said, and that one does like this and that—thanks to God, well now I understand. I pretty much understand everything, but before no. I only spoke Mam. People before only spoke pure Mam and they didn't know Spanish. The person who knew Spanish was rare. There it was pure Mam... .

More or less it was nice at that time how the people understood one another in marriage. It was nice. Yes. I remember, it was nice. People married, they respected each other, everything. It's not like it is now. Here, now he has, the man has two even three women. Before no. They respected the woman...

[My husband] keeps threatening me. "We go back to Guatemala, and I'll kill you." Here no, because the law isn't like in Guatemala. There I would be dead. I think that he, that perhaps he will do it to me when I get to Guatemala. Well right now, I don't think about going. I'm not thinking of going [back to Guatemala].

My children support me.... Why am I putting up with him if he doesn't help me in anything? It's better that I live only with them. Yes, that's what they can tell me. Now that they're grown, that I worked for them, so, it's better that I separate from him and live alone. I'm not going to be embittering my life, suffering; I suffered so much, 25 years.

Yanitza Delgado (pseudonym)

Yanitza Delgado is from a rural area of Tacana, Guatemala. She came to Georgetown in 1993 when she was 20 years old to work in the poultry plants. Yanitza has several other relatives in the community. When I tape recorded her story in the spring of 1999, she was torn about whether to return to Guatemala or remain in Delaware. She expressed nostalgia for her home and especially her parents. Recently, however, she purchased a house with her sister, where she lives with her husband and two children. Yanitza provides a view of the motivations, aspirations and conflicting feelings of the younger immigrant community members.

Having become involved in Sister Rosa Alvarez's support group for battered women, Yanitza began to exercise leadership among her peers. In the summer of 1999, she organized a Mother's Day party for Sister Rosa to thank her for all she had done for women in the community. From there, community organizers encouraged her to provide leadership for women in other projects. But with two small children, no English, and very little formal education, Yanitza explains that it is hard to do much. When I spoke with her in the summer of 2000, she said that the women's support group was no longer very active. Conflicting loyalties among the women themselves make it hard for them to maintain the group without the galvanizing presence of Sister Rosa. For her part, Sister Rosa has found her work increase astronomically as the number of women in the community has steadily risen.

Childhood Work Life

Well, my name is Yanitza Delgado, and I'm going to talk a little about my life, what I have lived, how it is there in my country. Well, I'm happy with my two babies. I have been here in the United States almost six years. I have my two babies born here. I came from Guatemala in '93.

Yanitza Delgado with her children. August 2000
(Courtesy of Katherine Borland)

The country [is] different here. I like it. I'd like to be both here and there. It's nice there. I like it there, because, because of what it is. And my family is there, my mother and father. And here I have my children, and my children's future is here. I hope that if they have a chance to be there for a time, it would be nice. I don't know what's going to happen (laughs).

Almost always we were working in parts of Mexico, in the town, in the highlands of Chiapas. We always maintained ourselves working in homes. Domestic work. We went only to visit my father and mother, and we came back to work. Almost always we worked from the time we were very small–this is what happens there in our country. Perhaps, for the economic situation one goes to work very young, at 8 or 10 years old–it's not heavy work but one goes with one's parents, helping them. I left home at 16, I left to work.

Yes. Because my sister, and my cousin went to work in the capital of Guatemala. And we one day went [there] with another sister, but we didn't like it. I don't know. And perhaps because we came late, but while we were in Tapachulas, I found work.

We always went with a sister or another friend. Three or four. We'd go. And we'd see each other on Sundays, on Saturdays. And there in Tapachulas the woman where I worked was very good, she liked me a lot. Yes. They say that there are people, when one does this kind of work, that one has to eat separately or… But with her no. Almost every place I worked, everything was nice. I felt good there.

Saturdays we'd get together only for a while in the afternoon. Well, there are girls who have Saturdays free. I didn't. I only went to see my sister, or she came to see me in the other house. Sundays, we had Sundays free. Or also, on Saturdays, if we could go out, we'd go and stay with our friends or to a farm to have a picnic, as they call it, that's it.

Before, when [my sister Evelina] was younger and alone, she made, wove belts, for the seamstresses. And I tried to do one, but it didn't come out. And the majority of people didn't use those anymore. Now everyone is wearing dresses. And so the belt,

127

well–because if one makes a belt and buys one of those [*cortes*] it's too expensive and also the cost of making it is very expensive, and there are very few people who use it. People wear dresses. Even though it's the prettiest, now they don't use it.

The Crossing

It took us almost a month to get here. That is, where there were guard houses, we had to stop short and go another way. We had to sneak in. Well, there were seven coming together. Since we had heard that various people were here. And that's why we crossed there. We had to cross a marsh. Do you know what a *pantano* is? It's a puddle of pure mud. Yes, it was a little difficult, but we did cross. And then we came here. It was a Tuesday, I don't remember the date now. We came men and women.

[My parents] never prevented us from having friends–yes, there are some, even today who, if you have a friendship or you're talking with a boy, they challenge you, "No, it's that, no," but my parents weren't like that. For me they are divine. I believe that all parents are divine for their children. My father never told me, "No, don't hurry, because you are there,"[65] No. He never forced us to do this or that. But we–I don't know. Understand that when we told him what we were going to do, we always helped our father in everything, in work, well we worked like men and women there.

And my other sister and my sister-in-law who I just heard from, we always worked in the fields. To fertilize the corn plot, plant the corn plot, and then in turn to raise the corn plot–we had to cut it, detach the cobs, carry it, and put it in the house. Because there is a *tampan* where you tie the cobs. And we put them there, and the corn lasts us a season, understand, because it is aired out. We plant a lot of corn. We don't buy corn–beans it depends how much beans we get, and if we don't have enough, we buy some. And always at our house, my mother always planted vegetables, and so we were able to eat vegetables.

---

65 The sense of this phrase is, life is fine at it is. Don't look to change it.

That is what I like about my little rock where my father's house is. Because it has water. And so, my mother, during the summer, has her greens. And so we eat fresh vegetables. All the time, normally, she tends them well, they have leaves, cilantro, herb, blackberry, and she plants potatoes, and my mother always harvests hers–although it's not sufficient, we do get it fresh.

Yes, how would I say it? Food. For example, beans or vegetables as I said, we had corn, it lasted the season. In other words, we still had some when the new cobs were ready. And so–I guess, yes well it was a dream for us to leave and to become independent of one's parents, and dress oneself. Because one is now older and no? One wants to dress according to one's taste. Because, now if one's fathers buys something, no well, he's going to buy what he likes and not what one likes, because and, and (laughs) one can't wear the same shoes as one's mother, no. And that was the reality. And we helped my father out, with money, yes.

Education

I went to school, but, I don't know, my own ignorance, well, I didn't like it much. Or also because there the teachers, a little thing (pause) there they hit you. They punish you. They hit you with rulers, and there was a teacher who hit his students with a belt. Yes. And well, there it happens, there's violence because there a person can't defend oneself. For example, because there, if a man hits his wife, if she wants to defend herself, she has to go it alone. If not, she puts up with it.

Yes, remembering my schooling, I went only two years. Because I also didn't want to. If not, well, perhaps, I don't know what would have happened. I wouldn't have gotten that far, but–I didn't want to either. My mother wanted me to continue studying. She told me, "At least go through to 4th or 5th grade, and then you can stop–bear it." But I didn't want to, and you see here. There are (Guatemalan) teachers, and we're all working in the poultry factory (laughs). But there are ways in which one needs [schooling]. Now, I know how to read and write. Not much, but a little.

My mother, yes, she knows how to read. My father no. My father doesn't know how to read or write. My mother knows only how to read, but doesn't know how to write. My mother didn't have any schooling. She learned by herself. They taught her only the alphabet, and that was what guided her. Then she knew how to read.

Well, I was there with my parents, and what I did, now at just eight, nine, ten–working, helping my mother in the kitchen or my father in the fields. That is what most people do there. They help out at whatever. I did that too.

The Difference Between Farming, Domestic and Factory Work

I don't know--we have different thoughts. One day a person was saying to me, "look, I just started to work, and you can buy a house, one day be an important person."

"Well, perhaps," I say, "but if I could, I would be there, but if not, it would be enough to be happy."

I say, "my stomach is full. I'm happy with my children."

It's a lot of work here.... For example, in Guatemala, it's one's own work. No one is going to come and say to you, "No, but you have to do your job, what you have to do in a minute, or in an hour, no. There we have to be at work at 8:00 in the morning. At 11:00, or 10:30-11:00, they give a *refaccion* as they say there, like a break–a glass of *pozole* or *atol* (grain drinks) or a bread to help you--20 minutes or a half hour--you know, since it's family. It's not, "no, just drink the *atol* and pun! to work." No, well, sometimes they begin to converse, being there [together] and "let's go another few moments!" It's your own work, and no one is forcing you. You don't have a supervisor, no one below [sic] you. That's it. But here, it's completely different.

Although, yes, sure one, one earns money. It's almost the

same. Because it comes and disappears, because at the end of the week, you have to pay this, to pay that. And that and that." Now nothing! Because there are people who come planning to, "I'm going there to earn money, no but, I'll do something, and in a little while, I'll send money, and this and that." And then being here, it isn't like that, because one has to pay for so many things. And with children, one has to buy things because it's one's own child.

Here in the poultry factory, at times you have to do what they tell you to, that you have to put at least seven, six pieces a minute, well, then you have to do it. Because, you're under a supervisor. It's not like there, when you're fertilizing the field, if you want to do your work more quickly and finish more quickly, you yourself have to hurry, and look...

We used to work together, my cousin Yvonne, my sister Sandra, and I. We had a mare which is a horse. We carried a *quintal* of fertilizer. We put it on the mare, and arriving there, we unloaded her. One person has to go and make a trough at the edge of the field. The other has to go spreading the fertilizer, And the other covering it–in order to work more quickly. We would go [indicates very quickly]. And to the other line. And then to the other line. And that way, one worked more quickly.

Or to say, "look but this isn't done correctly. You shouldn't do it this way." Or something. No. We ourselves organize–we'll do it so, in order to do it more quickly, and we'll go at such a time, or because we're doing this, or we won't go tomorrow, or we'll go the next day. And there's no problem. Because it's your own work...

Differences in Social Life

[Here] there were dances, movies, everything. But what happens is, we aren't accustomed to going. The truth is my sister has never danced. I went dancing once only. Because, I don't know. How can I tell you? Because, where we lived, understand that people are very religious, very stuck to religion. And if someone does that, it's a sin.

131

Dancers at opening of Gomez International. August 2000
(Courtesy of Katherine Borland))

But also there, they have parties, but they are spiritual, they are religious. They don't have parties there with dancing and all that. For that reason also, there wasn't any opportunity to dance. If there had been more of that, perhaps there would have been.

In our rural area we also have a church on Monday afternoons, but it's not Mass. It's our own preaching amongst ourselves. Yes. Mondays, it was in the local [Catholic] church, but if one wanted to have one in your house, one says, I want a service in my house on such and such a day–well, all the congregants would go. That's all that people did...

There everyone goes walking. To work, walking. Shopping, walking. Doing errands, everything is walking, since there aren't any cars. And so, that's how people get to know each other. You like someone [laughs]. If you want, then–my father also in this regard never told me anything–don't go out, don't have boyfriends or friends or anything. Simply since there, one–I had my first boyfriend at 16. Here everything is different. Or each person I think. For example, there one is dating, but it's only kisses and hugs, not sex. Nothing more. I was with a boy for 3 and half years, no sex. Nothing happened. I liked him he liked me. But he wasn't for me and I wasn't for him. He's also here, but not in Georgetown, he's in another state.

[Here] we were living out in the trailers. And there [I] met [my husband]. And something happened, and now I have these kids. He's from the same little town, the town of Tacana, and I'm from the rural area outside...

Residency

To be here without papers is very very hard. [If I had papers], I would faint from happiness. [laughter] So the first thing I would do, I wouldn't look farther, I'd go and visit my parents and come back, take charge of my children, without worrying about not being able to return. Having that would make things better. I would love it.

133

Delaware State Representative Joseph E. Miro and
Actor Edward James Olmos at Del Tech, Georgetown
Summer 2000
(Courtesy of R. Flores)

Carmen Garcia

I met 23-year-old Carmen Garcia in March of 1999. At that time she was both a member of the parents' advisory council for *Primeros Pasos* and a member of the battered women's support group organized by Sister Rosa Alvarez. Not surprisingly, she was much more outspoken and outgoing than many of her fellow Guatemalans and was willing to frankly share her experiences as a young immigrant. Unlike many Guatemalans in Georgetown, Carmen is a *mestiza* from Juliapa, Santa Rosa, in the southeastern corner of the country. As a consequence of her grandparents' farming success, Carmen was able to attend school and even received some professional training before adventuring north. She explains that in Santa Rosa the army posed no threat to the community and even helped in community service and charity projects. Her decision to emigrate then, was more personal than political. She was looking for ways to get ahead as an individual and as a woman, something she said was difficult to do in Guatemala.

Carmen emphasizes that she is alone in Georgetown, abandoned by her family and the recent victim of domestic violence. When I met her, she was looking for work, a difficult proposition for someone without documents. She lived with her daughter in a very basic house where each family rents a room off a main corridor and shares a common kitchen and sitting area. Nevertheless, Carmen was still in Georgetown in 2000 and appeared to be doing well. Her story clearly articulates the dual themes of culturally sanctioned domestic violence for Guatemalan women as well as the sense of freedom that young women experience upon coming to the United States.

Childhood and Training

[After I was born] my mother separated from my father; each followed their own life. My father has another woman. My mother is married. I have four siblings on my mother's side and

135

three on my father's side. And I don't have any full siblings. My mother, shortly after I was born, left me with my grandmother and left. I'm not sure why she left; she abandoned me. And since then, I lived with my grandmother, so now I call my grandmother my mother.

And then, when I grew older, my mother (grandmother) allowed me to study. Thanks to her–she worked very hard during that time–she sold tortillas. She sold corn, beans–what the people had to buy, my grandmother had it. My grandfather harvested it. My grandfather has a farm. My grandmother has cattle. My grandfather is self-sufficient. My grandmother has been also for the last 15 years. All her children grew up and made their own lives. I was the only one who stayed in the house. And so, since it was only me, my grandmother helped me to move ahead [in life]. She paid for my school. I studied mechanography, typing...

I went through sixth grade. I began secondary school, and at the same time, in an extra class, I began to study nursing. I've got six months of nursing. I got my basic primary and basic secondary diplomas... Someone who is in high school is someone who has money. There are many expenses. And sometimes what my grandmother gave me wasn't enough. So I stopped studying and began to work. And for a while I worked and studied, so I could be independent.

[I worked] in an office from 8:00 to 4:00, and then from 5:00 to 10:00 [I was] at school. And then I finished that period of working and study. And then I worked to maintain myself. I married at 15. [That's] normal... It's shocking when a girl becomes pregnant at 13 and has no husband or boyfriend and nothing happens, no one to take responsibility. But I married. I had a civil service, not in the church. And at same time, I worked and studied.

I worked for [a] pharmacy for almost four years. And I began to know many people from many places. I talked to the people. And when I had time, I went to help the young people who were collecting money for a good cause or project. Weekends I worked for the community. We always tried to help the poorest;

who didn't have enough to eat, who had many children, because many couples have five, six children there. [My] town [is] pretty large. It's got a first aid station, a hospital, it's got banks, a health clinic, schools–primary, secondary, kindergarten, all separate. It's also got a courthouse, it's got a private clinic, called IX. That's where all the people who work for the state go. It's got a first aid station thanks to the government and all who've cooperated, thanks to the [community organizing] committees.

We worked for the committee for abandoned single mothers, looking for assistance for them. We tried to help them. We tried to help them educate their children. There was a time when we taught people to read. We worked with 300 people. It was on weekends. We went to the rural areas outside the town, trying to help the people, and we never had a problem, thank God. Sure, there's always someone who attacks you, who says that what you are doing is not good. They always insult you. Because people insult one another there. They exercise their own justice.

Yes, once they tried to assault us. We were coming back, we were already close to town when some men came out and attacked us, and it was shocking because we were not accustomed to these things happening. Sure, in Guatemala, robbery and assaults are common. Very common. And then they saw that everything we were doing–and we were a group of all young girls–helped people older than ourselves... Literacy. It's a very good project. When the parents are interested in learning something, they learn. When they aren't interested, it doesn't work. It's like when we're here, and we have to learn English. The parents who need to learn, learn. And the others no.

Motivation for Emigrating

There are many people who come back from here, and they tell many stories, good things. And one thinks, if she could get

137

ahead, why can't we? And that's why I left there. Sure, I didn't ever have a bad experience with the guerrilla or government or anything because, on the contrary, the army helped us. The army never, never harmed us. When we talked to an official from the military zone to ask for assistance for the community, they always helped us. When we had the list of the people who were pregnant, the people who had many children, and we had to get them clothing, sheets, things for the bed, they helped us. For a time those from the military zone helped us a great deal. For us, the army isn't bad. On the contrary, they helped us with aid that they'd collected in other places where the military *had* molested the people, aid from the United States. They also gave it to the single mothers.

Yes, the reason [I emigrated], perhaps it wasn't economic–but because of my husband, the abuse–there were many reasons why we had to separate. For example, he never hit me, but he abused in another sense. Yes... When I told my grandmother, she said, "Look, this is your decision. If you want to leave him, leave him. But you must consent to do it. Because, I do not order you." They helped me in the sense that when I had my daughter, I was alone, because we already had many problems. I divorced when my daughter was six months old. Six months. And from then to now, I have not remarried. But we can't give up on life. I decided to divorce, and five days later I decided to come here...

The good thing is that my grandmother never tried to become her mother. She tells her, "I'm your grandmother, and the one out there is your mother." She always respected me that I'm her mother. Even though I'm so far away, though there are miles and miles of distance, she knows and respects me as her mother.

I was 19 [when I left].

In Georgetown

How did I get here? I came by car, I walked. I didn't encounter immigration [officers]. We were five people. An uncle, my aunt's husband, and three of their relatives. My aunt lived here. My aunt has been here nine years. She's gone now to North Carolina. She left a few months ago. I was left alone. I only have a [female] cousin here, but she doesn't help. She has a husband and child. She's distanced herself. Yes.

[When I got here] I felt very free. I felt I could make my own decisions. And because I felt free, what happened to me, happened. Not seeing my aunt. Their not having done what they said they would. It's that I lived far from Georgetown. During that time, I was very closed in. I wanted to get to know the community. I wanted to know the United States. And trying to get here to the center of Georgetown. Here I met many people–friends. I worked for Mountaire.

Even here, life is hard. Not only at home, because when I was left without work, my aunt and uncle left me. They abandoned me, and I had to look for other alternatives for how I was going to get on in life. I met the father of my daughter, I tripped again. I became pregnant, and after having my second daughter, we had problems. Being very different culturally, different in a lot of things.

When I started having problems with the father of my baby, through a friend I met Sister Rosita. I met the others there. And since that time, 1996, she helped me in everything. I wanted the father of my daughter to meet her. I didn't see him anymore, but she continued helping. At that time, I was in great need, as I am now. I didn't have a job. I had a lot of problems. I'm not working now. I need to work. And that's how I was when I met her...

[The father and I] had a lot of differences that we couldn't resolve based on character. Living with his family, his family attacked me. They said a lot of bad things about me, that I was doing [bad things]. I was working for a Mary Kay company, selling cosmetic products. I had to go out in the street to sell to get money. The jealousy started and mistreatment. The mistreatment began and lasted a year and a half. He broke things. By then I was pregnant, and we separated. Then, he came to visit, to see how I

Carmen Garcia and Sister Rosa
at the opening of Gomez International
(Courtesy of Katherine Borland)

was doing. He wanted to take responsibility, but he didn't say it in the manner that one should say it.

And then after we were separated, he attacked me. It got to the point that I decided to go to court. I wanted him to pay $20, $30 for the baby. He was making money–$300, $400 per week. And so, I decided he should give me something. While I was all the time spending, paying $60 in the day care, paying for diapers, for food... While on Saturdays, he would go to the dance, to drink; it was a sure thing, he wasn't going to come and pay me the money. The last time he came to visit, he destroyed the door, he hit me and made my head bleed. That was his character.

Nobody here helped me. They saw, they heard what was happening to me, but no one gave me a hand at that moment. They didn't even call the police while he was attacking me. Basically for them it's normal that a man hits a woman. It was a Saturday, June 2nd or 3rd, at 7:00 in the morning when we last saw each other. It had been three weeks since we'd seen the father of my daughter, because he'd hurt his leg. He couldn't work. I left it that he didn't have to help me, since he wasn't working. My work helped me, and then it was Saturday (pause) and after that, he came angry, drunk.

And so I thought it best to lock myself in. He didn't respect the closed door. He kicked it. And no one called the police. And they heard he was assaulting me. No one. Ay, I felt for my daughter, my daughter was in between it now.

"I've forgiven you the first, second and third times." I always forgave him. "Now it's over."

And he said, "If you call the police, you'll never see me again."

And I said "if it has to be that way." But even though he mistreated me, I loved him. Even now I can say that. But it hurt me what he was doing to me so I left him many times.

I left. I don't even know how but I left, fighting, while he was fighting with me. And I said, "you've passed the limit now." I left my daughter, I forgot everything. I left my daughter in there crying, yelling. She was not even ten months [sic] old. I left. I went to some friends' house. I called the police. But by the time they came, he'd left. He escaped. Now, if he touches me again, I don't know what's going to happen, because he's furious with me.

He comes. He's come twice, but I'm afraid of him. Because I don't want any more violence done on my person. So, it would be better for me to go. But I don't want to go, because I don't know–here I have friends, neighbors. I don't know what's going to happen. The day I'm most afraid is Saturday. I feel anguish about what might happen to me. It was a Saturday, like today, that it happened to me. And I'm very afraid...

Then, there's another person who works with Sister Rosa, who would go to the court to assist me. And up till now, things have gone well–not so well, but I've been able to keep going. And now with the day care program, that was also through Sister Rosita. She informed us and helped us get our children in.

[At the day care I am President of the] Parents Council... If they hire a new employee, we have to agree. If they dismiss an employee, we have to agree. Or we have to discuss–if there's something the center needs, we have to agree. We make decisions for the community. For example, we have another meeting regarding one of the employees, and we're going to discuss–it appears that they're going to dismiss her. So, if we agree, they dismiss her, and if not, they don't. It's composed of five mothers because no father wanted to share with us–none! And two community coordinators: Juan Perez and Gonzalo Martinez. They're the two who've helped us. And the director of the day care.

I like to be in this program because I see that it is a benefit for us. And of course, if we can't also bring in the men, as women we can do it. There are lots and lots of fathers, and not one of them wants to help! None of them collaborate. There are a few fathers that I know who aren't working and still they don't help; they don't want to feel that they also are important in this community. Here, we're all important, but if you don't do anything, they don't consider you important.

Because some of [the men] always say, "I'm the one in charge." That's one reason. And the second reason is a lack of will. If there's no will, there's nothing that you can accomplish. And we women are dedicated to helping one another.

Right now I'm taking classes at Del Tech. I like them. And I'm learning as well. On Tuesdays, we have [English classes] sponsored by the day care, just for the mothers. Five or six out of 50 mothers [attend].

Work

I work with borrowed papers. That's how I can work. I've worked for the Milford Perdue, for Mauser, Townsend's, Eastern Shore, Vlasic. The most basic is cleaning. At Mauser, I worked packing. At Townsend, I worked in the evisceration department where you clean the chicken, and then it goes to another department to cut up into pieces. There are other families that have helped us. Because they know we don't [have] papers, because they know we need to work. They know that the Hispanics are never going to do a poor job. Yes. We have the desire to work and we feel competent to work in a chicken factory.

[My reason to stay] is for the money, because in Guatemala, it's very expensive. It's very difficult to make any money. Here they pay every week. There it's every two weeks or every month. The same with debts. The only people who don't pay bills are those who live in the country... [My grandmother] says for the moment she's well. But she hopes that I will send her money. She hopes that we will help her. Because another of my aunts has arrived. She's in New Jersey. We're going to arrive and move things forward. Because each month, [my grandmother] will receive a small amount of money, which is a great deal of money there. [My other aunt moved to North Carolina] because they say there is better work there, because there are more opportunities than here. I don't know if it is true.

Here the community has helped us a lot... Here we try to help each other out. People help you. In my country, it's not that

143

way. There, each person looks out for himself. I see that there's a great difference.

Here you feel free because you have the right to everything. In my country, no. In my country, if you feel free, it's because you are already an older person, whereas here no. There, you are not free at 18. Here, whatever age you are when you arrive, there's no one to order you around. There's no one to shout at you. There's no one to hit you. There's no one to treat you badly. You aren't afraid of the thieves. You aren't afraid of someone abusing you if you're a woman. There you have to walk; here, everything is by car. Yes. I feel very free. Here each person makes money and spends it the way she wants. There no. There you have to think about how you're going to spend it without fear.

There you have to look at all the necessities there are. Because, sometimes, one's mother has six children. You've got to share among your six siblings. If your mother doesn't work for whatever reason, she's sick or she's lost a leg or arm, or for a physical defect, she can't work, the oldest child is the one who works for the other siblings, while the father goes out, wherever he wants, forgets about his children. And here, the mother can go out and work and fight and maintain her own children. And since there is no law there as there is here that helps women confront domestic violence, each person makes their own justice. And we can't get involved. Because the day when someone tries to intervene is the day they kill him. That's our problem.

Marta Chavez, and her children Saulo and Marisa

I first met Marta at the North Georgetown Elementary School at a graduation ceremony for the Summer Migrant Education Program. She was among a small group of adults who were graduating from Allison Burris's ESL class. Marta arrived in Georgetown in 1997, reuniting with her husband, who had emigrated nine years earlier. The family is from a suburb of the capital city, and so benefited from greater educational opportunities than Guatemalans who come from more rural areas. All of Marta's five children were studying in Guatemala and have continued to study and excel here in the United States. Her son, Saulo, even received recognition for academic excellence at the end of his first year in high school. And Marta herself is currently attending classes necessary for her certification as a child care worker.

The family's migration story reveals little of the political turmoil that affected so many rural Guatemalans. Financial difficulties led the family to consider emigrating and to endure years of separation in hopes of a better future. Mr. Chavez obtained his residency under the mid-1980s government amnesty for agricultural workers. Currently he works at the Vlasic Company and is trying to start an import business for typical Guatemalan handicrafts. The rest of the family followed the necessary legal channels to obtain visas and establish residency, but Marta explains it was a long, arduous process. I interviewed Marta at her Georgetown home in the summer of 2000. Her son, Saulo and daughter, Marisa were also present and contributed to the family story. This situation, as it turned out, was quite fitting since one of the strongest values in the Chavez family is unity.

In Guatemala

Marta: We come from Gueguetenango, which is a municipality of the capital city. We've met few people here who are from the city where we're from. Because the city has outlying rural communities and little towns, and yes, there are people here from the little towns, right? But I think those people have come here with the goal of coming, working, being here for a time, and leaving. Right? Because some have already left. And even if they have the money to go back and come back and work for another stretch, that's very lucky. I think others now aren't thinking about returning, because it seems the situation is that it's difficult for them to go back...

[In Guatemala, Marisa] worked in a bank, the other one worked in a store, a hardware store we call it, where they sell tools and construction materials for houses. He was already studying automotive mechanics and he worked in the afternoon in a mechanic's shop, a place where they fix cars, right? The other two were smaller. They weren't working yet. They were all in school and the three oldest were working...

I didn't get to take a lengthy professional career, because we were seven brothers and sisters, and I was the only girl, and the others took the basic course, that is, like high school. Then they continued at the University when they were already married. Because there one works more than anything. One works. At an early age, one works. And so I took other courses. I took technical courses. I didnt complete a degree. I worked in offices there as well.

And so then when I married my husband, we had livestock. We had a chicken house, with laying hens. We had a bakery. In sum, a flower shop, a barn with animals, cows, like that. A fully equipped barn. There were people who took care of the barn, people who made the bread, right? ...and the people who took care of the chickens and the hens. I mostly had to be concerned with receiving all those eggs that came into the house and putting the price on and packing them in boxes, so they could take them to the towns. That was my work. I always worked like that with [my husband] for a long time. But then in a flock of chickens, he lost almost six hundred chickens or a thousand, I believe, chickens that were already six pounds. So, that disappointed him. And a friend told him that he could work here, and without having to invest

Marta Chavez and her daughter, Marisa. August 2000 Georgetown
(Courtesy of Katherine Borland)

anything. Right? Because, what could we do? So, that's what made him come here.

It was rough. It was rough for us, because he left us. We even have our little house there, right? But he wanted us to stay with his parents. But I preferred to stay in my house alone with my children, because I have my mother and my brothers there in the city, right? And I knew they would help me–that we would see each other more often. And yes, when he left, it was very, very sad. After two years he came to see us for the first time, because, while he was here, when Bush was there I believe, he helped the immigrants to get the opportunity to get their residency. All the people who worked in agriculture. [My husband] worked in agriculture.

The Crossing

[My husband worked] picking crops. He tells us that picking is really hard. It's very hard. And so that's where he had the opportunity for them to give him his residency. After being here three years, he obtained his residency. That's when he filed all those papers. He claimed us, and it took nine years for all our papers to be processed. Right? Because he's been here eleven years now. And well, it wasn't a dream of ours to come to the United States. Because whether we liked it or not, we were accustomed to being there. And when he comes and it comes out– the residency, right? My residency is approved, and I want my children to come with me, and they say no. I have to enter by myself, because I had to come to work, and I had to show the embassy four monthly checks where they could see that I was earning enough to be able to allow them to leave the country.

And I had to do it. I didn't want to come, but my husband says, "Come and you'll see that here we will all struggle together, because it's not like we're together." And that's how I came, crying for them. I left them with my mother. And they stayed there another five months. Understand? Look, I worked here. I entered the poultry plant, working from 7:00 in the morning, when

I went in. I did my whole shift, which was almost eight hours. Right? I just came back to the house where I was living to eat something, and I went back [to work]. Because I left work at 4:30 in the afternoon. Understand? I started at the poultry plant at 7:00; I left at 4:00 or 4:30. I came home to eat something, because at 5:15 I started with the other evening shift until three in the morning. I worked one month like that. Because I had to send my checks to the embassy, [to show] that I was earning well so that they would let my children come. So, I was dying, then. I got really skinny, really skinny.

And so now, sending those checks–and another chunk of money, because they charged a lot of money to allow them to come here. So, that's how they finally gave them the way out. I did it mostly because I wanted them to be here then, because we had never not taken care of them. I was always with them. We were always together, always. If something happened to [Marisa], I knew about it. If it was a joy, we all enjoyed it, if there were a problem on the table, we all discussed it, including even the youngest. Because I said, "Even though you are small, God willing, you will someday be big, and from the time you are little, you are going to know what comes up." And that united us a lot.

Because I think that has helped us being here as well at [my husband's] side. It was my husband's dream, and now that we are here, well I think he feels satisfied by having accomplished that, because he thought a lot about it. Many of his friends told him not to bring us up here, because here [the children] would all become undisciplined. Right? But thank God they're going a little carefully–as I say, thank God. Something that has helped us is our roots and the way in which our parents raised us to be united. That's why we are all here together. If not, one would have not wanted to come. Another would have stayed there. It wouldn't have mattered to them, right? But we've always struggled together.

We spent nine years alone without their father, and with the effort he was making here, so that each of them would make something of themselves there in Guatemala–that helped them to take heart and to reach their goals–that one day they would do something, now through their father's efforts here. They have realized that it's not just through effort but they also know what they need. Right? For the future, more than anything. While God gives them life, they will continue struggling, because here the more you study, there's better work for you as well. Because I've noticed that. And the more one excels, well then, one is a little more comfortable. Right?

Choosing Delaware

My husband was in Florida, but while he was in Florida, he felt very contented as well. He worked in a store like Wal-Mart. And he hoped that we all would come to Florida, yes? To Homestead, I believe it was in Homestead. I believe there was a hurricane in 1993. I think it was Andrew, yes. It was so tremendous that from there he went to a friend who was in North Carolina, and from there, he came here. His nephew was here. He told him to come here. So, that's how he ended up here. He liked the little town very much. And that was another thing I asked him about–where was he going to bring my children, because I didn't want my children to come to a perverted place. Because, yes, there are parts that are very perverted, right? And he said, "No, I recommend it to you. I'm telling you the place where I am" because he came to live here—"is very peaceful," he says. That is, it's a very healthy atmosphere for them. Because, there's New York, there are all those cities where he had gone to see if they were–they were incredible!

And so when I came here, my son sent me a [letter], and [my husband] put it here [indicating her pocket]. And there were Black people from there, from the apartments and they thought he had put money there. But inside, he read the letter, right, from my son, and so he folded it and he put it away, and the thieves believed that it was money and they stole the letter. They hit him and they bloodied his forehead, and they opened the skin here, because they hit him with a rock. And when I came in, he went to the post office to look in the box. It was 6:00 in the evening, like that. It was still light out, and he went. And in the time that it took–he went to see a friend, and it got a little darker. So the people, the thieves followed him, when they saw him go by, they threw a rock that hit him here, in the spine. But that was the only time [we've had trouble]. So, then the police started to patrol there, because now more people reported that area right there, and now there's always a patrol car stationed there. That is, they've cleaned up the area; it's very peaceful now. Only that one incident [occurred].

The Poultry Plant

Because I did work in the poultry plant as well. I worked three years, and I was really sad to leave. Because I liked the work I did. I worked in "cut up", and I liked the whole area where I worked. They sent me one place, and I went happily, because I liked the whole area, and I worked at all the jobs there. And a time came when they operated on my hand. And so I just did work where I could move my hand then. While I was there I applied to *Primeros Pasitos*. I applied one Friday and then Monday they called me to work, that is, I left there then, I signed my resignation, and I began at Primeros Pasos.

When they examined me, the doctor said that they were just going to take off the callous and cauterize it, but when they looked at it, I believe that it had gone down into my bone. So they took skin from my wrist here. They took skin from here and they put it there. I didn't go to work for three months. But yes, I've seen that they do make other kinds of difficult operations on people. You see–a fellow worker paralyzed her tendon here from working so much. They operated on her shoulder, and it was a failure. It wasn't successful. There was this constant, constant pain in her arm, and that's how she was left, coming to work all the time, all the time.

Views of Other Poultry Workers

And I think they are American people with English, and I think that they could be working in something better and not there. Right? But I also think that they don't have the push to set themselves to study, or they've left high school and they don't like to study now, more than anything. Right? Because there are a lot of people there who could be working in something better, right? Earning more too. I asked fellow workers if they already knew English, why didn't they work in–but some didn't have their high school diploma, and they remained there, nothing more, and speaking good English and all. Right?

Marisa: For us the difficulty when we came to the United States was that we didn't know English. And when I see those people who work in the poultry plant, no? It isn't the worst job there is, because its a job, but one sacrifices a lot, and one gets hurt, because the meat is cold, really frozen, and it damages your nerves, your hands, and all that. But in reality, for many people–for us, as I say, its the difficulty of no English, but for them, although they know how to speak English, they have other situations. They didn't finish school, they don't like to study, or they simply adapt themselves with a little check on Fridays, and that's it...

Studying

Marta: I was making $8.00 an hour there. Here I'm making $6.64, because right now I'm a teacher's aid. Right? And God willing, when I finish my CDA then I will be earning like a certified teacher with a salary of $9.00, something more or less. Right? And it seems like—yes. There's a raise. It seems like going forward there are raises. I know. Apparently, the work looks easy, but it's a great responsibility to work with little babies. They bring you a two-month-old baby–you have to be watching it constantly, sitting it down, covering it up, like that, right? It's a great responsibility to work with little babies! But I love it, and well, I have the talent for it, and I like it. And there at times I don't just watch the babies, but also those who are walking, and those who can play, and all of them know me there now...

So in order to do my work well in a day care, that is, the State suggests that the teachers who are there should obtain the CDA. And so to do that there's a lot of training that you get. Right? Everything about the child. And that, well, I'm not worried, since I've had five children already and, as I say, nevertheless, I am pushing myself to get ahead. As I said before, I leave here at 5:30, 6:00 in the morning and I leave there [Washington, D.C.] from class at 4:30. That is, I have classes all day long. And in addition to going to class all day, they give me projects that I have to do every day, every day to pull them all together on Saturday and take them all the work that they assign. Written work and materials as well.

Saulo: Well when we came to the United States, the first year, in spite of the fact that I didn't speak English and my difficulties in understanding the teacher, I got straight As [in high school]. And for the same reason, there was a–I think it still exists–what's it called?–a Latino Association that helps Hispanics when they are excelling, and they give prizes. And yes, so they recognized me at an event in Wilmington, and they gave me two medals, and they had a really, really nice party for the people who had excelled.[66]

[Now] I'm the "Paper Work" guy at [the ESL/GED program], but I'm practically like a secretary. And I helped them make copies. If a teacher doesn't show up, I try to give the class, so the students won't leave, so they'll stay there. And that's everything I do.

Just recently, I started to work at a hotel in Rehoboth Plaza. And the 24th of August I'm starting college also, Del Tech [Georgetown]. I want to take a general business course. Optionally, that will allow me to be a director of some large

---

[66] This event is sponsored annually by the Latin American Community Center in Wilmington.

business, or I don't know. But it will open the way, and that's what I want. I want it to open the way for me.

I asked many of my friends who graduated if they were going to go to college or the university. They told me they simply weren't interested. Just getting high school was more than enough and right now they were simply thinking of working. And of all those who graduated, I think there were only two going to college, and the rest were simply going to work and to see what else they would do with their lives.

Marta: I believe that perhaps if there was some way of maybe helping them–sometimes there are scholarships, right? I know that there are scholarships to help them, but perhaps what counts is that they need good grades as well. That is what happens. Because if not, I think that with scholarships they could [go] as well, they would continue their studies. Yes? But since they are very, very simple people–like I said, they work at whatever job they can.

Saulo: And nobody helps them. For the same reason...

Marta: And nobody helps them. Exactly. In addition, they send whatever money they can to their countries, and they live here with the other half, That is, it's a very meager life for them. To continue studying above all in college, as I say, if they don't have a scholarship, they have to pay for college...

Marisa: When I came to the United States, and after three months of trying to learn English, I worked as a cashier in a Thriftway store, in a grocery store. Then, but it was part-time, and then they needed full-time and I still didn't have enough English to get a more professional job. And I went to work at Townsends, which is a poultry plant also. I went to work in the line there. With time I learned more English, and I was studying in college. They promoted me to line leader. After that, they promoted me to supervisor, and I was a supervisor of production in Townsends. And I entered the management-training program. After that, I worked for a time, and I was now studying business administration. And I saw that there wasn't any higher place for me to move up there.

So, I began to look around for some other kind of business. And that's how I found an announcement in the newspaper that comes out in English and Spanish, that is *Hoy en Delaware*. And I found an announcement from the American General Company. They were offering an opportunity for someone bilingual to work in life insurance. And that's how I spoke with the manager, who is Mr. Transforth, and he hired me, and I had to study to get my license in the State of Delaware–the license for life and health insurance. And after two months of studying, I went to take the exams. I passed them, and they gave me the license, and I began to work with the company as an insurance agent. They were trying to get into the Spanish-speaking market, and that was their purpose. But I also have English speaking clients. That is, I assist whatever client, in Spanish or in English in the different needs they have, like changing beneficiaries, increasing the coverage, and all that...

More often than not many families come to the United States not with the intention of staying permanently or making a career or thinking of the future. Many come to work for a time and, well, the children go to school, because it's a government rule that they have to go to school, and they go because they have to. Since we arrived, we came with permanent residency status. We thought that the change from Guatemala to here cost us so much that we weren't going to return in two years and make another change. So, we had to remain here for a time, and well, I was at the University over there, and I had to finish my university education in one way or another. So, when one has a goal, right? One has to work to achieve it. So, with us, I think that has also pushed us, that has also helped us to push ourselves to reach our goal. My brothers also have to finish high school and go to college to reach that goal.

Watching soccer with friends, April 15, 2001
(*Courtesy of Esteban Perez*)

Pedro Colon, Maricela Muñoz, and Reina Muñoz (pseudonyms)

I first met Pedro Colon, his wife Maricela Muñoz and her sister, Reina, on a visit to the Roxana apartments with former apartments manager, Pilar Gomez. When we arrived, they were outside visiting with another relative (they have several living in the same complex). Having lived in the Roxana apartments for ten years, they were about to move into a house in Georgetown. This means that they will begin commuting from Georgetown to Selbyville, where they both work in the Mountaire plant. The family articulates many of the sacrifices rural immigrants make on coming to the United States and the common problems they face here: dangerous border crossings, substandard living conditions, working without the chance of moving ahead, inadequate child care, and the costly struggle to attain legal status. When they emigrated, Pedro and Maricela left their two children with her parents in El Salvador. They have two smaller children with them who were born in Delaware.

Unlike their relative, who works in construction and has therefore picked up some English, both Pedro and Maricela get by without English in the poultry plant. They are concerned, however, that their young daughter learn English, as this will help her have a better future. Since this interview was conducted with Pedro and Maricela together, I indicate the different speakers in the transcript that follows. Maricela's older sister, Reina Muñoz (pseudonym), who joined the household two years ago, was also present and contributed towards the end of the interview.

Reasons for Emigrating

Pedro: I was born there in Canton Guaripe [El Salvador]. I came here because of the guerrilla. Also I am very poor, all that. One has to live—to look for another environment but, that's why we wanted to come. I came here to Delaware, and now I've been in Delaware for ten years. We were in Miami one year, but [moved] from Miami to here. Anyway, Miami was also a little more difficult, because at the time I arrived—I went there in 1989—it was very cold, and all the work got ruined. There wasn't any work so we came up here to Delaware. We had a cousin, and he was doing well here. He told me there was some work here and we came. We were given a job very quickly. I worked in what used to be Perdue.

Maricela: In Perdue, Showall, it's a poultry plant.

Pedro: Yes, in Maryland. I worked there for five years. Around 1995, I started here in Mountaire.

I have been here [in the Roxana apartments] for ten years. I have a lot of friends. I can go everywhere. I go to Georgetown, and many people know me. Since I like soccer a lot, and I go to the playing field to watch the soccer matches, I make a lot of friends there too. I like the place a lot because it is very tranquil. In contrast, I was a year in Miami, and I didn't like it because it was more dangerous, a lot of violence, and there are lots of thefts, there are a lot of gangs there still. And here, there isn't any of that. Here you can walk unafraid at night, and people are more tranquil, because everybody works here. Almost nobody robs here. I like the place.

All the people [who live] here [at Roxana] work...

Many people [have emigrated]. They have just come here, because El Salvador is a very small country, little, it must have about...

Maricela: There are 14 provinces.

Pedro: Yes, but very small, and I think that it has around 6 million inhabitants now and, out of them, there are like two million here [in the United States]. Yes, yes, there are many people here because of the same situation, because of the war that was going on. The situation got really ugly. There was lots of violence, robberies, kidnappings and all that. Later, the guerrilla movement, so people had to find a way to escape, because, for fear of

158

whichever side, the guerrilla or the military forces. The best thing for people to do was to look for another country. Since then we haven't returned to El Salvador.

Maricela : Well, as one says, we came here for two or three years, but once one is here, you don't leave. There, women don't earn money because they don't work, only men. And one sees that here one can work and get a check, and if somebody returns, that person wants to come back here again. And the travel through Mexico is very difficult now. And many people who are coming, they just end up dying in Mexico. On their way they are killed by Coyotes. Sometimes, even the Coyotes hit them, sometimes the Coyotes themselves kill them.

And for that reason one sees—one misses one's kids and all that. When I first came here, well when he came, my oldest [daughter] was two and the other, three months, and now the oldest is 13 and the other one is 12.

Reina: They don't know him.

Maricela: They don't know him. When they talk to him on the telephone, they say "Daddy, come back, because we only know you through a picture; we would like to know you in person." And so one has to cope with it, because one is doing this for the children. I am doing this for the girl, for Cindy,[67] right, so that she can learn a little bit more of English, so when she is grown up, she can come to the United States, and she will be able to work and know her English even for working and all. She'll know English to go work in a store, whatever. That's why, because if I take my [third] daughter to El Salvador, she is going to forget everything...

Also, because now we don't have a mother, his mom died, when was it?

Pedro: She died in October.

---

[67] Cindy is Maricela's third child, born in Delaware.

Maricela: In October it will be a year since she died.

Pedro: I couldn't go, because the return is difficult. I didn't risk it. Also in the same month I was sick. I had to have two operations. She had already died, and I didn't have anything else left there.

Maricela: People in a better economic position just come here with a visa, just to know the United States and later, they leave but not like we come, from the country and needing to work. The difference is noticeable in the fact that here one can work and earn money and back in El Salvador, there's work but only for the man and it's rougher work as well.

Pedro: Yes, because there in our countries, what they earn as a family is very little, and it is very hard to maintain the family. Also in these countries, people have very big families. They don't have three or four children, but most of them have 10, 12 or 15 children and to maintain such a family is very hard. That's why one does leave the country in order to survive because it is very hard back there. And the situation is getting worse every day. Everything is getting more expensive, and money doesn't have any value there, and our labor is not valued highly, because they pay very little. Yes, because what one can earn there a day is around two dollars or three dollars or four, and you cannot live on that. Yes. That's why you feel obligated to leave the country and abandon your family.

We are from small villages. Maybe with the people from the towns we can find [craftsmen], because in the town, the person who has a little bit more looks to open a business–setting up a store in order to get ahead. And finally, as you said, they become shoemakers, carpenters, anything–or they open a repair shop. But there in the villages, there is nothing else than to work in the field– to plant corn, rice, beans, and later the harvest until it is finished. From there you store some and you can sell some. So that you can go and buy your necessities. But then, what happens is you add it up, and you are going hungry now, because you can't pay, because you're working to pay off your debts, so working to pay your debts, then you can't be earning anything. There you endure hunger. Yes.

The Crossing

Maricela: When I came here, I spent three days and three nights in those trailers, in those big white boxes that one can see. And in order to be there, they had placed banana boxes in the back, so they could show these boxes or even to drop them if immigration stopped to take a look. Because the boxes were placed behind only, and we were placed in the front, and 125 of us came like that for three days and three nights. Once I got out, I didn't know what it was day–or night, nothing. And how, well, the peels! When I got out of there, everything was peels, because we were eating the green bananas, because I was hungry, and I had been without food for that period of time. That's why we came. Because we had a permit only to work.

Pedro: That's why one has to say goodbye to everything.

Maricela: When I came here, my dad told me "Look, daughter, are you decided? Will you come back or not? Will you see your daughters again?" But, since one is on the way, you have sold your life because, anything can happen. Just for any thing you can get killed, one doesn't know the cause but one can die. I told him "Well, only God is with me." But he was worried about my two daughters–that I left my two girls alone, and they were small.

Problems with Papers

Maricela: I worked for four years. [He] went to Montaire on January 26th, 1995, and I joined them in December, 1995. But, there is always a problem. Whenever the immigration permit is due, the personnel doesn't give you more work. As I told you, immigration always sends a letter. Immigration says that there is no expiration date for that. That's what they say, but here in the personnel office, no. They put you out, fired. Whenever my permit was due, the personnel dismissed me until the moment a new permit arrives. If the permit takes longer than three months, then I have to join the plant as a new employee again. And I will have to make less money again, because I lose all the time that I have been working there, and they don't take that into consideration.

Like the job where I am now, it is very tough. I have to work with a knife for eight hours and all my colleagues say, "No," they say, "they see that you've got a hard job. You will get a raise, won't you?" When I had an interview here in Georgetown, there were several people. Pilar was also involved but she wasn't there that day and there were several of us, and they asked us what the minimum salary was[68]. And there were several who said $5 and $4, but here at least where I am working, I make $7.40 an hour. But the other department where he works makes $6.50. But since he has been working for a long time, he makes $7.80.

But as I tell you, my job is not easy because I have to cut with a knife. Well the meat is already cut in two halves. We have to remove all the fat from the meat, and sometimes after using the knife so much, your hand gets tired. The work is very hard. The supervisors say one should hurry, but well, since they are not doing it, they cannot know. If they did this, they would know how difficult that job is…

Maricela: It takes effort to bring up children. I tell my husband, they are precious but…

Pedro: Yes, it takes a lot of effort because…

Maricela: They need a lot of care.

Pedro: They do.

---

[68] Maricela was one of the employees interviewed by the Department of Labor in their investigation of the poultry industry. In January, 2001, the DOL found that poultry industry standard practices result in underpaying workers.

Maricela: They cried because they didn't want the baby sitter. They cried and they told me "Mommy, don't go to work." I left them, with all my pain, but I had to. I spent some days working at night, but it was very difficult for me, because, when I left my work around 1:00 or 2:00 in the morning, I came here, I went to bed, and at 6:30, I woke up and got my daughter ready to go to school, and when she returned, she said "Mommy, don't sleep any more." I was tired. I closed my eyes, and I tried to open them, because I was afraid that they could leave the house...

Pedro: Later, when our daughter came home, and we didn't speak English, she didn't receive any help. The only [place] that she could learn was at school. At least now she is progressing. She forgot even what they said to her. Well, she could say the alphabet, the numbers, well with the numbers she has some problems.

Maricela: Yes, she changes [things around]. For example, she writes the letter "B" upside down.

Pedro: For the same reason that we cannot teach her either. We have to tell her how to pronounce the letters in English. How can we do it?

Maricela: They offer [adult English] classes in the little school.

Pedro: But very early, around 5:00 or 5:30. Then there aren't many people there. We should be speaking English, because we are in an English-speaking country, but I have problems with it. I have had many problems. To call the telephone company, the electric company to ask them to turn on the electric. I always have had a lot of problems, and I have been here for quite a long time, but I only know certain words...

I am not good in English, and I didn't have any education in El Salvador. There are many people who previously had their education, and they come here and start learning English. For example, my cousin, even without having an education before, he is speaking English, from his work, from the conversations with the people at the work, but I can't. When I had to call the electric and telephone company to cut the service, I couldn't do anything.

Other Kinds of Work

At least around here, there are people who like to work in restaurants, or like his brother, who is doing some construction work in the country. Because there are many people who don't like to work in the chicken factories. When I started in 1995, there in Montaire, I was making $5 per hour, and the ones in construction are making $8.50 or $9 or $10. That work is also very tough for them, right? Because in hot weather, ufff! But there are many people who like restaurants. I myself haven't worked in a restaurant, because I can't speak English, and you have to know it, because you may need it for something. At least his brother is working in construction. More or less, he is understanding how to do things.

In construction, they'll take a man like that, or in any store. But, as I told you, when the immigration permit is due. Well, not all of us work like this, right? Some of us have to buy *Tejana* papers, or other ones. But lately there are many problems with that because immigration is showing up a lot. Yes! They say that immigration was here the other day again, and they took Arturo's brother-in-law, well, several of them, they say.

And it's for that same reason, you see, because there are many people here who get in a lot of trouble or they like playing baseball, and they have fights and they themselves denounce each other to immigration. They say "This person is here illegally." Yes! It's a serious problem, that they are the ones creating problems. Among the same Hispanics, there are fights. If one has papers, the one who has papers says, "I am going to denounce the other one who doesn't have them," and in that way immigration officers come here.

They say there is a young girl who is from Mexico, and she has been arrested for a month. [Immigration] asks for $6,000 for some people, and they have asked $8,000 or $9,000 or $10,000 for her to be taken out of custody. Another thing is that if I have my little permit here, and one day immigration arrests me, and they ask me for $10,000, where am I going to get $10,000 or $6,000? I don't know how I would make it, and this girl is arrested in Philadelphia.

Well, I had an interview for immigration matters because my interview was in New Jersey, and the immigration judge was at the court, and I didn't get [political] asylum from immigration. I had a lawyer, and my lawyer charged me $3,500 for this. Imagine. Then I went to the court, and I didn't get the asylum. Then my lawyer made an appeal, and I am going to have to pay him $2,000 more.

Pedro: So the final sum came to $5,500.

Maricela: I had deportation orders, and they told me if I didn't pay....

Pedro: From the little we earn, saving and saving. We have to pay only $1,300 more.

Maricela: Yes, $1,300. We gave him $700 yesterday. Because here, when we don't have to pay for bills, we just make little deposits to the bank, $50 for example, and we have our little saving for any thing which may come—we deposit $50 or $100. When one doesn't have to pay for bills, you know.

Pedro: I already gave him $4,000.

Maricela: Yes, and then they told me that if I didn't pay for that bail, I would be deported, and if I paid $500 to immigration—that wouldn't happen. If I hadn't paid that, and immigration had caught

165

me, they would deport me. But this way, I have the right to leave voluntarily. I left voluntarily. When I went to the court...

There in immigration they have a Black woman working. I went that day, and I paid the $500 and she did nothing, nothing–and we were waiting. I was there waiting for at least a receipt, so that one day I could say that I had paid, and he asked her, and the lady said "Ah, I am working, you have to keep waiting," and we had spent the whole day in Philadelphia. We left there–well we had the court around 9:00 in the morning, and we just came from Philadelphia around 5:00 in the afternoon.

Yes, they gave [the receipt] to me, and what I am waiting for now is that–since my permit is due in November–I am thinking of going to have it issued again. I didn't say that, because I didn't want to have problems, maybe if I said it during my appeal, they could cancel my immigration permit. But I hope to get it.

Housing

Maricela: There were problems. We were living in an apartment and whenever we paid the rent, he discounted $21. Nowadays, he is not discounting us money, and he says it is because of the trash that he finds outside, but the trash comes from the people who get drunk. And as I tell my husband, "we are not responsible because the one who drinks is the one who leaves the trash outside," but he gets tired because people don't understand him right–but I think he should have contracted someone, a guard, all that–it would be good, right.

Maricela: You've seen on your right side a lot of little houses, right, a little before the prison, you know in Georgetown?... Well, for instance, the owner of those houses lives here in Maryland, she is the owner of the apartments in Selbyville the ones around the cemetery. She is North American and she is good. As I have told you, I have been living here for nine years and the problem is that here if something gets ruined and you report, nothing happens. For example, the air doesn't work well. And also, do you see this room? We have been here for a long time and they don't paint it, they don't do anything. Well, Guillermo wants to discount that from our rent, and when the cold weather comes, he charges us more for gas, around $30 or $40 more, because you can see how we are living here. [Pedro] has a brother, and he used to live here, and as you can see, the rooms are very small.

Pedro: Two rooms.

Maricela: Yes, two rooms.

Pedro: Well, [we are] five...Then [my brother] also slept at the house. There had to be a room for him too.

Maricela: Yes, because the children sleep with us.

Pedro: And also this area is very reduced because here the kids can't play because it is packed with cars.

Maricela: Yes, there are many useless cars and they never...

Pedro: And of course it is very dangerous because there are many people who get drunk, and they are close to the kids, and also the kids go there with their bikes, and can be killed by a car. And the other place is very tranquil and looks very nice. It is very tranquil.

Maricela: And there is a nice backyard for them to play.

Pedro: Yes, there is a lot of room for them to play.

Maricela: And the water is O.K, and here we have to be carrying– with those gallon tanks, we have to go and buy water,

Pedro: Water for us to wash ourselves, to drink and cook, because one cannot cook with this water.

Maricela: Yes, they say that they have talked to the Health Department but the Health Department never…They have a system so that whenever the health inspectors comes, the water is okay.

Pedro: Yes, I have been carrying water for ten years.

Maricela: Well, I have been doing that for nine years, that I completed on June 16th, because I left El Salvador on June 4th, 1991, and I arrived here on the 16th of June. I have been carrying water for nine years. I want to wash my children, and I have to buy the water and later, after washing them, and they go to bed, their whole bodies itch, probably because of the chlorine.

Pedro: But one goes to wash [clothes], and one is already prepared to carry water.

Maricela: I am going to wash and I am washing and I am bringing my water from [the Laundromat]. One has to do whatever is necessary, because if there isn't water, one has to go get some.

Pedro: The good thing is that there is a launderette here, and one can go and wash the clothes, and one can bring water, nobody says anything if you take water.

Reina: Well, now it is different.

Pedro: In other parts, they don't.

Maricela: At the launderette, they don't like it.

Pedro: There was water but they cut it off, because they didn't like people bringing it to their houses.

Maricela: Yes, they cut the water. They did that here too…

Pedro: Well, the other house, the one we want to rent, has four rooms and we will pay $600, but it has four rooms. It is much better because each of us will have a room...

Maricela: And the grass is already tall but the landlady is going to cut it for us, because we are going to move, and we are going to live there, we have to cut it.

Pedro: And the water problem is going to end, because the water is okay there.

Maricela: And we are not going to be limiting the water so much. And if you are washing something, you will be able to run the tap, and the water will come out fast and abundant. But here, if you are washing or doing something, you have to take the water out of the gallon...

Back in El Salvador

Reina: I am the eldest, I am a year older than her. There are only two of us in the family. So my mom is there. I came here to help them, because they don't have any help, only the little help that I could give them when [Pablo and Maricela] were there. And I have lived with [Maricela's] daughters for seven years, because she left them in my care. And once I saw that they were grown up, I decided to come.

Maricela: That's how we did it before, because she was in El Salvador before, and we worked to send them money for the whole family. Because my mom is going to be 64 years old on the 17th. My dad is going to be 63 years old in January, and they are already [old]. Well, my dad loves working. He wants to come here to the United States. We wanted to get a visa for him, right? But he didn't want to. But you know why? Because if he comes here, he is going to like it, and he is going to be working there in the fields.

169

Reina: And that's what I don't want for him.

Maricela: He works from 5:00 in the morning to 5:00 in the evening.

Reina: He is already old.

Maricela: But he said, "No, maybe I would work even longer."

Reina: But he doesn't want to come because he has her two daughters.

Maricela: Since my two daughters are there, he doesn't want to come here.

Reina: And her two daughters are already grown up. They need some respect and old people also at the house. When there is no respect in a house, there is not a man, an adult person. Well, the truth is that he is fine there. The important thing is that he is healthy, so he can work and fight for them.

One is in the fourth grade, and the other one is doing fifth grade. I went to fifth grade and [Maricela] stopped at fourth.

Maricela: Oh, but then my Dad only permitted [studying] to fifth grade, because there was no money, and he couldn't pay for that. He was the only one working, and he didn't receive help. So he took [Reina] out of the classes. If she had continued studying, she would have been at least a secretary or something similar.

Reina: I knew. I liked it, but we couldn't.

Maricela: No, she couldn't. Well, when we were children, younger, there are people who....Reinita doesn't like cooking, washing or ironing, and there, people already asked me if I wanted to go and wash or iron. If there were more like us, because we did it on our own, we worked in the kitchen for well-off people. I went there, I said goodbye to my mom....Yes, and [Reina] stayed with my mom. I got the money and we bought for all of us.

Reina: And we bought our own clothes.

Maricela: Yes, we bought our own clothes. We never had a party, or we never bought a ring, a chain, because my dad didn't make enough money with his work. So we didn't buy anything like a ring, a chain, not even a watch because we needed the money...

Maricela: [Here] at least, whenever I get my check and the money, I give them to [Pedro], and he carries the money. Because I am not used to wearing handbags. I have one around there and my daughter plays with it, but I don't like them. I have this because Reina gave it to me, but I don't like them. I never used those in my country. Then only people carrying more money use them, but we weren't accustomed to that.

My mom, as I say thank God, since we are living here, she is in a better position. Now that her birthday is coming soon, I already sent her a pair of shoes, I sent her a pair of earrings. She sent her a chain, with her name on it. Now she is living much better than before.

Joe's Market. Georgetown. August 2000
(Courtesy of Katherine Borland)

Nevy Matos

A good number of Dominicans have settled around Seaford. The first, Mister Arizmende and his family, originally came here by chance. Arizmende was a professional, who was hired by the DuPont Company in the 1970s. He remembers being in Delaware and missing the foods and products of his home country. At that time, Hispanics might have to travel as far as Baltimore or Washington to get specialty items. Seeing a need, Mr. Arizmende opened a store in the 1980s, JAR Groceries in Seaford. Recently, he has opened another in downtown Selbyville. These stores serve not only the growing Dominican population but also other Latino groups. Arizmende says he carries a bit of everything with regard to foodstuffs in addition to providing Spanish language videos, music and newspapers.

Nevy Matos, who lives in Seaford, says that when she arrived in 1994, there were about eight Dominican families in the Seaford area. Now there are, Nevy estimates, ten times as many. Nevy explains that many come from New York, fed up with big city life. Delaware seems like heaven to them in comparison.

I first met Nevy Matos one summer Sunday at Dios de la Maranatha Church in Seaford. She is a vibrant woman, gracious in welcoming strangers. Nevy was born in Santo Domingo, capital of the Dominican Republic, in 1958. She emigrated first to Puerto Rico in 1987, where she lived for four years illegally, before obtaining her residency. In 1994, she moved with her husband to Delaware where she now lives. Her husband, an upholsterer by trade, now works putting in insulation for the DuPont Company. Nevy works at Vlasic Company in Millsboro as a machine operator. She regards the storefront evangelical church as central to her sense of community here in Delaware, although she became a Christian only last year, after a long struggle with her husband, who was brought up in the church.

In her description of her early life in the Dominican Republic, Nevy stresses the severe poverty she and her family endured. She emphasizes the great difficulty of emigrating to a place where one knows no one. Nevy gives a detailed picture of the risks of crossing the notorious, shark-filled waters of Monkey Strait, between Puerto Rico and the Dominican Republic. She identifies schooling as an important factor in her adjustment to her new environment. Nevy completed secondary school in Santo Domingo, even though she was poor, had married at 13, and already had a child when she graduated. She describes herself as a lifelong learner and has taken advantage of English Classes at Del Tech. Here, then are excerpts from Nevy's story.

Early Life

Yes, well, my name is Nevy Matos. I come from a very humble family. My mother died, and I was left in charge of my brothers and sisters. We were five brothers and sisters. I was the oldest of the girls. And when my mother died, I was already married, because I married when I was 13...

In my country it's normal that a girl marries at 12 or 13, it's normal—at that time, not now. Now the person prefers to train a little. If I had had that experience—if I had had that mental maturity, perhaps I would have prepared myself mentally, physically and also economically with a profession or something, but I didn't think of it. Often, necessity impels you economically to do things that afterwards, when you mature and you say to yourself, "*Caramba*! Why did I do it? And why didn't I wait?" But it's inexperience that makes you do those things.

And I had married thinking that I could study, because I didn't have the economic resources to study, and with the man I married—I was 13; he was 40—I thought that I could give myself a better economic position, especially for me and my brothers and sisters who were the ones I was looking out for. My family, my brothers and sisters. And I was thinking about that.

But when I married, everything turned around. It wasn't what I had in my head. And then my mother died, and I was left responsible for my brothers and sisters by force. And then, getting ahead with my brothers and sisters, because my father abandoned us, and I was left responsible, when I was still very young for all those kids. They were four—three boys and one girl—and I alone had to go forward. Because, regrettably, with my husband that I married, he was an alcoholic as well. But I didn't realize, and then I saw it, because then, after one shares one's life with someone, you really get to know him. And I hadn't known him [before]...

...I worked sure. I worked because that's how I supported myself. I worked. I sold juice at the school. I made—I don't know how you call it—but in my country they call them "Johnny Cakes..." I got to where I had a little *colmado,* I don't know what they're called, but it's where they sell food...

To make enough to eat, to take care of my brothers and sisters, and my children, you would say to me, "Look, come clean for me, and I will give you a plate of food." And I went and I cleaned for that plate of food, to take it back to my family. That's how I worked in my country. I never worked in my country for the government, [as] a government or private employee, because I found it difficult to get [that kind of job.] When I applied, for one reason or another, well, because I didn't have experience, because I didn't have schooling, because I didn't have a profession, for whatever reason, they didn't give me work, they didn't give it to me. So, well, I had to build a life as best I could, look for [a way], because I had to survive.

The Passage

When I decided, when, when I decided to take the boat— I'm 42 right now, and I came here in 1987—and I remember, I remember it like it was today that it was May 17th when I decided to make that decision. It was curious because I really wasn't thinking about it. Instead, a boy came and he said, "There's a trip in a *yola*[69] and I'm going to go."

---

[69] Yola refers to a small motorboat used to transport people across the open sea.

And I, "Well, I'm going with you," and so, "where is it going?"

"Puerto Rico."

I told him, and so he said, "No, we're going today."

I said, "Good, I'm going today."

And he says, "No, if you don't have the money, you can't go."

And I, "How much do they charge?"

"They're charging 1,500 dollars." 1,500 Dominican pesos from my country, and they're charging that.

So, I said, "I don't have it, but I'm going to look for it."

And he said, "No, you're not going, because we're going right now."

And I said, "I'm going, I'm going in that *yola*," I said.

So, he left. He left that night at about five in the evening, and I left at eight in the morning the next day, because I didn't have the money to go, and I got it, I got a loan. And then I went to the place he told me, and there were all the people together.

But now that *yola* had come back three times, and that meant that each time a *yola* returned, each time it went back with 50, 70, 75 people. It was that they took money from those people each time, because each time it came back, new motors had to be bought, because they couldn't go back then with those motors they had, they had to abandon them and buy new motors. Imagine the number of people! Since they had come back three times, more than 200 people, like 300 people had been able to leave, who wanted to go on that trip, because they'd gotten their money together....

It was very difficult. It was really hard because they were fighting with sticks, with knives, with rocks, with bottles there. There they were fighting with one another, because everyone was fighting, wanting to get in the *yola* to go, to come here. And the trip was to Puerto Rico. And it was really difficult, because I, I never thought that things were that way, to that extent. What I did—it was about six in the evening, and I said, "Wow! and what is this?"

176

And that's when I said, "No, because they're going to kill me here." And I grabbed and I pulled myself up into a tree, I pulled myself up, well.

I said, "No, I'm going to wait until this commotion settles down," because they were fighting with knives and bottles and everything. I saw it in the air, and it was getting dark, and I saw the machetes like that and the knives in the air, like that they grabbed you there (laugh/sob) and they were dying!

I said, "Lord, well, my God. What is this?"

And I climbed up, but I'd already given the money to one of the people that one had to pay. Because they made a list in case the *yola* capsized, they drowned or something, so they would know the number of people who went in that *yola*. And so that was already written down and all, and I paid. But when I saw that, I climbed up and I say, "I'm not going for them to kill me, not like that!"

But the one who was the captain of the *yola* saw me, and he said, "I'm not going to leave until that girl gets down and you bring her to me." So, because the *yola* wasn't anchored at the shore; instead, they anchored it about 15 meters out, because it couldn't be on the shore, it had to be away from the shore, and and and—the *yola*. So, they came to get me in what they call a *cayuquito*. It's a tiny little *yola* but with oars, those that you row. They came to get me and another pregnant woman, and then they put us on board and we left.

In that crossing, I think we spent, uh, two days in the water, because—on the high sea, what they call Monkey Canal, that's always—when the weather is bad, that churns and all, the waves get bigger. A wave came over us and broke two planks, and it was filling up with water. That's when they, the captain and those others there tell us to bail, that is they tell us to get the water out. They say, "Bail, bail!" And that we get the water out of the boat, until it is all empty, because if not, we start sinking. So, two or three men came and they put nails in and they managed to close up the water hole that was there, the leak, but it was serious because it was two planks, and they were planks of this width that just flew up when that wave took us up and threw us down. That's when the planks broke, when they came loose.

So, well, that's how we managed to keep going and we arrived, and I remember that we arrived in Puerto Rico. We arrived in the afternoon; it would have been around five in the afternoon. But we couldn't disembark, because immigration was there that day, we couldn't disembark, and we disembarked at around ten at night. And anyway, immigration grabbed a lot of us, because at that hour three disembarked, three other *yolas* that came from other points of the Dominican Republic...

From there I didn't know which way to go. Imagine arriving at a strange place where you don't know anyone and where you don't know what you're going to do or what is going to happen to you, at that hour, it was ten at night when we arrived, and we threw ourselves into the street to walk. And we came across two people who picked me—us up. Because my eyes were all red, my eyes had gone red from the exposure to the sun, from the sea and the water, and I was totally burned, and my skin was like that from the sun, because it was an uncovered [boat] that I took.

And a woman took pity on me and said, "Let's go to my house. I will give you food." And she provided me with clean clothes, food—milk and cookies—that's what we ate. And then, after, we continued our route because we were, let's say, from Wilmington to here, that's the distance we were going, and then, well, when we arrived there, I arrived at a house I didn't know, because—I had set out and I only had the telephone of a woman who I didn't know either. That woman. They gave me a reference, a woman who is like my mother said, "You can go to that house in confidence, because I am sending you."

I arrived at that house—that is hard. It's hard, because when you leave your country looking for progress, looking for a better life, for yourself and your family as well, it's hard when you arrive. And if you find someone who gives you their hand, who tells you, who gives you, even if it's just a roof to sleep under and some meals, so that you can get fixed up with some work or something—it's nice. And I thank God a lot, because, well, when I arrived here, I found that outstretched hand, the hand of a friend. And I got to know a woman. I said that she was my mother, even she—when she saw me, "Call me Mama Celeste." And I called her Mama Celeste...

At the bus stops, they took away people, immigration, but I never had that problem because I knew my condition, that I was illegal. So, what I did, I worked in people's houses as a sleep-in [maid]. I stayed there. I didn't have to be walking around, catching buses, going out, coming in, risking my life and at the same time having a bad time. So I stayed in people's houses working as a sleep-in [maid]. After that, when I became legal, when I had my residency, then what I did was, I got cleaning work where I went in the morning and came home at midday or whenever I finished my work. Then I would go to my own house, but then, by then I didn't have any problem...

I spent four years illegal because there was a law that was the amnesty. And the Amnesty Law allowed the people who had been illegal for "x" amount of time, could become legal....

It's very curious, what happened was, that at that time, when I married—I don't know if it is all right to say it. But I married there in Puerto Rico and I obtained my residency. It wasn't something that I was looking for, because when I married, I didn't think that things were going to come out the way they did. But, I think that the person I married, what he did was very damaging. He did a lot of damage. He even got to be a drug addict. And he took—he robbed, we're going to say it that way—he stole a lot of money from me...

In Delaware

I left. I determined to leave Puerto Rico—there were three reasons that motivated me: in the first place, I lived all the time in San Juan Santurce in Puerto Rico, and life—everything was still really hard. And I had already brought my two children, who were adolescents by then—from the Dominican Republic. And I had them studying in a school in Puerto Rico—public, that's called *Facundo Hueso*. In that school they were studying and they came and attacked my son there and they really beat him up. Then, afterwards, they went to my house to attack me, and in Puerto Rico they use–the houses have to have those bars, to be barred with iron bars, the windows and all, because there is too much delinquency and robbery there. So, they went to my house to attack me.

My [third] husband had already decided that he had to leave Puerto Rico. His work was getting really difficult by then—he is an upholsterer, what they call in English an upholsterer, that furniture, chairs on boats, planes and all. And by then it was getting difficult for him, because there was a lot of competition with the Hispanics that were arriving there illegally. Anybody was opening a workshop, and they did the work for nothing. And so, my husband said, "I'm not going to throw my work away. I'm getting out of here." And that's when he decided to go to Louisiana. A nephew of his lives here and his brother lived here in this state. And when he arrived in Louisiana, he called me and said, "Get everything ready and put it, put it on a ship going to Louisiana." He gave me all the instructions, and I called a company, I got everything ready, and I put it on that ship for me—that was going to Louisiana. And suddenly, when the ship—I had sent—the ship had already come to pick up the shipment from my house, and he calls me, "Did you put the things on the ship?" I say, "Yes, they already came to pick them up." "CALL IMMEDIATELY and tell them to send it to Delaware." And I said, "But I don't know if they take that route." And he says, "No, call, call, because it can't come to Louisiana. I'm going to leave Louisiana today. I'm going to Delaware. They called me that there's work there and we're going there." I said, "Ay, my God!" But I don't want to go, really, I didn't even want—in spite of everything, I had my doubts about going, because my two children were born in Puerto Rico, the two small ones, and I had my doubts about leaving Puerto Rico, for the same problem that they spoke—everything was spoken in English. And I said, "And then,

Nevy Matos at Seaford
(Courtesy of Katherine Borland)

how am I going to speak there, if everyone speaks English and I speak Spanish, who's going to understand me?" And that was my concern about moving from Puerto Rico to here...

And even when I went to buy my ticket at the agency, I tell her, "Delaware," and she says, "Delaware? And where is that?"...

It's something that I value a lot, for me it is very valuable, to arrive illegal, through great sacrifice to get your residency, and then with more work to make yourself a citizen, because all this requires sacrifice...

Learning English

When I came here in '90, '94, I came in 1994, I didn't even know how to say, "table" in English! So, wherever I went, I had to find a person to help me to interpret.

And I said, "No, but from here I have to go forward; I can't stop short in this way!" And I asked around, and I found out, they told me that Del Tech gave free English classes. And I went there and took two hours, two days a week. And that's how I began, little by little, little by little, until today, I can fend for myself, and I have work where they raised my position. I went to ask for a change, to be a machine operator, eh, I can write, I can read. I can understand in English whatever thing they say, not perfectly, but now I don't have to go around looking for a translator to translate for me. And speaking and–some things that I don't understand, well, I can go back and ask about what I didn't understand, what was it they told me? And I can understand what they tell me. And today, I can say that I'm a citizen, that in this state I did it. This requires thanking the Lord a lot, and thanking President Clinton as well and so many people from right here, Americans, who have extended their hand to me, and who have helped me so that I can move ahead.

It's what helped me a little, because there are a lot of problems here with many Latinos, or let us say Hispanics, who come from Mexico, Guatemala, and that was their problem, not knowing either how to read or write even in Spanish. There are many people who don't even know how to sign their own name. And there isn't a school here or an entity that can help this type of person who emigrates. And often because they're afraid—because they're illegal and they don't dare look for help, because they believe that immigration is going to catch them or something. Many of them go to private doctors even, because I've gone with many of them as an interpreter. And they're afraid of going to public places because they're afraid immigration will catch them.

And that's because they don't have an orientation to direct them and tell them they have rights, simply because, if they get sick, to receive medical assistance. If they need some economic aid, to look for a place that can provide it. But since they don't have that help, that understanding, many of them get stuck. And they don't open themselves up, as they say, to ask for help. But because of that fear and ignorance, of not understanding, that happens a lot. And I have talked to many of them. I tell them, "No, it's not like that. You can ask for help. They have to give it to you. That's separate from immigration. That doesn't have anything to do with the fact that you are in need, you are sick, and you go to a hospital to look for the help you need."

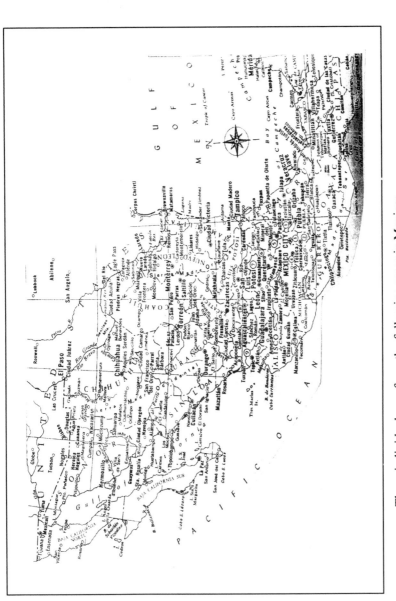

These individuals are from the following areas in Mexico:

Margarita Gonzalez .... Juarez, Chichuahua
Rosario Hernandez .... Cuacoyula, Guerrero
Maria Lopez... Zacatecas
Maria Martinez .... Matamoros, Monterrey
Maria Mendoza.............................. Rio Bravo, Tamaulipa

ENTREPRENEURS

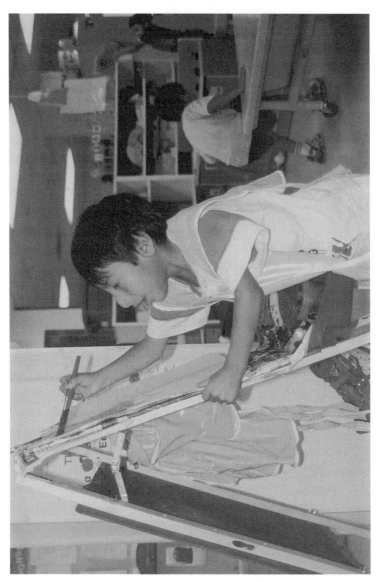

Hulisis Perez, August 1998
(*Courtesy of Allison Burris*)

Wilson Hidalgo

I first met Wilson Hidalgo at his small store on Pine street in Georgetown. The store carries clothing, some basic foodstuffs, music tapes and other small items. Apart from being the only Cuban immigrant in the area, Mr. Hidalgo is also a poet. He dedicates himself to the love of poetry, an avocation that he shares with a few other Spanish-speaking residents in the area. He is a particular fan of the Cuban poet and 19th century nationalist, Jose Martí. Mr. Hidalgo has a small sign posted in his shop window advertising literacy instruction in Spanish. When I asked him about the sign, he said that, being from Cuba where education is a right for all people, and being a former teacher himself, it pains him that many of the new residents in Georgetown cannot even write their own names. Therefore, he not only provides services as a writer, but tries to encourage young men and women to learn to read and write in Spanish as well.

Mr. Hidalgo's immigrant experience is unusual for the area. Since Cuban immigrants receive special status under current U.S. immigration law and since he arrived with a visa, he has had few problems obtaining legal status. Ironically, however, Mr. Hidalgo freely admits that he did not come to the United States to escape communism. Rather, he fled the worsening economic situation that has obtained in Cuba since the collapse of the Soviet Union. The father of four grown children, and thrice divorced, Mr. Hidalgo is worried about helping his children back in Cuba, whom he misses terribly. A strong thread running through Mr. Hidalgo's narrative is the belief that with faith and sacrifice, anything is possible.

Life in Cuba

I was born in the country, from a peasant background. I find nature fascinating, I love the countryside. With the revolution,[70] I went to the capital to study. I was able to study. I studied a little of everything, although I didn't finish anything. Before that I was in the army. From there, I studied education. Then I was studying nursing. And then I was at the Naval Academy of the Merchant Marine. And after that I left my studies and went back to my town to begin working. I started my teaching career, and I did that for eight years. After that, I developed a vision problem, and my doctor recommended that I change jobs, and I went into business. I come from a family of traders, and I like business...

In Cuba I didn't have a store. In Cuba I worked for a government business, even though I grew up in a trading family, because my dad and my uncles did have businesses, but they had them before the revolution. It changed with the revolution. Everything belonged to the government, to the people, and so then, a life of independent employments didn't exist anymore. Small businesses remained, in the countryside the agricultural fields remained private, but in general, the rest of the businesses became government property.

What can I tell you? I have a beautiful family. I have four children. My mother is still living; my father died many years ago. My children are more friends than children. I have always assisted them, whether I was close by or far away. Right now, I'm helping them from here. I send them money. I send them what they need to fulfill their lives, because they are working there as well. They each have their job. I have two who have professions, who are married, and the two younger ones who aren't married. Really, I never thought about coming to the United States. I am a very family-oriented person. I like to be home close to my family. So one always feels good being close to them.

---

[70] Cuba experienced a socialist revolution in 1959, led by Fidel Castro and Ernesto Ché Guevara. One of the priorities of the revolution was to make education accessible to everyone.

Decision to Leave

In 1995, I had the idea of coming to the United States. It was like an explosion for me, because I had never thought of coming to the United States. Moreover, many people in Cuba took four, five, ten years to get out after they decided to go. My case was completely different. I had never thought about it. One day I gathered my children together. I told them in the month of December in 1994. I told them I would come to the United States, that I was going to travel to the United States. That was a decision that my family didn't believe at that time. Because I didn't have any possibilities to come here. I don't have family here. I didn't have any way to get the money for the trip. Nevertheless, I made up my mind. I arranged my trip between December and August 1996.

In 1990 the country's economic situation really got worse when the socialist camp fell [internationally], when that tower that nobody thought could fall, tumbled. I think that not even the United States itself nor any other developed country in the world thought that socialism or communism was going to fall on an international level. In our country we had all our help from the socialist camp, and so then in 1990, it got worse. And then in 1991, 1992, the economic situation in the country became unbearable. So, due to economic problems–because I never had any political problem, I never got involved with politics–I decided to leave the country in 1994.

Look, in those years the United States had already approved 20,000 visas for Cubans a year. So, in the year that I left, 26,000 people left, because the group leaving from Guantanamo was also included, and they were counted among those who entered the United States that year. Logically, in order to leave the country I had to get all my papers in order, go to the American Embassy, request permission to leave from the Cuban government. Well, for me it was a little difficult. At that time they were only charging $250 to leave the country. So, the Cuban government raised the quantity that one had to pay to $900. Since I didn't have any family in the United States, where was I going to get $900?

I think it's worth telling. I had a revelation. Do you know what a revelation is? My situation was so difficult that one time my mother called me and told me to give up traveling to the United States. She said I had my family in Cuba. I had my children, I had her, I had my house. I had work, really I had everything. I should give up going to the United States, given the situation that she saw that I wasn't going to be able to get $900. So, I told her to stop trying to make me give up, because I had already made up my mind to come to the United States. I had faith in God and I was completely decided that I was going to resolve that problem.

And I had a revelation. I did everything that was shown to me in my vision, that I was dreaming. I was asleep, but I understood that it wasn't a dream. And truly, my answer was just this: "My God, if you put this in my path, even if I have to fulfill your command on my knees, I will do it." (I am a man who has always refused to beg. Moreover, I have been here in the United States for five years. I have my store, and I have never asked for money from anyone. I have succeeded in everything little by little through my work and my effort.) So, then I had to go and call at the doors of the churches, and I truly submitted myself. I called at the doors of several churches, even though I knew that they couldn't [help me]. So, then, well, I went to the Bishop of the Catholic Church. And it wasn't easy.

I think I had three meetings with the bishop, and they were very tough. But I felt supported by something, and I knew that it was much more powerful than me. It was supporting me and speaking through me. Actually, the bishop told me twice that he couldn't help me but the third time he told me to come the next day, because he had thought about what he should do. There were even moments when we crossed words, not swear words, but persuasive words. And I think he came to understand, and he signed a check for $900. I had all my papers in order already. I had the visa, the passport. All I needed was money to pay for the medical exam, the ticket, and travel fees...

Let me tell you, I was traveling to the United States with five dollars. I was going to arrive at the Miami Airport with five dollars that my sister had given me. But I also give thanks to God, because the Cuban government lowered the fees by $100 out of the $900, just at that moment when I hadn't yet paid all the fees. So, I was left with $100, plus the five that my sister gave me to travel. With those $105 I came to Miami. Two days later, I apply for a work permit, and with that $105, I pay for the work permit. That's how I started my life in this country.

A friend came to pick me up. He had gotten here a month earlier, a little more than a month. And he picked me up, and he had me at his house for four days. In four days I found work, and I found a place to rent. I started living and paying my rent. I was only in Miami for six or seven months. After those six or seven months, I moved up to Maryland to plant pine trees. With the tree farms I went from Maryland to the Canadian border, as far as Minnesota. There I was, in the country, jumping around like a goat among the bushes, planting pine trees.

There was a Cuban contractor. I came across him here. He lives in Pocomoke. So, he came from there and we went all the way to the border in Minnesota, planting trees. I came back. I didn't really like the work. Because you earn a lot of money, but you spend a lot of money. Really, you earn a lot of money today, but in a hotel you have to pay a great deal of money to stay. So I didn't like that situation. From there I went to work in Perdue in Maryland, but not in Salisbury, here in Showall. I worked in Showall almost two years, catching chickens. There I got medical insurance, so I could have an eye operation. They operated on both eyes. And everything came out well, thank God.

Cataracts. Because I had had vision problems. I had had a chronic illness in 1980. And so the medicines they gave me to cure me of the chronic illness caused my cataracts. That's why they were so advanced so quickly. They operated on me here, and everything went well, very well. I got that problem fixed.

A Business

After the operation, which was something I wanted to have done, well then I decided to open a store in Salisbury. In this store, everything was going well, even though I didn't have a lot of buying power. I became partners with a Mexican afterwards, but not there. I closed the store there to go into a partnership with the Mexican in Milford. We didn't agree in Milford, and I had to pull out. It was called *La Fiesta*...

The result was I ended up alone. And I had to start again by myself. And thank God, I moved here to Georgetown. I opened my store here in March of 1999. And now, with the little buying power I have, the store has been growing, and my work. Because when I started here, I worked at Purdue here in Georgetown. I worked at Purdue from 7:00 in the morning to 2:30 in the afternoon, and so I ran the store from 2:30 in the afternoon to 10:00 at night. Then after I had worked about four months in Purdue, I stopped working for them, and I decided to dedicate myself to the store only. And now, I'm doing that, based on the little that I make. I believe it's progressing and it's going well.

I'll tell you something. I left Cuba with goals. I think a man has to have goals. Because as I told you, many years earlier–I even had the opportunity to come to this country in 1973–I married the daughter of a man who has lived here since 1960. He lives in Miami now. I married his daughter in Cuba. And he offered to have us come to the United States, and I didn't want to go. The situation in Cuba at that time was pretty good, and, well, I didn't have any intention or interest in separating from my family. I have always felt that they are my greatest gift. I think that for a father, for a mother, to separate from one's children is something difficult and serious. Because we can never recover the time that we live away from our loved ones. And it's even greater when they are adolescents. They really need our company, our guidance, our love, our advice, all the help that we can give them. And well, I saw my children grow up, and I believe I made my decision in an opportune moment. Sure, if I had come in 1973, I would have been a lot younger. Perhaps I would have been able to struggle more broadly, and in other circumstances.

But, as you asked me, how is it possible to begin a life with five dollars? Well, one has to lay out one's goals, and one has to have faith in them. Because if I hadn't had faith, if you ask yourself what would have happened to me, when I really wasn't able to get $900? And [if] I hadn't had faith, and I hadn't had courage, what would have happened? Well, logically, I would have had to stay in Cuba with my papers, with my visa and my passport. But my faith and my decision were what allowed me to triumph. And I believe that same faith is what has accompanied me during five years in this country. Because I have achieved this victory alone, without a wife, without children, without any help. And what can I say, except that yes, it's possible.

My first business, which I started with very little money, I started after being here two and a half years, not even three years. I started the Salisbury business with $4,000. But you can imagine how much came from that $4,000. I rented the place, I paid the security deposit, the electricity (since it was for a business, the deposit was $300), the telephone (since it was for a business, they charged me $125). So, I had to buy some shelving where I could display the goods. And I only had $4,000. I couldn't use any more than that. My first purchase for the store was $1,006. I put something in each corner. A little something in each corner. And so I continued working in Perdue. When I opened the first store, I was also working in Perdue for several months. That salary helped me pay the rent, at least to cover my bills. And to keep the key for what would be my own business.

Of course, my decision to become a partner brought consequences—it was a defeat. But it was a temporary defeat, no? A material defeat. But it wasn't a spiritual defeat, because spiritually, I was prepared to begin life again. I think this is the most important thing a man should have—that spiritual determination that he can get to where there are no longer any obstacles. Really, the only thing that has set me back sometimes has been the language problem. Because I haven't been able to study the language. I think I could have done it. I am capable. I know how to develop it, how to study, but one always needs a teacher. There are a lot of new things one has to learn, things one has to relate in a language, at which you by yourself are not going to be able to succeed. And I believe that if I had been able to go to school, I would have succeeded. But really, it's the only thing that bothers me right now. I have no other difficulty. I haven't encountered difficulties.

Even when I got that $4,000 together with the purpose of opening the store, I still sent money to [my children], small amounts, but I sent it to them. I have been sending money mainly to five people: my four children and my mother. And sometimes I send a little help to my brothers and sisters when they have a particular need. For example, now a sister from the Church in Cuba has a problem, and they told me about it in a letter, and I also sent her some money. Because I have a little box in the store for special cases. I also think that I can resolve certain needs that certain people have. Even though my store is not making a lot a money, I still think it's possible to create a fund, so that at a given moment, you can help someone out.

On Poetry

Well, I think I began to write poems, stealing some arguments from the pages of Jose Martí. Because I remember that more than thirty years ago I read a book of his. And then I tried to write something, and I think I even digested some of his words. That's why I say I think I stole some of his ideas, no? Later, I stopped writing for several years. I really hadn't discovered yet at that time that I was going to write some day. At that time they were inspirations, they were moments, perhaps my relations with other people made me want to express myself in a certain way, and I guess I thought that the simplest form would be [poetry]. But in Cuba I wrote once in a while, on certain occasions, but I never gave it much importance. There are people in Cuba who have saved much of what I wrote, when I didn't really have any

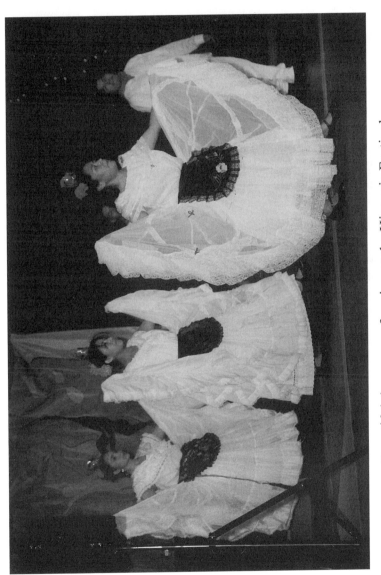

Beautiful dancers performing at the Hispanic Festival
(Courtesy of Rocio Flores, *Hoy en Delaware*)

experience. I know those people have kept those documents, those poems, those writings.

But it wasn't until I came to the United States that I decided to write. When I got to the United States, I met a Dominican woman, a beautiful woman in every sense of the word, a very simple human woman. And I wrote my first poem to her. But after that first poem I decided never to throw out my poems, never to let them go. So I would save everything that I have written since I arrived in the United States. I have the idea, the purpose, another goal is to publish my own books, not because they're mine, but I believe they have a message that can touch people. We are a world without love. We are a world that–we're living in the cosmic age, and really, this takes us practically to the simple things, the little things, to that which can move us. It might be a flower. It might be a sentence. It might be a poem. It might be a painting. But that's not really how we are thinking.

We're thinking about world catastrophes, about the travels of leaders, about the progress of wars, about the problems of our countries. And really, I believe that the message, this message of love, ought to be sent, because it ought to go to every generation, to every system, to every people, to every language...

I don't write for myself. I write for humanity. Everything I write has a message from the heart. I have felt it. I have lived it. Most of what I have written, I have lived. I always look for motifs. There are diverse motifs in life, because I have written–my poetry is not centered exclusively in love, but everything contains love. But it's a diverse poetry, a poetry of nature. It's a poetry for Woman, who deserves so much. Woman, who is so beautiful. She is the only natural flower that exists among us. And we men generally don't appreciate her. I tell you, a man without a woman is nothing. A man without a woman is worth nothing. And a woman truly needs a man. That's the reality. We are made for each other.

Rosario Hernandez

I met Rosario Hernandez one summer afternoon in 2000 in her new sports store in Georgetown. I had actually been directed to speak with her husband who has been actively involved in organizing the soccer leagues for many years. Rosario, however, was happy to talk. Her store specializes in expensive soccer equipment and paraphernalia, products that appeal not only to Hispanics, but also to North American sports fans. When I spoke with her, Rosario was in the process of moving her business from a stall in the Laurel flea market to a small building on the west side of Georgetown, close to route 113.

Rosario shared a detailed account of her border crossing along with an equally harrowing account of her encounters with immigration..[71] Rosario and her family had apparently allowed an acquaintance to stay with them temporarily without knowing that he had outstanding warrants against him. When someone reported him to immigration, immigration surrounded Rosario's house, and entered flourishing their pistols and badges. The adults, children, and even a visiting American child were thoroughly frightened. Ironically, the wanted man, who was at a neighbor's house, came over to see what all the commotion was and was apprehended. Nevertheless, the Hernadez family, unable to produce legal documentation were remanded to the newly established immigration office in Dover, where their case is under consideration.

What is amazing about Rosario's story is that the family initially came to the United States in order to earn money to pay off a business debt. In five years of working in the poultry plants and farms, they were able to save $50,000 and achieve financial solvency in Mexico. Yet, like many immigrants intending only to stay in the United States for a period of time, Rosario and her husband have been enticed by the greater opportunities available here, especially for their young children.

---

[71] This second story unfortunately was not recorded on tape.

In Mexico

I was born in a little town in Guerrero. Guerrero is very well known because it includes a lot of tourist places like Acapulco. I was born in a little town from there called Cuacoyula. I was born in that little town, and after a year they took me to Mexico City. We were in Mexico City for ten years. My family was very close knit. I went to grade school there. After that I went to high school. We moved back to Guerrero, to Iguala. That's where I finished high school. After that I started studying for a career. I got my diploma as a teacher in Iguala. I graduated. I took my professional exam and I passed it. I have a teaching diploma. Later I traveled to another city, called Cuernavaca, where I studied one year at college to be a Spanish teacher.

But what happened was that I got married (laughs). I got married. When I got my teaching certificate, they sent me to my husband's town, a little town, to work as a teacher. I worked there for two years, almost two years and about six months. After that I married my husband, I had my daughter–the one who is around here somewhere, Cristal.

Well by then the economic situation back there–I was a teacher, my husband was a trader–it was a little hard to pay the bills. He started having economic problems with his family, because he worked in the family business. They started owing money, and well, one of my husband's brothers was in New Jersey, and he proposed that we move here. Later he moved to Delaware. He started living here in Georgetown actually. Then we moved to Delaware. Do you want me to tell you how we came here?

The Crossing

Well, the journey–I was pregnant. I was seven months pregnant when I came. We were at the border for almost a week, trying to cross. We were in a hotel for a week. We ate very little. We didn't have a change of clothes. We were worried about finding the way to cross over. And we met a man who supposedly helped us, a taxi driver. He directed us to someone who could take us across. And after a week there, well, the desperation, it was hard. We had already spent the little money that we had brought with us. I couldn't eat well, and being pregnant... The family got desperate, and the first person they found–they offered to take us across...

But the way we crossed–now that I think about it, I feel that I would never cross again in the same way. Those people offered to take us across, in two inner tubes that floated on the water. And they proposed to take my mother, excuse me, my mother-in-law and my father-in-law across in one and my husband, me and my daughter–because I brought my one-year-old daughter in the other one. But we realized that one of the tubes was leaking air. And they decided, "No, we are not going to use that one. We'll just use only one." What they did was to make my mother-in-law lie on the tube first, it was a big tube. They put her in first. Then, they put me in, pregnant as I was, and my daughter came on top of me. We crossed the river around noon, and you could see people from the other side, in Mexico, and we could see people from here, who were crossing the bridge very naturally. But at that time, I think it was lunch time, I don't know, they were inattentive.

Ay, in that moment I felt scared, but finally, I say, "Here we are in the river." Then when we were almost halfway, just about across–and my daughter started crying. She was very small. She was barely a year old. She started crying, because she was afraid of the river current. And my father-in-law and my husband and the other man who was taking us across were swimming pulling the tube that we were in. And she started crying, and the person who was crossing spoke a little rudely, he expressed himself very badly, vulgarities. He said, "Make that girl shut up." And on that occasion, I had in my pocket, I was wearing a shirt, and in the shirt pocket I had some chewing gum, and I gave it to her. And then she stopped crying. But after that, the person who was taking us across said, "Do you know what," he said, "Now we're"—he said something vulgar, he said, "Now we're fucked."

We weren't going to be able to cross. It was all over. And my husband said, "Why?" He said, "Because we didn't come out at the spot where we should have come out," the river was carrying us, and we were frightened. And well, my husband and my father-in-law who knew how to swim started swimming...Finally, my husband swam away and he took hold of some river plants but on the other side, in United States. Then from there, we could get out of the tire quickly. We were able to get out. We ran, and–before that, the person who took us across said, "On the other side there is going to be a person in a car waiting for you so that you can get in and they will take you away." And yes, we got out–with our clothing all wet, with our sneakers all wet, we got out quickly, and right then, in less than five minutes, we got in a car. From there, they started taking us to another place, farther up inside Texas.

I forgot to tell you that when I made the decision to come here to the United States, my family didn't approve. They said, "Daughter, I gave you an education. You can–with your teacher's degree–you can work here wherever you want, in the Mexican republic..." My family had always been very close. I have two married brothers, two sisters, and I was the youngest in my family. I have my dad and my mom, and it was very hard for me to come here and leave them. And I thought, "If I go to say goodbye to my family, they are going to say, 'Don't go.' They're going to cry. And I'm going to feel sorry, and I won't want to leave them." From my husband's town we traveled to Mexico City. I could have passed through Guerrero to say goodbye to my family, but I didn't. And we came here, and those ten days when I was there, I wanted to call them and to ask them "What shall I do? What shall I do," but it hurt me to think of their learning how I was going to cross. I said to myself, "I'd better not," so I left it like that. We were there ten days, I tell you. We crossed. A person from Texas picked us up in Waco, Texas.

We paid. We paid $700 for each person: my father-in-law, my mother-in-law, my husband, my daughter and I came. There were five of us. $700 for each person to risk our life in the river! They even charged $700 for my daughter, to take her across, in that way–swimming. Well, as I told you before, we didn't think of anything but finding a way to come here. Finally, we came. Thank God, nothing happened to us. We came out [of the water] and the person who picked us up there in Texas took us to his house to rest. But we were wearing the same wet clothes.

But before he took us to his house–to pass through the whole of Texas... There were five of us plus the person who was driving in a very small car. And they told us, well "We are going to travel in this way, or maybe you want me to drop you here, because I don't want the police to come by and see you." So they left my husband and my father-in-law–they told them they had to decide which ones would go in the car to rest and which ones would be left in the middle of the desert for two or three hours. So my husband said, "Well, my dad and my mom should go with you to rest, and later you can come to pick us up." And my daughter went with them. They left us around two or three in the afternoon at a place. The place looked nice, with many trees–it's dry but with trees. It was hot, with trees and everything. And they left us there for three or four hours. But then it got bad, because there wasn't any light. It started to get cold, and I with my wet clothes, my husband in wet clothes waiting there. And then suddenly we heard animals moving around. We had a bad time then, because we were taking the risk that they wouldn't leave us stranded. But he told us, "When I come to get you, I am going to give a signal, and you will come to the car, so I can take you away." And yes, he came. And once again I said, "Thank God he didn't leave us here," with the danger that an animal or someone would come and find us.

Finally, we got to the place, and we rested until the next day. Those people are from Texas. Supposedly, they are Americans, no? And what I remember about them is that he said, "It's about time that you wake those Indians up!" He was referring to us, that we should get up because we were going to continue the journey. He said, "Come on, hurry up, wake those Indians up!" And I said, "Okay, we are Indians," Right? They are also Indians, because Texas was part of Mexico and Mexico was an Indian territory. He treated us in a very despotic way.

Then, we continued the journey. When we crossed [the river], we bought new clothes–we thought, so we could get changed. That person stole our suitcases. I brought my daughter's clothes, an extra pair of shoes for her. When he took us across, he said, "Well, I will bring your clothes tomorrow." And we brought a lot. We brought clothes for the five of us to get changed: tennis shoes, very good ones from here supposedly. And no, he never gave it back to us. He stole our clothes. I brought my perfume, a little bit of Mexican money there. He never gave it back to us. He stole it.

Finally my brother-in-law traveled to Waco, Texas, to pick us up. He picked up the five of us, and he picked up another two young men. There was a guy who went along with my brother-in-law to pick us up [in] Texas, from the state of Delaware. It is like 72 hours. In a Monte Carlo, in a Monte Carlo car. It is not very big, but well, it was comfortable to travel in. They came and got us. We didn't know–we were fine in the car, but we didn't know that we were going to pick up another two people in another little town. Then, there were two people driving from Delaware plus two people whom we picked up there. There were four adults plus my father-in-law, my husband, my mother-in-law and I. That was another four adults, plus my daughter. So eight people were traveling in the car, really uncomfortable. I was pregnant, as I told you, and sometimes–it was 72 hours! We didn't stop even to sleep, because two people driving took turns. And what happened was that I sat squeezed on one side so that the other person could stretch his legs or feel comfortable. And then my husband had to sit on the floor, so that my mother-in-law could stretch her legs and also feel more comfortable. So that's how eight adults and a child traveled in a car, on a 72 hour journey or more, from Texas to Delaware.

Arriving in Milford

I repented, but I say, "Okay, now I'm here. I've moved forward." I had been ten steps away. Now I've advanced two steps, and if I go back two, it would be returning to the beginning. I've already moved up two steps, and I'm going to advance another two. So finally we got to Delaware. My brother-in-law was prepared for us. He has a very nice apartment at Washington Street here in Delaware, in Milford. We opened our eyes. We said thank God, because we're here now safe and sound. We were in a comfortable, pretty apartment, but we didn't have anything, not even a chair to sit on. We didn't have T.V., nothing. The place was spotless, but without furniture or anything. And that's how we got here.

We arrived and my brother-in-law had been here for awhile, like five or six years, and he knew a lot of people here. Because my brother-in-law was the person who paid for our crossing, the food, the gasoline, everything to bring us here, and well, his economic situation wasn't very good. People started bringing us used clothes, bags of beans; they brought us potatoes.

Then, I went to a church, St. John's Church, that first Sunday. We went to a church, and we met more people, and I met a woman who helped me a lot, her name is Eloina... She liked helping Hispanic people a lot, because she is from Arizona, and she speaks Spanish, but she is married to an American who worked at the base in Dover. She was very moved by the fact that we had arrived without clothes or shoes...

Yes, well it was very difficult, but when we arrived, we met very good people who helped us. This woman, Eloina, I remember her a lot because she helped us a lot. She belonged to another church in Dover...it is an American church. And she announced to all the Americans that, well, she knew a family who had just arrived and couldn't even buy shoes. That church helped me. They brought me mattresses. They even brought a television. They brought me clothing for my daughter and clothes for me, coupons to use at Acme for food. They helped me a lot. They helped me a lot. Even toys, because she didn't have anything and she was one year old. From that moment, we started pulling ourselves up.

My husband went to work with my in-laws. When we first came, I worked as well for a week. I worked for a week in King Cole. It was a vegetable factory. I was working there for a week, because they hadn't realized that I was pregnant. Since I had been at the border ten days, plus the three or four or five days that we traveled–I was pregnant, and I got anemia. I was very anemic. My son was very small, when he was born. So they hadn't realized that, because my stomach was not very noticeable, and so when I applied, they didn't realize that I was pregnant. And I was already seven months pregnant. But they noticed it later, and they told me that I couldn't work. Because one has to go to the bathroom all the time, whatever–a pregnant person implies more [problems], and I stopped working.

After that, I stayed at home. I went to two doctors, and they didn't want to take me, because my pregnancy was very advanced. And a friend of mine told me, she said, "I am going to take you to Dover, so that a doctor can take a look at you." But, she said, "We will go Monday," but by Monday I had already given birth. I went to Dover to give birth, in Emergency...My baby was born in good condition, maybe a little anemic and small.

[My husband] worked in King Cole for a week, but since we didn't have a car, he had to change. They were hiring at ConAgra, in Milford. And, yes they started working there. They worked there about five years. It was a poultry plant in Milford. Before it was called ConAgra, and now it's Purdue in Milford. And then from there–well, we started covering our bills–my son had been born–and now we finally got established. But the reason why we came here is because my parents-in-law owed like fifty thousand dollars in Mexico. Then they started working. They put all the money together, everyone's checks. They sent them to Mexico to pay for that. Otherwise they would have lost their house and some lands that my father-in-law had, some fruit orchards which he didn't want to lose. That's why we came here.

My brother-in-law, my husband, my father-in-law and my mother-in-law worked. The four of them were working, and at that time we couldn't–we weren't–we couldn't say, "I am going to buy some shoes, because I already worked for it." No, all that money was collected and sent to Mexico. They didn't keep anything, only a little for food. After the first four or five months, I started working. And now I could buy diapers for my children. I helped–I never helped them send the money to Mexico, but they sent it, and I bought food for all of them. I paid the bills with the money that I earned. That's how we could resolve [the debt], and after five years of their working very hard–they did double shifts–they worked in the poultry plant in the morning, in the afternoon. Then, they went to the night shift, and in the morning they went to [pick] blueberries, here in Millsboro...picking blueberries, peaches, nectarines...

In Mexico I had never worked in a poultry plant. I wasn't used to arriving and having to punch a time card. You have to be on time, because if not, either you lose some minutes, or they send you home for the day as a punishment. I wasn't used to that, and it's really different. Yes, in fact when I came here–the sadness of having left my family, the sadness of seeing yourself doing some work that you'd never done before, but the need was great. And after five years of hard work–my parents-in-law, my husband, my brother-in-law worked very hard for five years–they could resolve the debt they had in Mexico. And after that, each one worked, and they started saving money, and once they stopped paying their debt, they took their money and went back to Mexico, my parents-in-law. My brother-in-law started working now for himself. He went to New Jersey and he worked at a paint shop, painting cars and he was making good money, so he took it all, and he went back to Mexico. So the only ones who stayed here were my husband and I.

The Decision to Stay

We stayed because we had already done what we had come to do. And it wasn't fair for us just to come and to pay for their debt and to leave empty-handed, after having spent so much time here. After five or six years, why should I go back to Mexico? They weren't going to give me my teaching position back. So we thought, "Let's stay here." My parents-in-law didn't have family here. They had daughters in Mexico, and they wanted to go back to Mexico. But, apart from my family in Mexico–my mom, my dad, all my brothers and sisters–I had already created a new family. And my family was here now. My son had already been born, they were already going to school. My daughter had grown up now. She was going to school. She had already learned English. So I said, "It's not good for them, if we have brought them to a place where there are many opportunities, now we're going to pull them up by the roots, and we're going back to Mexico, to do the same thing that we did before–if we can have more opportunities here." That's why we decided to stay...

English

I worked at ConAgra at night. I worked at night, so that I could take care of my children during the day. But I only worked six months. Only six months because they were very small. My son was just one or two, and my daughter was about four or five. There is one year between them. But well this was the age when they wanted to touch everything, they wanted to eat, they needed attention. And working nights, my parents-in-law working day and night, and I only slept for a while, and I took care of my children. I fed them, and I went back to bed again. I couldn't sleep well. It was terrible...

I said to the director of the day care [in Lincoln]–I didn't speak English very well. I don't know how she understood me when I told her that I was very tired, because I worked at night and I took care of my children during the day. Then she said, "Well, if you want, here we are." So first, I took my children to the day care, and then I worked, but it didn't work. I decided to leave my job, and I told the director of the day care that the children wouldn't be coming, because I wasn't working anymore. I didn't have a way to pay. And she said, "If you want, you can come and help us with something, we will give you work, and your children can stay here." Because I liked that place, because my daughter–my daughter learned Spanish first–and there she could learn English. So I said, "Okay," and I left all kinds of work, and I went with them. I went there. I took care of my children–the children stayed there–and they paid me. There I learned a lot–because my daughter–I didn't know what scissors were, or what glue was. I didn't know that. I had worked in Mexico with children, but I had never spoken English. I didn't know what Play-doh was. And she at only 3 or 4 years old helped me, and I asked her in Spanish, "What's this, sweetie?" And she answered me in English. So little by little, I told the kids, "Let's play with Play-doh now." Why? Because I had already learned the word Play-doh. The next week...They were learning and I learned from them. I learned from the people with whom I worked. I learned from all of them. I can speak a little bit of English thanks to the fact that I worked in that place.

The people there, the director, the teachers, all of them helped me, and after two or three years I learned a lot. They realized that my English was better, and they gave me the responsibility of taking care of children, but they gave me the responsibility as a teacher. I started as a teaching assistant for two-year-old children. And finally, I was a teacher for the same children, the two-year-olds. I have many memories of that, many pictures. In Mexico, I liked working with children a lot, and I couldn't do it very long in Mexico, but I did it here. I taught my children, the students, how to use scissors, the basic things–the colors. For a two year old that's very good to learn, and they learned. And it gave me a lot of satisfaction that they learned, and I learned with them. I was there for five years. My children were already at school. I came home from work really tired, because with so many kids there, I got home and my two children were a handful. All children are a handful... After that, I left and I worked again, this time at Purdue. I worked for a while.

A Business

I worked there awhile, and I helped my husband pay the bills, because before we got a house for $600, because my parents-in-law and my brother-in-law were living there. But when they finally left, they left us alone, and it is a lot to pay. I helped my husband. We could cover the housing expenses and all. Then, we saved a little money to start our own business. Then finally, we started our business at a flea market in Laurel. There I started my business with the same things: I have sport shirts, soccer shoes. We networked with companies. Some people helped us. They gave us telephone numbers for companies. We called. They sent us catalogs, and we started working. And now I have my small business there in Laurel. We met another person who helped us with the money orders. And now thanks to that, we have the opportunity to open another store in Georgetown. And now I am not working. Now my work is my own business, and I even have my children here (laughs).

We knew about that flea market [in Laurel] because my brother-in-law had some friends who invited him to go once, and he went. Later my parents-in-law were invited and they went, and later they told us, "Let's go to a flea market," but there were hardly any Hispanics there. The people who have businesses—most of the people there are Koreans. So, they just have clothes for the people here. I had never seen a person who sold boots, hats, sports shoes. Many people like soccer, but there was no [equipment]. So my husband likes sports very much. He plays soccer. He is always involved with the Latin Soccer Leagues. He has always had his own team, he's trained them. My children have played soccer for three years now.

My husband has been their coach. He has trained them. So, he said, "Well, if this is my life, and I like it, why shouldn't I bring this?" We went to the flea market in Laurel in those days, and we saw a spot but we were afraid that we didn't have enough money to invest and open. But finally, we kept saving from here and there, we invested. And we said, "Here and now, yes we'll start it." And I thought, "If I am not going to work anymore, I can man it, because it was only Fridays, Saturdays and Sundays." And I quit my job. I ran my business on Fridays, Saturdays and Sundays. All week I am with my children. I do orders, I do other things, but from my home. And now I have the opportunity to open this business.

Ah, when I arrived, the last house where I have lived, I've been there almost seven years now–I came to that house, and since I've always met very good people as well as people who are either envious or they don't like us because we want to get ahead. But we hadn't been able to open it, because we didn't have the money. But later when I met this friend of mine seven years ago–she is an American Indian, born here in the United States. She was intrigued to know what Hispanic people were doing in United States. She was very interested in us, and we talked to her a lot, and she has helped us a lot. She is the person who rented us the house, the last house where we lived. She has helped us a lot–she loves my children very much. We pay her $500 rent. Before we paid her $600, but now we pay her $500 because my parents-in-law and my brother-in-law are not living with us anymore. It's just my husband, our children and I. She says, "Well," she says, "I know that you have intentions of doing something. I love Rosa very much"–they call me Rosa—"and I love the children. I have always thought of them as my own grandchildren." She loves me a lot, she says that I am her daughter. And we have never taken advantage of her. She has always helped us. During Christmas, she doesn't allow me to pay her the rent, and she tells me to use that money to buy presents for the children. She is a very good person, and on this occasion she told us, "I am not going to charge you rent for this month. Get going with it. I know you can do it," and thanks to her, we are here in Georgetown…

Rosario Hernandez
Laurel Flea Market. August 2000
(Courtesy of Katherine Borland)

My daughter now–after everything we went through–my daughter now has many opportunities: she knows how to use the computer, she helps me with the accounts, she helps me counting all the goods that we receive and pricing them. My son too. They help us a lot. And I think that, as my parents told me, they didn't leave an economic inheritance. They gave me an inheritance, which is my education. I didn't know how to profit from it, because I left it in Mexico, and I came here. But God willing, I can leave my children–apart from their education–also some ways to get by, not just crossing their arms and waiting for things to come to them. They know how to work already. They help me. And if I want to reward them, they know that everything they have or everything they wish to have is going to be through work. It is a lesson for them, and in the end–if something happens, I don't know what, one never knows–this business is going to be theirs. If they let it grow, or let it fall down, it's theirs. It will be theirs. Therefore, we are doing everything for our children, even staying in the United States...

Decision to Stay

My husband is a company administrator. He has administered hospitals and he came to work here, and the only problem, the only obstacle that we have had is just that we have never made the time, or we have never felt like going to school or finishing a career linked to the things that we did in Mexico...

My daughter likes computers a lot. Possibly she will become a very good secretary, a lawyer, a nurse. She likes playing soccer and her dream, apart from having a career, is being a professional soccer player. And in Mexico–well here, school is also very expensive–but in Mexico women are not as highly esteemed as here in the United States. Here a woman can play soccer, can play softball, can box, can swim, can play tennis, anything, and in Mexico, there is no league. Well, just this year a women's soccer league appeared, just this year. And it was because they accepted it after a long struggle, but there is already women's boxing! Yes, that's Mexico's culture, my people's culture. They think that a woman cannot do certain thing–of course, if we think about it, as long as it's not too heavy, right–but a woman can swim, she can play tennis, she can be a professional soccer player. But in Mexico things are different. They think that a woman's place is in the home. It is difficult. In Mexico it is difficult to find a good female lawyer. Well, there you don't find very good lawyers or female presidents of very good companies. So you have more opportunities here than in Mexico, and also a better economic situation [laughs]...

My husband was president of the Latin Soccer League for two years. Through sports he is involved in the community, not just the Hispanic but also American, because he was the coach for some American kids in Harrington. It was a YMCA league. It is a league from here, but since he likes being wherever his children are–we wanted to be, we were going to the trials in Milford, and a friend, who was a coach in Harrington told him, "I could still accept them in Harrington. Take them there," and then they started playing there. The first year, the American was surprised at how the Hispanic kids also wanted to participate, and American football is different from soccer, and they liked it. And I think that because of that they are still playing on that team. They are appreciated now, and the coach knows that they play well and all of that. On that side, my husband and I try to get involved in everything related to sports...

Around three years ago, actually four years, I participated for two years in the Hispanic Festival. Since in my teacher training I was taught to do arts and craft, I did all of that in Mexico with the children, and I love to do that. I participated in the Hispanic festival with a demonstration for the American people. I taught them to make *piñatas*. I made a *piñata*. From the first step until the final step of breaking it. I taught them to make paper flowers. In Mexico, whenever there is a celebration, we make paper flowers, with different papers and colors. I taught people how to make flowers and *piñatas*. I had great success, and I appeared in the newspaper. People liked it a lot. It was what they liked best. I participated for two years...

Before, one year ago, no, around two or three years ago, it was unusual to see Hispanic people in Milford. Most of them gathered around Georgetown, in Dover, over by Bridgeville and Seaford. Now in Milford there are a lot of [Hispanic] people. A lot. You can see them in the schools. There are many Hispanic kids...

Legal Status

Well, immigration came to our own house because of some bad people who possibly didn't like us. We didn't appeal to them. I don't know. But immigration knocked, and well, what could I do? It was immigration. They brought all their pistols. If I refused to open the door, I wouldn't like to have them pointing the guns at my door. "Come on in." (laughs) There were two very good people, people who spoke Spanish, but a very rude Puerto Rican started insulting us. He didn't insult us but he talked coarsely. I couldn't make him leave my house, but he behaved very badly. He's Puerto Rican and he is Hispanic. What hurts is that he's Hispanic. Puerto Rico, thank God, the United States likes Puerto Rico, and they have [residence]. But if they hadn't been Puerto Ricans, they would have been in the same situation as the Hispanics. Well, several people came. They gave us an appointment. We went to that appointment at the Immigration Office at Dover.

We were the first ones, I think—we inaugurated Dover.[72] And they called us in, and we went. We explained our situation. Immigration showed up, and there's nothing else to do. We know our position. We went to the appointment immigration gave us. They opened a file for us. At the beginning we didn't have a lawyer, but now we have a lawyer who is working for us. We

---

[72] The 1996 Illegal Immigrant Reform and Immigrant Responsibility Act (IIRIRA) mandated an INS presence in Delaware. An INS field office was opened in Dover in the Fall of 1997.

went to the second appointment. They gave us a year in order to prepare for the third one, which will be the last one. God willing everything will come out all right, because with all the sacrifices that we are making, all that we went through. It was our own fault to come here and all. But all that we went through, I think, merits something.

Zenon Perez

Zenon Perez came to the United States from Guatemala in 1987, when he was eighteen. Born in Tacaná, he moved with his family to the regional capital, San Marcos, when he was ten. While he attended primary school, Zenon also worked to help his family economically. He and his two brothers were traders and in this capacity they visited many parts of Mexico. Political violence prompted Zenon to leave Guatemala, while the promise of political asylum brought him to the United States. Once in the United States Zenon joined the migrant stream and eventually found himself in Delaware. Nine years ago, he married a Mexican woman, who was a guestworker for the crab picking industry in Maryland. They have two children, an eight year old boy and a four year old girl. Zenon's wife is Pentecostal and attends the Soldados de la Luz Church in Milford.

I first met Zenon when I heard that a new international courier business was to open on Race Street in Georgetown. This business, which Zenon plans to manage along with his regular job as a line leader at Purdue and GED classes, provides a window in to the fascinating issue of immigrant remittances. Remittances from persons residing in the United States now form a gigantic portion of Central American and Caribbean economies. Zenon has managed to identify a local market for courier services and convince the Washington-based company, Gomez International Courier, to act as an umbrella organization for his business. In the process, Zenon has had to learn to use a computer and work on the internet, two areas in which he has had no previous training. Despite this progress in business Zenon and his wife have not yet resolved the question of their legal status. While they applied for residency only a year and a half ago, their lawyer assures them that they will receive it within the next few months. Currently, Zenon is getting by with a work permit.

In Guatemala

...My father was a carpenter. My mother had a food stall, like a restaurant, like "Little Mexico."[73] My father made tables, bureaus, shelves, cupboards, everything. He would make every kind of furniture, but he's gone now. In five days it will be two years since he died...

...I was at school for a few years, but that's not to say I'm educationally prepared. No. But yes, I went to school. What happens is that in my country–before, not now–before we didn't have enough money to study a university course or a preparatory course. Now, yes. Now anyone can become college-educated or a doctor, or I don't know, something else, so that they can prosper more quickly than I have done. But yes, before people did study. They became teachers, but it required sacrifice. Well, I'm talking about seventeen years ago. I don't know about now...

We were three brothers who traded. I traded from the time I was small. We came to Monterrey, to Puebla, Veracruz, Mexico City with my older brother, who died in an accident. He was very well known, the man was well-known, but he died in an accident. And the other one, who is also here in the United States, he also had a business. But I came here by myself, without any group, because I already knew Mexico, okay? Crossing over, it's like anyone can pay someone to take them across the border. Once I was on this side, I went to Miami. At that time, there weren't many Guatemalans. There were just a few. People were mostly Chicanos, but there weren't enough Guatemalans to say that yes, there are a lot. Now there are.

The reason I came is that before they were killing people there. So, once I was in a school. I was studying when they came to shoot at the school. After that I didn't go back to school; because I was afraid, I didn't go anymore. So, the thing is they asked me, "Why don't you go to school?" "No, because they can kill me." Because they killed a lot of people. They killed children.

---

[73] A small three table restaurant on Race Street specializing in Hispanic food.

Before, they didn't have compassion for anyone. So, that was my decision, "No, I'm going to the United States." Because by then we heard the people saying in the neighborhood, "No, it's a very good place. No, because you can earn money, since they are giving refuge there to the illegal Guatemalan immigrants..."

In the States

In Miami they were giving immigration papers. It was a white card. So, since I had my car...when I arrived, I bought a car. I was taking people to a lawyer named Sofia in Miami. And the woman told me, "Don't charge them. I will give you a tip for the gas and your trip." And no, I took them. Then I stopped transporting people, and I went to New York to pick apples. Then I went to Pennsylvania to pick apples also. I went to New Jersey to pick blueberries. That is nice. I think it's the best work there is in the fields. Just that you have to pick the ripe ones. It's easy, easy.

In Virginia I was driving a truck checking the young men who were working to see that they were working well, but I didn't stay more than three months, and I didn't like it, because I thought that ordering the people around was...I was going to have problems. So, I left and I came to Maryland, working in Allens in Cordova. I began working on the floor, and then they put me to watch the people as line supervisor.

The reason I came to Georgetown was that in Maryland I had an operation for cirrhosis. So, I had an operation, and they gave me three months rest, and then I didn't have any other way to work. So, I came here. I believe there were a lot of people, and the people told me, "Give me a ride. I'm going to Florida. I'm going to renew my papers." And I would take them to Florida. I'd take them, and that's how I earned food money. That's it, and then when I recovered, I went to Mountaire, and I was working there for three years. I came to Purdue, and I'm working there now in Purdue. Right now in Purdue I'm a line leader.

[To be chosen as a line leader] I believe the first thing is one's ability to do the work. The supervisor is watching you, he sees what you do, how you do it, and how much time it takes you to be able to do it. So, that counts a lot. One's ability, how fast one is, how active one is about doing things. So as not to get tired, you have to find a way to do it. So, that's my way of doing it, and for that reason I've been working seven months at Purdue, and I've spent almost three months as a line leader. Now they want to send me to be a supervisor, but I still don't have the GED to enter a supervisory position, so that they give you decent wage, a fixed salary...

I've thought about going after the GED. The faster I do it, the faster I can find a job, not just there, but any place. I think they'll give me an answer this week whether I will start to take classes, but I haven't decided yet...

A Courier Business

The reason [I'm working with Gomez International] is that my ability to open a business with my own name–let's say Portillo Company, or Zenon Perez Company, wouldn't work, because in Guatemala one has to register things with immigration, pay taxes, pay for all that. I was looking for a way to do it with my own name, but I couldn't. So, that's why I looked to Gomez International Company, and they were willing. I will use their name, they'll take care of things, they'll go through immigration. That way one doesn't have to check things one by one, everything goes together...

I found their name in a book in Washington that was like a newspaper that I found. And I called him. I asked if I could speak with the representative of the International Line. He said, "Yes, I'm the owner." He spoke with me and asked, "What did you need?" And I told him, "My idea is to talk to you about a business plan," and he said, "Yes, wait for me in a certain place, at a certain time, I'll be there." He said, "I'm wearing a green shirt, and I'll be there." And I was waiting for him, and that same day that I called him, that same day we met, we got to know one another. And from that day, he told me, "Keep in touch, and I'm going to see if it will work." And for a year and two months I've been working on the business, and then in six months, less than six months, it's finally started to work. And the owner said, "Yes, now it's set. Now we're going to do it." It's not that I can't be independent or not that he won't try to help me, right. We've agreed that he will come out here and see how things are working, what services I'm offering to people, how we're helping people.

[At first] he didn't have the power to give me [permission], because he wanted to get to know me. He wanted to find out what kind of person I was, to what ends I would go, and if the decision that I had–I had to keep pushing, as I did do. And if I had been an irresponsible person, I would have said, "No, they don't want to give it to me. It's better not to continue. I'll retreat." So, that man would have viewed me as someone, let's say, who didn't have the interest. If I had pulled out, he would have thought to say, "No, no he doesn't really have the interest to do it. No." But I was after them and I think that's what made me win out...

It's been a dream of mine. It's been a dream that is now becoming a reality. And the owner of the company said, "Yes, we're going to give you an opportunity. You'll just have to use the name of the company: Gomez International Courier." It's nice because I've been to the offices in Washington, Maryland, Virginia. I've gone once to California, Chicago–they're in Chicago, Miami. There are so many people who send things and, thank God, in the computer records–because all the people's names are there, where they're from–there's not one person who's complained for the thirteen years that the company has been in existence. That's what I would like to do for the people, to help, but I'm fighting hard to do it. A business is not that easy to develop, it doesn't matter how small it is. If it's small, you struggle to get clients, and if the business is large, you struggle to get the money for your merchandise. That's how it is. But it's been my dream...

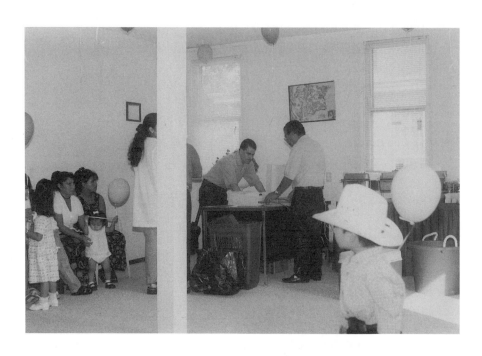

The Opening of Gomez International in August 2000.
(Courtesy of Katherine Borland)

I was looking for something more, and I don't know, it didn't come about. I wanted to open a bookstore, yes. My wife goes to church and she wants to open a bookstore and sell cassettes, bibles, Christian books. So that was my idea. I thought about it, and I said, "if this business doesn't do well, I will still open a bookstore. I'm going to open the bookstore." But what hasn't helped me in this moment is getting the license, having the license for the bookstore, because we already have the license for the other business.

I have to work probably three, four, five months so that the office, the business is functioning well. Then I'll leave the poultry plant. Then I'll be serving my people. Because it's not that easy to forget about them, leave them in such a way. They come and they ask if their package arrived or not. They have to come to the office or call me at the office. What's happening? And I will immediately communicate by computer, because we have an Internet line–what happened to that cargo? What happened with that letter? What happened with that money? If the person says, God willing it never happens, there was an assault or something. Well, we must pay the money back immediately to the people. Then one has to give them the account that's on the computer. How much was it? So then, please, we need to pay that immediately. That way people are going to feel comfortable. They'll say, "Ah, yes, even though they lost money, they paid it." Right? One can't put "buts"–"but they robbed me," but no, one has to pay the person. I don't think that will happen. Perhaps sometimes it's happened with other companies, but was it really bandits, or was it the company workers themselves?

...Tomorrow they're going to give me the key. The opening–we're going to inaugurate it–will be on a Saturday. What we want to do is let the people know about it, chat with them about the services we offer, the costs, how long the deliveries will take. Even if the people's houses where the delivery is going are far from town, maybe two or three hours from town, their things still have to arrive at their destination, and that's what we want. That's why we're going to inaugurate it, and offer them a drink, a taco, I

221

don't know, and let people know about it, speak with the people. I'm well known by everybody. I like to fix cars, I like to give people rides, I like to do a lot of things...

I don't have normal training. I'm going once a week to Washington, to the Washington office to train myself. The secretaries there show me how to find the names, to enter a client on the computer, other things. Using the computer is easy. What's a little difficult for me is the Internet. I've got the idea already. I've worked for a day. They left me in the Washington office for a day, and I worked, and everything went well...

Let's say you are Maria del Rosario Chavez or Perez, okay? Your sending something to Mr. Juan Perez. You send it. We're going to weigh it. It can't weigh one pound, it has to weigh two pounds or more, and 50 pounds or less. So, we're going to say if it weighs 22 pounds, we'll have to charge you $3.50 per pound or $3.00, to deliver right to his house. And if his house is close to the office, four or five blocks from the office, then perhaps we'll charge $3.00 a pound. And if it's less than 21 pounds, we'll charge $4.50 a pound, because it's low weight.

And those packages are leaving every Saturday night or Sunday night. You sent your package today, Thursday, or you sent it Tuesday or Wednesday, and there they'll be delivering it Tuesday or Wednesday morning, or even Monday, depending on how far away the house is. [I take the packages from here] to the central office in Maryland, and a truck comes and takes them from there to the airport, and the airplane takes them to the capital. In the capital, they are distributed. They go through the central office to the central office in Guatemala. They arrive Sunday, and Tuesday the person can already have it, or Wednesday morning.

That would [also be true] for the money order. Now for cash, because we also send cash, the people come here and say, "I will send $300 to my house. I want you to send it in cash." Okay, you have to send it by Internet, just as Western Union does. Okay, if it's $100, we have to charge $10, because that's the charge. If it's $200, we have to charge $20. Now, if it's more than $200, $201 or $200.50, we charge 8%, so now you're not going to be paying more than $20. You're paying about $22 [sic] for $300, but that money is going to be delivered immediately, in one hour in cash in dollars, just as you send it here. If your house is far from the office, it will be delivered the next day. If you send it today, your money will be received tomorrow around midday, because they're far from the office, maybe two or three hours away. But that is the service for cash. Now, a money order goes with a letter, and that will be delivered in seven or eight days, Wednesday to Wednesday. It's seven dollars including the letter. But your letter is delivered to the door of your house with the money order inside, and the person has to sign a paper and show a photo I.D. and that paper showing delivery there is then sent back to us, so that you know that the letter arrived at its destination. So, someone comes and the person over there says, "No, no I didn't receive anything." Okay, you're going to look at the signature of your loved one, your brother or your father, or whoever. You're going to look at that signature. "Is that the signature of so-and-so?" "Yes." "Then he received it, there it is." They can't, they can't say, "I didn't receive it, because there is his signature."

Money Grant and Western Union are [already] here [in Georgetown]. With Money Grant one has to go and pick up. If the people are from Tacaná, they have to go to San Marcos to pick it up at the bank. Apart from that, they don't deliver in dollars. They deliver in *quetzales*. And the person has to spend money on travel, food, hotel, and the return to his house in order to go and pick it up. And if the person here sends $100, how much is left? They are left with 500 or 550 *quetzales*. That's what is left for the person. But in this service, I'm not saying that it's going to be better, but I think that people prefer to have their money in dollars, like in a money order, so they can change it and they can know how much they gave them and what the [exchange] rate was. I think that is an advantage, yes.

On the Future

I think that Georgetown has changed a lot, it's not like it was before. Before, this was a very cautious, very strict place. But sometimes, one has oneself to blame for that, for going out, for not obeying the law. Before it was very strict. I always go out in the street, and I notice how much it's changed: lots of Hispanics, lots of people with families. Before, you hardly saw anyone in the street. Now you see lots of people with their kids in tow, couples shopping together, you know, shopping with their family, the children. Now, it's very different. I see a lot of Hispanics here in Georgetown. It's a pretty place. It's...sure the town isn't big, but I think it's the county where many people have found work, and rents. That's the advantage of Georgetown. They rent almost all the houses, not at a very low price, because you know, it's expensive, but it helps us, the Hispanics, to have rentals, to have work.

My hope for my children is to try to work more for them, because one never knows what life will bring. Try to work for them, maybe buy them a house or maybe leave them a business like the one I am starting now. I don't want it just for me, but I want for them as well. Try to give them the education that they prefer. I'm not going to force them either, saying, "you have to study this career," to make it that I decide for them. No, they also have to decide what university course they want to take, what they would like to study. But they aren't going to choose an easy course either. Because then later they're going to work somewhere and they'll tell them, "No, you're going to get minimum wage, because that career isn't very good." I prefer to give them a good career, even if it costs more. I think what's important is not what it costs, but that it helps them later to become a business administrator or other things. They should be at that level, yes...

My son is going into third grade this year. He hasn't lost one year since he's been in kindergarten. He's done well. Sometimes he complains. He says when he comes home, he tells me, "Dad, the teacher doesn't want us to speak Spanish at school."

"Why?"

"Because she says it isn't good."

"Yes, of course it's good."

"No, she says no. We have to speak English, she says."

"Well, okay, if that's what she says."

"Why don't you talk to her? One day she chastised me very badly" he says, "because I was speaking Spanish."

"Ah," I said, "She probably thought you were using bad words in Spanish. She probably thought that."

"No," he says, "I want you to talk to her."

"Okay, I'll go."

He asked me to do that twice. And I went to the school and I asked the teacher why he couldn't speak Spanish, and she said, "Not in class. When they're on the playground, yes, when they have their break."

Okay, so then I explained that to my son. He understands now. I don't think that's an excuse. In class they shouldn't be speaking any other language, because they're learning a language, but even so, now they're teaching them in Spanish as well. They're teaching them English, both things. But they have a schedule. My son has had four, five teachers. They've worked very well with him...

I think I would not [return to Guatemala]. If they give me the opportunity to live here, I think it's better to be here than to be there.

Family Literacy Class at *La Esperanza*
Yolanda and Jesus Diaz April, 2000
(Courtesy of Allison Burris)

Margarita Gonzalez

Margarita Gonzalez, originally from Juarez, Chihuahua, Mexico, settled in Milford, Delaware in 1987 and opened a laundromat there in 1995, which has become the most visible Hispanic business in town. Margarita has provided assistance to other Hispanic residents not only through her business, but also through a myriad of formal and informal roles. For instance, she helped form a local chapter of Working Capital, an organization that assists ordinary people interested in starting their own businesses by providing technical assistance and starter loans. She also collaborated in a short-lived project to provide credit union services to Hispanic workers. Margarita has been recognized for her community work by the Governor, and has served briefly on the Governor's Council for Hispanic Affairs.

In many ways Margarita is more privileged than her Hispanic neighbors. She came to the country legally, is financially secure and has never had to work in the poultry plants. Moreover, following a husband who had a military career, she traveled widely before settling in Delaware. Yet, in many ways Margarita empathizes strongly with their plight. She too came to the United States to escape wrenching poverty in Mexico. When she arrived in 1970, she was seventeen years old and spoke very little English. Much of Margarita's success in Delaware has resulted from her recognition of her own very real skills and talents despite her humble beginnings. Throughout our interview Margarita emphasized that what she most wished to provide to other Hispanics was the belief in themselves that, she says, makes everything possible.

Early Life

I grew up frankly with my mom. When I was four years old, my parents separated. After that my mom always worked in

Margarita Gonzalez, Owner of the Milford Laundry
(Courtesy of Katherine Borland)

the city.[74] She was a cook in restaurants. She did things as a waitress in hotels. So finally when I was 13, I started to work to help her...

So they paid me 75 pesos a week and then I earned 100, 125, 150, but I didn't get any more. So for that reason I wanted to work in El Paso. So by the time I was 15, I had been working for a long time in El Paso. That's why I didn't go to school. I only got to the fifth grade in school, because I felt obligated to work to help my mom, although I don't know why I saw it that way.

I had been working in El Paso as a maid for a doctor in a very big house all that time. There were three maids working in that house. And there I said, "I am not going to be a maid all my life." On May 1st, 1970, I went to Las Vegas. And it was a little bit before my seventeenth birthday. There I started getting jobs as a waitress in hotels...

I went on my own with a family who were going there. They were a retired couple whose kids had left, and they wanted to leave. They saw me as a kid, although I thought of myself as being very grown up, because I didn't perceive any kind of danger. I wanted to go to California; my wish was to experience California. I thought that I would never see the ocean, because in Juarez and the outskirts there was only a river, and sometimes it had water and sometimes it didn't, and that was all the water that I had seen. And I dreamed that we were going to see the ocean, and then I thought, "I am going to California and I will see it." Those were my greatest dreams.

But they were going to Las Vegas, and one of them, a first cousin of one of my uncles, told me, "We are leaving for Vegas on this day. If you want to come with us, come." So I made up my mind, and I packed my bags, and I left, because I didn't want to work in El Paso as a maid all my life. I went to Las Vegas and of course I missed El Paso a little bit. But I have always been a person who felt the responsibility of working and working and working. I knew that I had to do something to take care of my

---

[74] Margarita refers to El Paso, Texas, just across the border from Juarez.

family. I always had that determination to take care of the whole family. So, for three or four months it was hard for me but later, when I started working and I was doing well at my job, I got used to it...

When I was in Las Vegas, I heard some people talking. We were in the dining room eating one day and one of them, a colleague, was making some comments about people crossing the rivers and about coyotes. And I didn't know what a coyote was, so I told them that I didn't know what that was. And she said, "Have you already forgotten the river you crossed?" And I said, "Through a river? Why am I going to cross a river if it's full of water? Where I come from, people don't go through the rivers, only over bridges!" And they turned and looked at me, because they thought I was illegal, and I didn't know that the people who were there could be illegal. I thought that all the people who were there were in my same position. I hadn't any idea of what was going on. I didn't have the slightest idea, in the same way as my daughters didn't know anything about that. So now everything that I hear frightens me. Mentally I get scared from knowing about all those people–I don't like hearing that news, I don't like reading books or special reports in the newspapers about tragedies, because I cannot take it. How is it possible that people have to go through that? I don't understand it. That's why the people here struggle a lot and I really encourage them to get their paperwork done, if they have that opportunity...

After that, two years or a year and half later, I met my husband. I had a friend, and both of us worked together in the same hotel, and one day she came and told me, "Gonzalez came to my house to visit me. He is in the military. He is around, but he is always out with his plane, always out." I didn't pay attention. The only thing I did was work and work, and she saw that I wasn't paying attention, and she said, "You know one thing," she said, "since he is not Elsa's boyfriend any more" (Elsa was my friend Gloria's sister) "he said that he is coming on Wednesday to pick us up." He had to give me a ride too, since we were always together.

So if he were going to give her a ride, he would have to give me a ride too.

When that Wednesday came, when all the employees left by a side door, he picked us up. I told him I wanted to be dropped at my place. He told me that he wanted the three of us to go out, but I refused. I told him that I wasn't used to that. I told him that I wanted to go home, that I had to be at home because my sister, the one after me, lived with me. And I didn't know what was happening, and he insisted on not doing that but taking Gloria to her place first. And Gloria was a little bit annoyed because of how he, having just met me, wanted to drop her first and then drop me off. Why did he want to know where I lived? Finally, he got his way, and first he took Gloria and later he took me home.

The next day in the early morning, he knocked at the door and he told me, "I am coming to take you to your job." He barely spoke Spanish. He spoke English, only a few words in Spanish, but I could understand him very well. So he told me, "You don't have to take the bus." And he stopped by, and I said that I was used to taking the bus. The bus stopped at the corner, so I got to and from work on the bus. But he said, "No, no, no, I am going to take you to your job," because at that time he was on sick leave, because he had had an accident and had an arm in a cast, and he wasn't working. So he came in the morning and he took me to my job. And I said, "And Gloria, why didn't you pick her up first?" and he answered, "Oh no, she can take the bus." "That's nice of you!"

And that's how I met him. He took me there, and he went there to pick me up in the afternoon. Several months passed, and he asked me to marry him. I got married at 21. Then I only worked for three more months. After that, I never went to work. He was second generation. His parents had already been born here and brought up here, and he was second generation who grew up here in the U.S. If they went to Mexico, it was to visit a cousin or a relative there on the holidays, that was all. So in his family they almost never speak Spanish. His mom speaks to them in Spanish, but they always answer in English. I have a son who does the same too.

Around 1975, we left Las Vegas, and we went to Guam. I lived on the island for three years. We lived in the U.S. again from 1978 to 1982. When I came back, I was pregnant again. From here to there (Guam), I was pregnant, and from there to here, I was carrying another baby. From 1975 to 1978 we lived in Guam, from 1978 to 1982 we lived in New Mexico–that's where my son was born–and from 1982 to 1985, we lived in Guam again, and from 1985 on we have lived in Delaware.

When I had my son, the second time that we went to Guam in 1982, I was bringing my newborn baby, two or three months old, from New Mexico to Guam. And I couldn't be at home without doing anything. I always felt responsible for helping my husband economically. So I was at home, and I am not like those women who just sit on the sofa or go shopping. I couldn't do that. So I told him "I want to see if you can get me some houses to clean. Tell me where I have to go and what I have to do." And he said, "You are crazy."

"Why am I crazy? You go to work and I can go two or three days to clean a house." Because there are empty houses as big as these, totally empty where you have to clean the walls, to clean the fridge, the stove, the floors which had to be very clean, without dirt or anything and the inspector came. The yard has to be mowed. I earned my $300, sometimes even $500 for each house. I cleaned a house each week, and I got my check every week. At the beginning, he was a bit reluctant, but when the money started pouring in, he liked it. Later he started imposing his will.

Well the first time that I went [to Guam], I didn't do much because he didn't let me go. The second time I told him, "When I went to New Mexico for four years, I was a person who still did something." I even ended up selling Avon–for five years I sold Avon. Five years! I couldn't believe it. Why? Because it gave me good results. There wasn't a thing that I didn't try that didn't get me good results. For a time I started making stuffed elephants, but I had to stop because I didn't have time to make them all because of the large number of requests. And everything started because I made one for my daughter, and people looked at it and said, "Oh, what a nice elephant, what a nice elephant." And I started making them so much that I said, "No, I am not going to make more, because I don't have time to make so many." So I said to him, "There is much to do."

In Delaware

[We always lived] at the military bases. We were at the military base here for two years but, since we knew that he had to retire, he only had five years left, we had to start looking for a house. From the very moment that we arrived, in September 1987 (that's when we started living in Milford) I started communicating and socializing with Hispanic people. From time to time in the military we met someone who was from Texas or Puerto Rico. My husband is a person who doesn't like to socialize with people, get-togethers, nothing of the type, always separated from the rest. That's why I hardly related to anything that was Hispanic culture. I remained by his side most of the time. He was more a person from the United States, brought up in the American way.

Then in 1987 when I arrived here, it was when I starting socializing with Hispanic people, because I had no idea that I was going to come across anyone here. I had never had contact with or seen people from Central America at all. So, it was something I couldn't believe how in this corner of the world there were people from so far away. And more than that they came to me a lot. They started looking for me a lot, because my husband started working for Delmarva Rural Ministries from 1989 to 1992 with the migrant workers. He was an interpreter for them, for the fields, all the fields around there. He worked there for approximately five years part-time. And it was then when we started getting involved with all the needs of the Hispanic population.

I thank God, who has been so great to me–and myself having come from a place where I didn't have anything, not even shoes and that's the cheapest thing. And that's why I sometimes wanted to do anything. I was the one who crossed the streets and went to clean those houses there, sweep here, take care of children, in order to get money and help my mother from the time I was a kid. And look where I am now. Why? I don't understand. I don't understand why. I am not an ambitious person. I don't like ambition. What I had was my husband's ambition, not mine, but from the moment that we got separated, and everything remained here with me, I had to keep it up. But if I were a person without anything, I would be very happy, I wouldn't have problems. I think so.

Then I see all these people who have so much need for everything. For them to have only a room to put their family is enough. But at the same time I consider them very intelligent, because they come, they don't care about living in any sort of condition for a short time–two, four or three years if it's necessary–and they return to their countries, and they live even better than here in the United States. So here, I have dedicated myself to help them: immigration issues, interpreting situations, courts, doctors, anything. Even sometimes taking care of their children, so that women don't lose their jobs. That's my way of seeing things.

A Child Care Business

When we arrived here, I started doing day care. I got my license for a day care at the base, as a military thing. But once I moved here, I said, "Where am I going to find children to be taken care of here outside the base?" Well, I was surprised, because there were many children to take care of, a lot, and many of them, of course, from Hispanic families. Do you see this big house here? I asked to rent it for them. Even at night I was taking care of children, because sometimes they called me to watch them. They knew they could bring their kids here. And that's when I started becoming aware of all the needs of the Hispanic families...

So there are courses that one has to take, that if I told you how difficult it was for me to pass those courses–now I wouldn't be well prepared to take that course. But a friend of mine named Julie encouraged me to go and get the license. She even told me, "You have to go in person-to-person. You have to go and bring your license back." And I said, "But Ms. Julie, I don't think I can get it." And she answered, "Why not?" And I said, "I don't know what they are going to ask me, and I don't know what kind of questions they are going to have, and I feel I don't know what I am supposed to do." And she said, "Oh, yes, you know. And you know what? I am coming with you." And I said, "Ms. Julie, you don't have to go." And she said, "Oh, yes." She said, "She is going to get a license too. She is going to open a day care, and she wants to talk with the lady in charge." And finally I got the license. And she encouraged me a lot to go.

When I was there, I was so nervous that my husband talked, because it was a whole day thing to see if I could be in or not and to prepare everything in order to take the courses in different areas. There were like three courses, and I had such a difficult time, because I had never been to school, and I felt incapable, very incompetent to do that. I thought that everything was going to be questions. And it was very hard at the beginning, but later when I had to go to the workshops, I was like, "What's this?" and my world collapsed. That was me, because I didn't have knowledge or any previous study. My head was always spinning. So I started learning to relax a little bit there and let things go without having anybody judging me. So I was learning in a new way in other words.

[Learning English] was part of my relationship with people, and especially television. I didn't just turn it on to watch it when I was at home. I turned it on even if I didn't watch it. I just listened to it. At the day care, the children heard their music on their tapes, and they also watched their programs on the television. Others played and like that. I don't know what happened with me, why I put myself to such a test, so intensively and so profoundly that everything seemed very natural to me as if I had been born here and grown up here. I was here, and here I would remain, because nobody is going to send me away...

Later, after I got separated, I continued running the day care. I had a very rough time, because in 1990, the same time my husband retired from the base, my eldest daughter got cancer. She went into the military, and when she came back from basic training, they discovered she had a cancer. She had treatments for two years. All that time, from the moment that she was told she had cancer to the moment they told her that it was very advanced, she looked the same. I always thought positive, and I thought that she was going to be fine, regardless of how bad she looked later. I continued believing strongly in her recovery, and thank God, she recovered. She is married. She has two or three children and there she is quite well, thank God.

Another thing, after that, since my husband and I decided to separate, he wanted to take my son, the middle one, with him. That was so brutal, very hard for me, and that was when I had to decide to close the day care because, mentally and emotionally, I couldn't do it any longer. And I left my job at the day care. That was when I decided to take a little time, about six months, to decide what to do next. So I said to myself, "I am not going to work at Purdue," and I started the business that I have now: a laundromat.

The Laundromat

Why a Laundromat? It's funny, because I didn't know what I was doing. I had no idea what a Laundromat was. I had never gone to one, especially after I married. I hadn't gone to a Laundromat for like 20 years! The reason is that when I was in the day care, the parents of the children that I took care of always came and complained about doing the laundry: about going at six in the morning to stand in line, about not getting their clothes washed well, about how long the dryer took, about all the money that they spent because the machine didn't work properly. They always had to struggle with problems there, because the people there were very prejudiced, a whole list of things. You cannot imagine how many things I heard against the Laundromat.

And I knew I wanted to start a business, and I didn't know what. And I wanted to join the Hispanics. It was my dream to have a Hispanic store with Hispanic products, but I had to forget about it, because I realized that on my own, I wasn't going to be able to make it because, for that, it takes many people to achieve success. And I said to myself, "At a Laundromat, you don't need many people, and you only need a person to run it and be responsible for everything. And that's what stayed in my mind: a Laundromat. And what's better than a Hispanic Laundromat? So everybody could feel comfortable to go, not only to go and do the laundry, but also for everything they might need, and that is very true. That's the reason why I decided to open a Laundromat. I didn't know where I was heading, but that's okay...

I got a loan through Small Business and thank God, I am still there. That's one reason why I work hard, in order to pay off the loan. And I make anyone understand that having a business, being self-employed or having your dream fulfilled, is possible. I describe the United States as the land where everything is possible and nothing is impossible. All that you can wish can be achieved with hard work and a lot of effort, with a lot of dedication and a lot of determination to achieve it...

It's going to be six years that I've been here. And that's where I usually live, spending every day, working sometimes 16 or 17 hours. But if you have ever considered what work can one do at a Laundromat. Well, you can do a lot. So from that time to this, I am still struggling. But when I look at the needs of other people, that's what makes me strong mentally, emotionally and spiritually. After all that, I have been very lucky, God has granted me a lot of luck.

The Governor's Council for Hispanic Affairs

It seems to me that [being chosen to serve on the Hispanic Council] was more a little of everything because, practically, at fourteen, I went on my own to the bridge between the U.S.A. and Mexico in order to get my passport. For me filling out papers was nothing at all, because I know that everything related to immigration is just paperwork and more paperwork and a lot of documents and proofs that you have to… And then I see that these people are very afraid of what immigration might tell them. And I cannot see why there is so much fear about that, to deal with a task that maybe produces a positive result. And I have always encouraged them to do that.[75] And I realized that many of those with a work permit, when they were called for an interview, they wanted to avoid it. And I couldn't understand why. I encouraged a lot of them, "Come on, let's go to the interview. I will take you. Let's go to the interview. You show your authorization where you prove who you are, and your curriculum also." And they would say, "No, they are going to take it away from me. They are going to deport me." And I answered, "No, you are not going to be deported."

So I worked very hard to make them understand that the best thing to do was to show up and prove their identity and their nationality, something that for them was like the end of the world. And then I wondered, "When these people have to go through these processes, why are they so close-minded, why all this fear?" When immigration officers come, for me it's something like going to the doctor and waiting for his diagnosis, but it has a cure. But they don't perceive it that way. They have a lot of fear and horror. When they go to court, it's the same. They have an enormous fear. They prefer to escape from the situation and get into trouble.

There are many people here for whom I have filled out forms. I push them to fill out and send in their forms. So for this reason, many people come to me. Then like five years ago, I started training my eldest daughter, because she didn't have the slightest idea about immigration. My daughters didn't have any idea about what it means not to be from this country. Then, my eldest daughter, Ana, as she is very studious, very intelligent, has

---

[75] That is, to complete their immigration paperwork.

knowledge and computer skills to fill out papers. I trained her to get familiar with immigration problems, and now she loves it. There is no subject that she doesn't know, or forms that she is not aware of, information that she cannot provide so that poor people can go on. They come and look for me, and they know that if they are going to ask me, "What shall I do here? What do you think I have to do?" I am going to tell them, and I am going to send them to my daughter, so that she can give them all the forms and all that.

I was even one of the people responsible for collecting signatures, a million of them, to be presented to the president so they can offer amnesty to my country. And even today, I was so surprised because every time that I asked anyone to sign for me, they looked at me in horror, because they think that we're getting signatures, addresses and telephone numbers in order to give information and get people deported. So this is the reason why they put me on the Hispanic Council.

The Credit Union

Ana started working with a credit union with Mr. Karl Hall. He is a very well-known man because he is very familiar with Hispanic people. He is a North American guy, but he spent many years in Cuba when he was young. He was living there and from there, he went to live to Central America, Nicaragua, I think. He gets along very well with the Hispanic population. His father started the credit union many years ago. He ended up being the president of the credit union, and his dream was to make the Hispanics understand the great necessity to save money, something that the Hispanic, I mean the one who comes to the U.S.A. for a temporary period, doesn't plan to do, because he is afraid.

They always think that if they open a bank account, the government is going to take away their money. They prefer to carry it in their bag, or they prefer to send it to their country every month. Lately, many cases like this happen that they change their checks, they put the money in their wallet and then the delinquents and low class people around are taking notice of that and are attacking the Hispanic more and more in order to rob him. Sometimes they beat them up too. So Karl wanted to start a program where they even went to Georgetown and they parked there at *La Casita* and their checks were cashed every week. At the same time they gave them the information, that if they were looking to open an account, they could do it with $5 or $10, and that they knew that they were going to be saving $5 or $10 every week in a savings account, and the day they wanted to leave, they had that money there, saved. And my daughter was working with Mr. Karl Hall, and he is an excellent person, very interesting.

There were 3220 Hispanic members who were new members in a [period] of four months, whose checks were cashed every week. They didn't have to be looking for a place to cash their checks. Many of them struggled even to get their checks cashed, and you know that.[76] That is one of the reasons why Mr. Hall felt so sorry about many of them working the whole week in order to get a piece of paper which they couldn't even cash. Since he was the president of the credit union, he presented this idea to the Board of Directors in order to see what the others thought. There were five votes against seven, all of them Americans, but once I voted, there were six against six and they had to consider the project, and he voted for this idea because he was presenting the idea and the other six had to go along. But those six who didn't agree from the very beginning were the ones who made everything fail.

They were afraid of the credit union growing too much and offering more facilities for the Hispanics. Also the credit union wasn't going to be run only by the Harrington community, because this was centered in Harrington. So we fought around a year and a half. Finally, Mr. Hall was under so much pressure that his health was deteriorating, and he said, "Let's do whatever they want. But you'll see, this is not going to stop here, because you are going to continue at your laundromat." I had great support from him. He

---

[76] In Georgetown, Perdue workers must pay a five dollar fee at the local banks to cash their checks if they don't have a bank account. The nearest branch of the bank upon which the checks are drawn is 80 miles away in Salisbury, Maryland.

stepped down and, since he stepped down, the credit union was over. It wasn't in Harrington any more. And he was president of the credit union for twelve years, ever since his father died, who was the one who founded the credit union in Harrington. But since it was a credit union created in the Harrington community, they didn't want any people from outside the area to join the union, and that was the way they paid. It's been three years now that they haven't had a credit union there.

[The mobile unit was functioning for] a year and a half. Well, on Thursdays it went to Milford, because on Thursdays there was a big company with many Hispanic people who got paid. But they couldn't go to Purdue here in Milford on Fridays, because they went to Georgetown on Fridays for the whole day, and they cashed about 2500 or 3000 checks. And people stood in line for the whole day.

And to make things worse, as I tell you, we Hispanics sometimes give a cold shoulder to ourselves. Because in 1998, a little before the credit union closed and was dismantled, prices were already bad, and that service was almost over, then Puerto Ricans came, because in Philadelphia they knew there was a mobile unit doing this. Four Puerto Ricans brothers came, and they robbed the unit, for almost nothing, because there wasn't even $2,000 there in cash. So that was one more reason to close it. They were Hispanics, but they didn't know anything about it, and nobody had told them about the benefit for all the people coming from Central America and Mexico. And that was a factor that also looked bad for the people against the plan, but all the time Mr. Hall said, "The dream is not going to end, because you are going to continue cashing checks at the Laundromat. I am going to help you in any possible way and, if I can help you in anything, I will do it." And that's what I am doing now. It is not linked to anybody or any association. It's just a service that I am offering for the Hispanics there, for the Milford community.

I was attacked one day, a Thursday night. They got inside because they knew that on Friday mornings, that is, on Thursdays, I get ready to cash checks on Fridays. Who were they? Hispanic people. But we moved on, because these things never stop. As I always said, "As long as they don't put me out of business, I will continue."

Working Capital

Well, I had my day care for years. I had made my dreams come true in one way or another, because for ten years I loved doing the day care–when one day I met Robert Blaid. He gave me this idea of creating a group, forming a group, and he asked if I could. He is a North American, and he has a building company, and his wife is Argentinian. So Robert Blaid was interested in meeting people who were interested in creating their own business, no matter what their dream was. He wanted to let them know what the state could offer them. I volunteered to help him, because, as I told him, "I don't need that, because I imagine that I already made my dream come true for years and, if I am still running, it is because I think I am doing fine."

This happened around 1993. At that time I had a very close friend who had just arrived from California, and he was very good at construction, and I helped him because he didn't know what was necessary, but he was working for a company. When he arrived here, his uncle came to introduce him to me, because he wanted me to tell him how to start looking for a house, how to buy a house. And that's how I met him. He told me he was going to work here, he was looking for something in construction. And then I started helping him look for jobs in companies, and I proved to them that it wasn't impossible, because there was a time when they got desperate and wanted to leave. So, I got the phone book, and I started looking for all the numbers related to drywall companies, and I started making phone calls. And I began telling him more or less where he could find the companies in Newark and probably in Kent. So in that way he could sign some contracts, and now he even has his own company. I got his license and his insurance.

To this he said, "No, that's impossible. That is going to mean a lot of money." And they said, "No matter what it will mean, you will be part of the company. Don't worry about the money. Money sometimes comes and sometimes goes." Let's see. I went and I talked to the company owners who wanted him insured more in a certain way and wanted to give him a hand. Frank Rubino was a very popular man in Delaware, and he got sick recently, and he just died some months ago. So he told me, "Definitely, Mrs. Gonzalez, if you speak to Germinio, and you teach him and tell him what to do to make his own company, I will support him a hundred percent, and I will give him a job for two years in advance so that he can cover his back with a good contract right now." And I said to him, "Are you listening to what this man is saying? Nothing is impossible." And I replied, "Mr. Rubino, could you be kind enough to tell me what he has to do?" And he gave me the list and said, "When you are done fulfilling all these requirements, come and see me, and I will go everywhere, even calling here, there and everywhere to help him." I even lent him some money. It's not that I had much money to give out, but credit cards. I told him, "Don't use your credit cards. I will use mine." Because, as a company, he had to pay a lot–labor, supplies, everything. And he only got his payment a month later, from the companies and from the builders too.

So, at that time in 1993, his two nephews and two brothers had come before him, because two stayed in New Jersey and two came to Milford. The ones in New Jersey believed that the ones in Milford weren't going to do anything and weren't going to achieve anything, because this town was dead, and this state was dead. There was nothing! And there in New Jersey, well you know what they say–there is a lot of work in New Jersey. Of course, they drove 50 or 100 miles every day to go to work, but there was work in that place. Now the ones in New Jersey have come to join him, and now all of them work together here, along with their friends. He brings more than ten groups of self-contractors run by his company, and it's interesting because he is a man whom I admire a lot.

He was the first one I enrolled in Working Capital. I registered him so that he could hear lectures, so that he could hear from other resources that it wasn't impossible, because I struggled a lot to make him understand that. It looked almost impossible to him. He, Jose Somalo, the one who is doing the newspaper now,[77] Eloina Alonso, who is responsible for the radio station[78] are some of the people who began our dream and sat down to discuss it. So they are people who managed to do something. [Germinio] comes from Mexico, from the interior of Mexico. His parents were farmers on a ranch, from what I heard, and he is a person whom I admire a lot as a Hispanic person. And he has made his dreams come true. There are several like him...

I am a person whom nobody can tell, "There is nothing to do. I don't have much more to do," because I look at him, and I don't believe it. No matter how poor you are, no matter what facilities you have. Anybody who wants to sew, who wants to do something: a little machine in a yard sale, something that you can buy, you can buy fabrics to do something. Now I have just encouraged a young boy who came from Mexico, and he is a tailor in Mexico. And I told him, "Why don't you continue sewing here? You don't know how hard I have looked for somebody who sews." And he said, "Ah, Mrs. Marga, but why?" And I said, "Why? I am going to look for a job as a tailor for you. Just leave it to me. All the people who come here asking for someone to cut their trousers, to fix something, I am going to send them to you. Is that okay?" "But how?" he said. " Yes, I am going to send them to you and you are going to see how." He couldn't believe it. Every day he would come to my door, knocking at the door for one thing or another. And can you see what I told you before? There is much to do but often these people need somebody to push them and open their minds to believe that you can do it and that nothing is impossible.

---

[77] Jose Somalo, from Spain, and his wife, Rocio Flores, from Mexico, publish the free bilingual-Hispanic newspaper, *Hoy en Delaware.*

[78] A supervisor at Purdue, originally from Mexico, who has a radio program on *Radio La Exitosa*, in Milford. Panamanian Rafael Orlando Dossman also works for *Radio La Existosa,* providing a combination of music and national talk shows of interest to Hispanic immigrants.

People cook on the weekends to sell, and I know because I give them change. They come early on Saturday morning and I give them change. They go to the parks, the fields, the soccer fields in different places. I truly don't know where, but I know that in the school, at the soccer fields they have been selling [food] where the games are, and people just order from them by phone, and I am even one of their clients. I call them, and I ask them what they are doing and if they can bring me this, and they say, "Oh, yes, we'll be bringing it to you right away." That's how I know that there are two people doing that. One is Mexican, and I think that the other one is from El Salvador. But nobody dares to open a restaurant here with something.

As I told you, I feel very good because I can encourage them to be on their own, to believe that they can do something. And I know that in one's country a person doesn't like to live without money, without food, and I, when I came to the United States, I didn't want to go back. I came here, and I will die here. The only thing that I like about Mexico is the way that they watch over their dead people. They don't take them to the funeral parlor. And I say, "If I knew the day that I were going to die, I would go to Mexico to die, not just to be buried in Mexico but for the wake that they have and the way they treat the dead."

When I was 14, I went to the bridge to ask for my visa myself. I was 14. I had my papers, my photos, everything, and I got my passport. I went alone, without my mom or any elder. I had to be separated completely from my mother, and we spent many hard times together. But I wanted to be here and, if my mother had gone with me to town to get my own passport, maybe I would still be there. And no way! Ever since I was a child I always dreamed of coming to the States, because I have uncles, who live here and cousins that were kids–many of them were born here and many came here as children–and I was always dreaming of coming here and going to California and seeing the sea. Because my grandma spent some time there: five, six months, depending on the extension that she got, and my grandma brought back shells, things, and I always wanted to see the sea. That's why

I tell you "God is so powerful." I wanted to see the sea, and not only did I see it but I lived by it for six years as well. I wanted a house and, not only do I have a house, I have several, and I don't know what to do with them. That's why I tell [other people] you can get anything by working, anything. Maybe not the spiritual, but something, although they shouldn't see this as impossible. I am not an ambitious person, because there are much more important things than all of this. And now I am very busy with my business, very much so, because I have a responsibility to fulfill. So the day that I fulfill that responsibility, for me that business is as if I had—it's the same or more than if I had a husband or a family.

COMMUNITY WORKERS

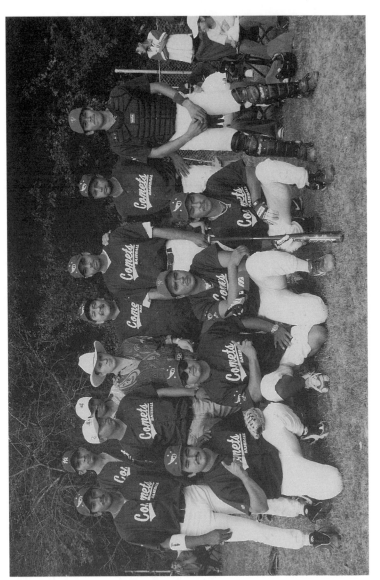

The Comets Baseball Team
(*Courtesy of R. Flores*)

Pilar Gomez

I interviewed Pilar Gomez in April, 1999, at the United Food and Commercial Workers Local 27, where she works as a special representative. Originally from a small fishing village in Spain, Pilar emigrated to the United States in 1978 at the age of 18, first to Baltimore and subsequently to Bethany Beach, Delaware. What is amazing about Pilar's story is the way in which active involvement in the community helped her break out of her personal isolation. Although she is bilingual now, she remembers poignantly what it was like to arrive in the United States with no friends, practically no family, and no way to get around or communicate.

Pilar first began to work for the Hispanic Community of Sussex County as an office manager for the Roxana Apartments, where many Hispanic workers reside. From there, she quickly became involved in the Strong Communities Program and the Hispanic Soccer League. Her support for the Mountaire-Selbyville wildcat strike in 1996 brought her to the Union's attention, and she was quickly hired to liaison with Hispanic workers. From the union office in Georgetown, she provides help of whatever kind is needed for community members, be they Hispanic or English speaking, union members or not.

Pilar was also a founding member of OGAM [Guatemalan Mutual Aid Society] and has worked closely with *La Esperanza* and the Delmarva Poultry Justice Alliance. She is one of the first people most journalists and researchers meet when they arrive in Georgetown, looking for information on the Hispanic community. Although Pilar's role in the community tends to be unofficial and supportive, her unbounded energy and willingness to sacrifice make her a very important organizer indeed. Pilar is a gifted narrator. Her story is full of illuminating details. She has also achieved a great deal.

Pilar Gomez at Local 27 Union Office, Georgetown, Delaware. August 2000
(Courtesy of Katherine Borland)

Life in Spain

I'm from Spain, from the region of Galicia and from a town that isn't even mentioned on the map, which is called Cillero. Very few residents. It's a very small town, mostly of fishermen–a fisherman's village–and all the people make a living from the sea...and my father was a sailor. Now he's retired. And most of the people who live there, well, that's what there is. There isn't anything else than to fish. To board the ships and go fishing. And the women stay at home, caring for the children or if not, well, working the land as well. Because that's what my mother did. My father went to sea and my mother worked in the fields...

He was actually the ship's cook. He cooked. He had the title of motorman–it's like an engineer. But he didn't like this. He liked cooking better. So, whenever he signed onto the ships, he would ask for the cook's position. So, he worked for a boss. The ship did not belong to my father. There are only certain people in the town who over the years became rich and bought the ships. And so in order to send the boats out, they need people. And so that's what it was—my father was a worker.

Well, the mothers cared for the children and they went to work in the fields. Well, if the child was young, they took it to the fields, sure. And the child there, covered in dirt. I remember when we planted the potatoes, the *papas*, what they called *papas*, we would go to the field and we brought what we called the *merienda* (snack). A sandwich, something to eat, and water, which we carried in a canteen. And we would go in a little cart, my mother carried me in a little cart, we'd go to the field. And there they lay out a blanket and we sat on that to eat or drink or something, while the women worked the fields.

And at times, when it was time to [harvest] the potatoes, they gave us a basket, and inside the basket was the potato that was what one had to plant. And so the women made the furrow–how do you call it?–yes the *rego*, and there they told us, okay, and they marked with their finger the little hole where one would plant the

251

potato, and so there we made the hole a little bigger and we planted the potato. [laughs]

[My mother] had two girls, my sister and I. Two died, we don't know why, but in towns like that that were so little and so remote, well–there aren't hospitals, there weren't at that time. Now there are. But at that time, there weren't doctors specialized in certain things. That is, there was a doctor, but probably he was a general practitioner, and he attended to everyone. So, from what my mother had told me, before the children died often. They don't know if it was because the woman worked a lot and in the end she aborted, with the heavy work that they did, or they didn't know– sure, because they never gave them blood exams to see if the blood was compatible, between the man and the woman.

Education

Especially being a country that was directed by Franco and well, the women were inferior, the women were considered well, inferior, in a word. And we couldn't talk about or comment on certain things that happened to us, because we were mistreated or we were looked down upon. We were prostitutes.

When I was in high school, in the second year of high school, my drawing teacher–I always liked to draw and paint, and I think I did pretty well…[the art teacher] called me, and told me that I wasn't doing well in his class, that I was definitely going to fail that class.

And so, I said, "well, what do I have to do. Can I do extra work or what? What do you recommend?"

He tells me, "Look, I will help you if you want."

I told him, "Okay, let's see."

He tells me, "Look, what you have to do is, ah"–and he told me but very quietly, in silence, obviously.

He tells me, "take this bus on Saturday, and it will take you to this place. I will be waiting for you there."

And I say, "but where?"

And he says, "Yes. On Saturday. If you want to pass the course, we'll see each other in that place."

And I say to him, "Ah yes? You can wait for me sitting down, mister." And I left his class and I never returned to the school.

My mother was angry, sure, because they didn't know why I had made this decision. I came home crying. And–my mother worked, and so when I got home, my mother was still at work. So, when she came home from work she saw that something had happened, no? So, I didn't tell her what had happened, but I did tell her that I was fed up, that I didn't want to know anything more, that my classes weren't going well, that I was desperate, that I wasn't passing the grade and I don't know. That I don't want to continue, and that this isn't for me, I told her.

"But no, you have to continue." I don't know what else–I told her, "Look, I'm going to go and waste my time. I prefer to go to work at whatever. But I don't want to return. It's not for me. It doesn't make sense for me. That doesn't mean anything to me," I kept telling her.

And so, well, sure, I was already, um, maybe 16, 17 years old, something like that. And so, obviously, it isn't that they forced me, but "well, if you are making that decision, well, we're going to help you, no?" And so, well then I never returned. And sure, the Institute sent a letter to me and my parents, asking why I wasn't returning. That is, missing so many days, no, they send a letter to the parents asking what is happening. So, my parents went and told them that I wasn't going to continue school anymore, that I had decided not to continue. So, having parental permission, one could leave. And then I didn't continue.

It was pretty common. For some circumstance or other it was pretty common, that they took one or two years of high school and then left, or didn't continue studying. Or there were many my age who finished the eighth grade and didn't go on to high school. Yes. A lot. Just as there were many who did.

There was work. You could work with your mother in the field, or my sister for example, what she took up, and she also didn't go to school very long, she took up embroidery. She went and took some classes to learn to embroider. And since before one didn't buy sheets, one made them, and the towels, one bought them, but then one embroidered the initials of the family. So, people like my sister who didn't want to go–because there were also some factories and–canneries, where they packed the fish in tins. And that work also my mother came to do. So, what she did was—my sister didn't like going to the factory, the fish packing factory.

So, my mother says, "Well, if it isn't that, you must do something else." So, she went to school to learn to embroider...

I'm younger than my sister, we're eleven years apart. And, so, I, well—I either had to go and embroider or I had to go to the cannery [laughs]. But I didn't want to do either one–I didn't like it. And so, I began to do a class in typing, to learn to type. And I began to go to those classes, and then I was going to take a class in computers as well. But then I met the man who is now my ex-husband, and so I left everything, and then he brought me here. That's how it was.

He was a sailor, and he was from the same town, but he already had spent many years here and he was a resident of this country. So, well, I was 17, very young, no? Ah, and, those things that happen that you fall in love stupidly, no? A foreigner, although one knew that he was from the town, but it had been years that he hadn't lived there. So, well, for a town, for a person from the town to come who had been in the United States, oy this was as if the Pope had come! It was an attraction that one doesn't see. Imagine...

In the United States

Arriving here, he has sisters here. But, I don't know why it should be, but his sisters never appreciated me, they never liked me, perhaps I was never good enough–since he's the only brother, the only male, perhaps they saw me as not good enough for him, I don't know. But there was never a relation–from the very beginning it was very tense. So, I was practically alone. I arrived in this country shortly after my eighteenth birthday. I turned 18 in April and I came here in June of the same year. That is, April, May, June, I was 3 months into my 18th year, and I came pregnant already. Imagine, you come to a country and you're 18 years old, pregnant, and with no husband, we can say, practically, because when I came to this country, he was at sea, he was working on the merchant ships...

And when he arrived, we began to look for a place to live, because we couldn't stay with the sister. So, we looked for an apartment there in Baltimore, and we lived in that apartment for four years...

I felt, sure, very lonely, because you have to realize that, I didn't know English, my husband had returned to sea, and I was left pregnant, because my daughter wasn't born until October, and I believe I moved into that apartment, it would have been I think in July or August, when I moved to that apartment. That is, I spent—and pregnant in a place where I don't know anyone, with no one to talk to, with no one to communicate with, pregnant, something happens to me, what do I do? I didn't even have a telephone. And I had neighbors on one side and the other, but they were Americans. If I wanted to talk to them, I couldn't. They didn't understand me, and I didn't understand them. Yes, they tried, and I did also, but pffff, it's very difficult.

I spent hours cleaning house, because there wasn't anything else to do. And I didn't even have a television in the beginning. There was only a bed and some plates for eating, and everything. And when my husband came, he did the shopping for the whole time when he would be away, so that I would have something to eat. Because I didn't even drive. And the stores were a bit far. I could have gone walking, but to carry everything. How was I going to carry everything. I couldn't. And so, when he came, we did the shopping so that it would last me as long as he was away. So that I wouldn't have to worry.

Sometimes two months. Now, I see my life and I say, "but how could I have gone through that?" That is, it looks very easy, but one only has to live it and you realize. Ah–I don't know. I don't know how I did it. I can't even explain it to myself. I remember, and then, I look back and see myself at that age, sure, and I remember. I was pregnant and I sang. The only thing I had were some cassettes of Spanish music, and they were by Julio Iglesias. I see myself, well, cleaning and singing the songs of the music of Julio Iglesias in the summer.

And so I opened the windows and come on! I put the music up as loud as it went, because I didn't know what else to do. [laughs] And I looked at the people who passed along the street and such, and I looked again and I went back to cleaning [laughing], and to sum up. I went to bed really early [laughs], because there wasn't anything to do. Ah, when night came I went to bed. And I got up, well, whenever I wanted to because there wasn't anything to do.

I remember that sometimes the postman would come with certified letters from my parents and it was maybe 12 o'clock, and I was still in bed. Because what was I going to do? I got bored. I didn't have anything to do. I didn't have anyone to talk to. Well, come, clean again. Oohhh! [laughs] My house was, you could see yourself in the floor. In the floor you could see your face [laughs]…

And so, when [my daughter] began in kindergarten, then I had to move more, and begin to communicate with the people. Now I had more contact with people. To speak to the teacher and all. That is, when my daughter began in kindergarten, she didn't know how to speak English at all. Only water, cookie and Mommy. That was it. And so for the teacher and all–there weren't any Hispanic people there where I lived. There wasn't anyone. I think I was the only one…

So, one day, the teacher called me for a meeting and she told me that she had to talk to me because the child wasn't doing well in the school and she was going to fail kindergarten. That is, they were going to keep her back in kindergarten. I, the little that I understood. So, I asked her what we could do. And she said, "leave off speaking in Spanish. And the little [English] that you know, you're going to have to speak to her and she with you."

And I told her, "well, let's see."

And so, what we did, and I believe that's where I began to go out a bit and develop. When she brought the homework, she brought sentences I remember they put, perhaps, and she had to write them, word for word, "The dog is up." And so, she had to write them over.

And I asked her, "Nicole, what does this mean?"

And she told me, "The dog is up."

And I repeated after her, "The dog is up."

"And what does that mean?"

And so she told me. And the next sentence was "The dog is down," in order to differentiate, the up from the down. And so, I repeated it with her. And so, little by little, little by little, I started to learn. I didn't want to say to my daughter that I didn't understand, so I told her, "Now let's see, tell me, how do you pronounce this?"

And she told me, "Red."

"How? "

"Red."

And I repeated, "Very good!"

Then I began to watch television. I began to watch the soap operas. And the soap operas–it doesn't seem so, but they taught me a lot. Because, even though I didn't understand, but just looking at the action, I was given to understand what was happening. Then, the next day, I had to return to see it, to see what happened. And so, little by little I caught on as well, phrases, sentences and so on. And then I began to speak a little more with my neighbors.

And sometimes when they didn't understand me, well, I drew pictures. [laughs]. Or with my hands. For example, one day, I remember, I told my neighbor that I had made a dinner and I wanted to invite her. But she didn't understand me. So, I made signs with my hands towards my mouth, I said, umm, yum, ummm! [pounds on the table] and I drew a picture of a house, and

257

I told her it was my house. And I put, afterwards a number. The number, which was the hour, and she understood me. And that's how it was, how I came out more.

And so, I was now managing better in English. Now I was, let's say, on my way. Yes. I, by that time, one could say that I was doing well. That is, five or six years went by before I could manage on my own more or less (in English).

And I asked [my husband] to help me, and I said, "But help me and so on, how do you pronounce that?"

But he would say to me, "No, no."

I even told him I wanted to drive, I wanted to learn, and he told me, "No, because you can't speak enough English yet. You don't have to drive." Well. One had to listen to him. That woman yes, but now no. [laughs]

Well, because, again one has to realize that I came to this country when I was very young. Without knowing anything, without having any experience. You come with a man, and this man is for you the protector, the father, the lover, the sweetheart, he's everything. You protect yourself with him. So, for you—at that time, for me, what he said was fine. Because for me he was everything. I didn't have any family here. I didn't have anyone. So, for him-- he was everything to me. If he said it was no good, well okay, it wasn't any good.

I remember when my daughter was small, I didn't have my son yet, and on several occasions I threatened to leave, because I didn't want to continue in that way. We weren't getting along. The little time that he was home, there were always fights and well—in short, a bad situation. So, one time I even took a little bag and put some clothing for me and for my daughter, and I went for the back door. And he detained me, he stopped me.

He stopped me and he says, "Where do you think you're going?"

I told him, "I'm going because I don't want to go on this way."

He tells me, "Where the fuck do you think you're going, and you don't even know how to speak English, and you can't defend yourself. Without me you are no one."

And so, I reacted, and I told myself, he's right. What am I going to do, where am I going to go? I don't know anyone. I don't speak English. I don't have money. I don't have anything. Where am I going to go with a baby? And I stayed. And it was like that. It wasn't just one time, but several. And well, I had to bear it. What was I going to do? I didn't have any money. He made the money.

Only if I called my parents and I told them, "Listen, send me money, send me a ticket, I'm leaving, because"–I didn't want to create problems for my parents. I felt that I didn't want–they didn't need that from me. Because I respected them, I made do.

Breaking the Isolation

When my daughter was around–I don't remember the exact age, but she was still young, that is, a girl, I remember that in Baltimore, I took her to an after school geography program. And so, there, the director who was in charge of that after school program, I spoke with him.

And he said to me, "Oh where are you from?" because he noticed, sure, my accent. By that time, I was able to defend myself in English. I knew it. And I tell him from Spain and all. And we had a good conversation.

And he told me, "Look, I am looking for a person who knows how to speak the two languages and who is amenable to giving Spanish classes to the children. It's a program that I'd very much like to have here in the center." And he says, "Do you think that you could do it?"

And I, I looked at him and with a strange face, as if someone–"But I don't have any notion," I told him. "What am I going to do. I don't know. I never worked," I told him. "I wouldn't know where to start," I told him.

And he says to me, "Look, if you are open to trying it, I am too, with you."

And I say to him, "But it's that I don't know even where to start." And he gave me a little orientation. So–and he gave me a lot of books to make copies and take notes and all. And from there, I took it and I began to make my own classes to later present to the children... And the Baltimore City Hall even gave me a diploma and an award for the Best Outstanding Volunteer, or something like that. I don't remember. I have it at home. [laughs]

And I felt, well, very good. Ah, because I've told you, I spent many years as if I were in a cave, let's say, shut-in, without doing anything, without knowing anything more, and that, well, it gave me the strength and the inspiration to be able to do more and to continue. Perhaps, that–there was where Pilar began to be Pilar. Because before I wasn't Pilar. Perhaps, I was Pilar but I wasn't. I wasn't acting, I think, the way I was. I was acting through the agency of another person. And that, well, it opened my eyes and my mind. And I liked it. And I continued.

And then, starting from there, I continued giving classes after school and at a private school in Baltimore, I think it was called St. Francis...

In Delaware

Well, the city where we were living in Baltimore was turning very bad. The neighborhood was changing a lot. It was becoming very dangerous. So, since we–our children were still young, we had bought a property, a piece of land here years earlier in Delaware. Because we had come here for vacations, and we liked it, and we bought a piece of land, and we had it there. And so, well, when the neighborhood began to get bad, we decided to come here. And once again, it was even worse. I ended up even more alone. [laughs]...

Yes, in '92 we moved to Delaware. And for awhile I was at home without doing anything. Not for nothing, well yes I was busy, sure, moving and organizing everything and all. And then I began to be interested in looking for something to do, sure. Because the children were older then, and they cost more, and I said, "I have to do something." And I applied at the high school to give classes to adults at night, to give Spanish classes. And I did that for a year, a year and a half also. And I had a lot of students.

And they were all–they wanted to learn to speak Spanish for different reasons [laughs]; one because she was a nurse, another because she worked in the bank, the other one was a mechanic, the other one was a politician. Well. The other one was a priest [laughs].

At the same time that I did that, my son had to move from 5th grade and he had to go to another school where he would take the 6th, 7th and 8th grade. But it was a school that was considered very poor; it wasn't a very good school. So, I had some friends and those friends informed me that they were forming a parent's group to make an alternative school, I think they call it. And they invited me to go to a meeting that they had, and I went. And I was very interested in what they were talking about and all the–the projects that they had. And I began to get involved with those people. And from there, well, we began to organize, organize, organize, and within four months perhaps, we opened–we called it, we ended up calling it the Snow School, the School of Snow, because we didn't know what to call it.

The person who is truly interested in his child's education, well, sacrifices something else and does what he can to give his child the best education. It was expensive for us. I'm not going to say it wasn't; it wasn't cheap, but it was very good I think.

Roxana Apartments

And then, I tell you, [my son] began high school and then afterwards, I looked in other places at the same time, and I got a job in a place called Roxana. There are like 47 apartments, and Hispanics were all living there. The owner of the apartments is American and he didn't speak Spanish and he had problems communicating with the people in questions of, well, the contract and whatever. And he found out that–I don't know through whom, I don't know, I can't say—he found out that I spoke both languages and he called me one day and he asked me if I would be interested in working two days a week for him.

I said, "Yes, why not?" I began to work with him. And in the beginning, sure, I didn't know, I had never worked in a community with so many people [laughs]. And especially to be in charge of 47 apartments! [laughs] It's a lot, no? And I went little by little, two days a week wasn't much. In the beginning, well, I felt lost, I didn't know. But the man taught me what the contract was, what they had to do, what the regulations were and all that they had to follow. Everything. He gave me all the information. And I began to involve myself not only with the owner and in what was necessary to direct the apartments, but I also began to involve myself with the people.

Because they looked at me in the beginning with mistrust. Because, perhaps I'm white or who knows, I don't look like–well, I didn't look like them, and they saw me, sure, Who is this woman who comes here, speaking Spanish to us, and telling us all this? No? And so, I began to get more and more involved with the community.

And I told them, "I'm here to work for the owner, but I'm also here for you, for what you need." And it took a long time for the people to get used to me and to confide in me. It took a long time. Perhaps now I say probably because they viewed me with distrust, because they saw me as part of management, of the rent director.

And I told them, "No, no, don't worry, no. I have to do my work, sure, but at the same time, here I am."

So, I said," well, how am I going to gain their confidence?" Because, I wanted to help and I saw many many problems in the community.

There were many men, yes. But already there were families, there were a number of children, a number of families. There were more men than anything, yes. The majority were single men…

Well, I became friends with various women and very good women, magnificent. I wish they were still here, but unfortunately they returned to Mexico, because they would have been very good people to interview. One of them was a very good organizer. And she moved people! She was called Maria, the woman. She's a woman of 40+ years, and she was very well respected there in the community, because she was like everyone's mother, obviously. And there they were. And she, whatever event, there she went– "Come on, get moving, I don't know what or when, this or that"– or whatever thing I needed, she was always disposed to help out.

So I began with programs. Through the agency of the Catholic Church in Bethany Beach, Saint Anne's, volunteers began to come. Older women, older retired women and men, and they wanted to work in the community, because they knew that there were problems there, and well, they told me, "What can be done?" And so, we gathered ideas together and we began to do an after school program with the children.

And afterwards, I continued with other programs. Then I began with the program, I called it Head–like a Head Start Program. I took the two-to-four-year-old children, because those children didn't qualify for the true Head Start Program because they didn't know enough English. So, I said, "No, we have to do something here. Here you aren't going to upset these people." So I began to get things moving again, and I began the program. And I took the two-to-four-year olds, and I myself began to give them those classes, also twice a week, for two hours.

I did everything in English. When certain of the children came time to begin kindergarten, when they went to take the exam that they give them–the test that they give them to enter kindergarten—the school found out that something was happening in the apartments. And they called and they asked what was happening. And I told them. Ohhh, how marvelous, how fabulous, because one notes that those children have [improved...], because there are some who come and they have no idea, and all. And so, I liked this, obviously, it's logical, no? I, without knowing anything, and to do that, well, it's something to be very proud of.

Two-year-olds at *Primero Pasos*
(Courtesy of Rocio Flores)

Afterwards there were many men, and I found out that there was a soccer league. And they like to drink a lot, unfortunately. [laughs]

I said, "Well, what can I do?"

So, I began to get involved with the men. But involved in the sense of [laughs] finding out what ideas they had. Finding out what was going on. So, I told them, I proposed, if they would like to form a team with the players that were there in the apartments. And they liked the idea. Oh, how great! And I don't know what, and they began to share ideas and more ideas. And we got together on Saturdays and Sundays to create this idea. And from there a team was formed. And they ended up calling it Hispanoamerica, and I got them the uniforms, the balls, I got them the money for the registration, and it was the only team in the league in any year that was more prepared than anyone in the question of regulations and laws and to have their written documents, and their identification cards ready, that is, all that.

And I liked that a lot also, sure. And the league began and they played every Sunday. And I was never absent. I think I missed only once when I went to meet my cousins in the airport. All the other times, I never missed a game. There I was supporting the team and bringing them their water every Sunday.

Oh, when I went to the soccer games I forgot to tell you that we put, I have a friend who puts programs in the Internet. He has the Internet and agencies or organizations that want to put the organization on the Internet, consult with him and he puts the page up and all the webpage, he designs it. And he went every Sunday to the soccer games, to watch the team.

He told me, "Pilar, I'm going to do something."

I say, "What?"

And he tells me, "I'm going to put the team on the Internet."

"Great, then do it." And he did. He even put photos and everything of the team...

And afterwards, I was sent several faxes telling me that there were teams from other countries including from Brazil who

Regular Soccer Match
(Courtesy of Rocio Flores)

were very curious about what was on the Internet about that team from Roxana. And I have the copies. [laughs] That is, they were very active years for me and for the Roxana community, because there was a lot of movement and a lot of action.

During the wintertime what do we do? There's no game. What are we going to do? We have to do something. Well, what do you think of having a Social Day? We'll call it, the Social Day. To share the day with the community. So, we got together on Sundays again, in one of the apartments where we gave the classes to the children, and there we got together the people who wanted to—and they brought movies, they brought card games, they brought dominoes and chess games. And there we were in the afternoons on Sunday to give people something to do.

Another program–it's that, ay–oh, the garden. The owner of the apartments–behind the apartments–has a lot of land and he doesn't plant it or anything. So, he asked me if the people would be interested in my making a survey of the residents to see if they would like to plant something. I said, "Oh, that's a good idea. I'll do it, let's see what happens."

And I began to ask the people. And they also liked the idea.

And, "when are we going to start and what can we plant and how much land and all?"

I said, "Well calm down, calm down," [laughs].

And so the owner collaborated very well. He gave us an enormous quantity of land behind. He cleaned it, he brought a tractor and turned the earth over. He cleaned it.

And then, he said, "Well, now each person should divide, according to his apartment, he should divide the land that he wants." All the portions equally. And they should mark them. They did it like that. They bought stakes and we bought rope and each one, and I have a tape, I have it recorded. You see the people working, marking their little piece and putting the apartment number on the stake. There, that's how one saw that it was theirs. And I got the plants free from a gardening store. And they brought me a great number. They brought me tomato plants, chile

267

Garden Project behind Twin Cedars, Roxana Apartments
(Courtesy of Katherine Borland)

peppers, cilantro, well, I don't know, a lot of things. And the people began to ask, "Pilar can we plant other things?"...

We also organized–well, there was a Mexican tradition and I don't remember the name exactly, but it was the coronation of the Queen of Spring, I think that's what it was, where they choose a girl, let's say the prettiest, and they make her a Queen's costume and with a crown. And they choose a companion who must be a boy of her age, and he also has to be in a costume. And, and they get the community together and they go and they put a throne, like a king's throne also decorated, and they have flowers around and the girl comes out, she came out of an apartment dressed in her costume and accompanied by the boy also all dressed up, and they got to the throne and there they crown her and they give her roses. That is something that they organized, that I well, I wasn't familiar with that tradition. I was there once again to support, help in whatever way necessary, but they organized it...

I was still married, but the problems became more intense because, perhaps I don't know if I ought to say this, but my husband didn't like where I was working. Because, since they were, he said, all *Hispanos*, that they were taking advantage of me, of my kindness, because I am too good, and they don't pay me, they pay me a shit and a half, he said, for the work that you do. And those shitty Mexicans are good for nothing, and—well! Because I felt good about the work that I was doing. And a person—my husband, who was supposed to support me, comes and tells me all that, it hurt me a lot. And it hurt me a lot. So, that, well, made the situation worse. "No"–I said, "no." ...

And then, afterwards, one thing led to another, the papers, I went to court, from here to there and, well, they gave me a divorce. Magnificent. Fabulous. Never had I felt so good in my life. I felt free. When they gave me–when the paper arrived in the mail, I think the divorce came in the mail, and then I didn't have anything that tied me to him. Ohhh, I felt really happy, but really happy.

15th Year Traditional Celebration at St. Michael's Church, Georgetown, Delaware.
(Courtesy of Rocio Flores)

The Wildcat Strike

Okay. I still worked in the apartments, and I will never forget it. It was a Sunday, and I told you, on Sundays I went–in soccer season–I went every Sunday. And it was a Sunday that the team was going to play. And since there were players who didn't have a way to get there, to the field where they played, well, I picked up and brought those who needed a way to get there, those who needed transportation. So, when I got there, well, I got out as I always did and [I was], calling them, no?

And a young man comes, named Pedro, and he stops me and he says, "Pilar."

"Well, hello Pedro, how are you, what's going on?"

He says, "I have to talk to you."

I say, "What's going on?"

"We have a problem."

I say, "Problems with who?" And he began to tell a story. It was a Sunday and the young man had had an accident a few days earlier. In one of the poultry processing plants a young man in one of the machines cut off a finger and half of another. And the young man, it appeared, had a very large family working. He has a lot of family working there in the poultry factory and a lot of friends. It appears that it's a very well known family, everybody knows them, and he says, "Look, the family wants to do something. They have the support of the community. They have the support of other friends. They want to do something. But we need help."

I tell him, "What do you want me to do? I don't know what to do. I don't even know what happened."

And he, "I told you," he recounted everything about the accident, and he said, "We want you to help us."

I said, "Okay, look, I will help you all I can, but I don't know where to begin. I don't know what you want me to do."

And he told me, "Just suggest to us what we might do. You, I know, have contact with a Priest"–they were referring then to Father Jim Lewis.

I said, "Yes."

And he says, "I know that he's very active in the community and I know that he comes here, you talk, and he even gives you ideas, and he helps you."

"It's true."

He says, "Could you get in touch with him to help us?"

"Yes. But, I said, there's a problem."

He says, "What problem?"

I tell him, "because I have to go to the playing fields to bring the players. It's a commitment that I made and I don't know what to do."

But there was a man who I had worked with for a while, and he would go with me sometimes to the field, not the one who had the internet, but another. And that Sunday coincided in that he was going to go to the apartments also to look for some of the players.

And so, I called him and said, "Look, now, this has happened. This situation has occurred, and something has to be done. But I can't stay. I have to go to the field."

He says, "Fine. You go to the field, take the players, and I will try to help him." The man didn't speak Spanish. But Pedro spoke some English. So, the man took it on and he got in touch with Jim Lewis. Because he knew, he also knows Jim Lewis. And so. That same day, that same Sunday they met it seems, in a church with Jim Lewis, that man, and fifty people. And that was Sunday.

So, I after–after I come back from the field, and I find out what happened, and they say they want to have a strike.

And I, "Great! Fabulous." I will be there as well to support them and help them. [laughs].

And so, they said that they were going to meet in the Church at Selbyville on Monday.

I said, "Okay, I'll be there."

And yes, we came together. But now it wasn't fifty people. There must have been like a hundred and fifty. And we met there. And all of them were workers in the same plant. And all with the same goal, and defying what—the action of the company? And well, I, well, obviously, wanting to or not, I got involved in that there with the people...

Okay, we met in the church in the area of Selbyville. And I tell you, when I got there, there were already a lot of people. So, we began to organize things more and Father Jim was there, with all the workers and all the workers with their boots on and the helmet and everything. That is, it was all very exciting. And we began to make the posters with different things in English and Spanish.

The Sisters were also there,[79] and they also, obviously, collaborated. They came to help us and all who were there, making the signs and putting down that they should treat us like human beings and not like animals. We demanded justice, ah, we want better machine safety. That is, I don't remember now, but that kind of thing.

And so, that was Monday, and we went in front of the plant, sure. Then the plant officials began to come out. And they were trying to convince the people to go in to work. But the workers, no. There were some who did go in. But the majority, no. And those who at times were going in, we would call, "Hey, come here, come here, come here, we're having a strike, don't go in." And you saw the worker going over to the group that was striking. And that's how the group started forming, and more and more until almost 300 people who didn't go to work.

And the strike lasted from Monday to Tuesday. And I remember very well, as if it were today, the parking lot in back of the church was full of cars on Monday night, and they decided to sleep there. Some slept on the ground, others slept inside the church, others slept in the church room, others slept in the cars, I stayed and slept in my car. From time to time, we took turns during the night, and one would come from time to time to call me. Pedro normally would come and knock on the window of my car

---

[79] Pilar refers to the Sisters of Charity—Maria Mairlot, Rosa Alvarez, and Ascension, who now work through *La Esperanza*. See their stories, this volume.

and he said, "Pilar, it's time again to picket in front of the poultry plant." And I would wake up and, "Come on, let's go!" And once again, boom, boom, walking in front of the poultry plant. And, and that was Monday night, Tuesday morning.

So, then one began to watch the television, the radio...because now it came out, I tell you, in the television and the radio and all. And the newspapers. They called the police. The local police. And they couldn't do anything because we, well, resisted. We said, "No, no." Yes.

So, they prevented us from being where we were, because they said that it was company property. So, we asked them, with Father Jim's help, we said, "Okay, if that is so, tell us where we can be."

So, they showed us where we could be. And there we were. A peaceful demonstration, but there we were in front of the poultry plant without passing into the property of the company, there. They sent for the state police as well. And they sent for an Hispanic policeman to control the situation. Hispanic or not, police, we went on in the same way.

Ah, and then, almost like, at 8:30 or 9:00 in the morning, some people from the Union appear with an interpreter, with another young man who had just started to work for the union. And they arrived there to the church room, and told them in English and in a very serious voice, they told them, "You have half an hour. At 9:30, if you don't show up for work, you're all fired," said the Union agent. "Because the contract says that you can't strike." And everyone was left with their mouth open.

And several of them say, "What contract?"

And the Union man, "The contract that you signed."

"We don't know what we've signed!" several voices say.

"Where is that contract?"

So, Pedro grabbed [the floor] and said, "Where can I get that contract?"

And they told him. So, he went and another one, to get a contract. And they saw there that yes, it was true that they weren't able to strike. But, they went on the same. Whether the Union was present or not, they continued.

"No, we aren't convinced, no, we're going to continue, we don't care what you say. I don't know what all else."

Well. In one word, they didn't pay any attention to them. For this, now a certain amount of time had passed. They said that they wanted the things that the workers wanted, the company had to address [those issues], if not, they weren't going to work. But they didn't pay attention to them, they continued.

And then it was, I don't know, but perhaps 12 in the afternoon, I think. So, the company decided to meet in a neutral place, neither the church nor the company, with the Union, the Company and the Workers. So then I couldn't go to that meeting. Nor could Father Jim. No one. Not the Sisters. That is, it was only the workers—certain workers, not all of them. The leaders, the company and the Union. And there, we don't know what happened, we don't really know. Because when they finished that meeting, Pedro came and he said, "Well, boys, we're going back to work."

That is, we don't know. Today I still don't know exactly what happened in that meeting.

I told him before he went, "Pedro, don't let them convince you. Be sure that the demands that you request, that they give you in writing or that they approve them."

And he said, "Yes, that's good."

So, when he finished and said, "Boys, let's go back. Let's go to work," I said to him, "Pedro, what did they tell you."

And he said, "Yes, they're going to improve the situation and they're going to make the changes," and so. And then, little by little they went returning, returning and in the end, everyone went back.

So, the Union, sure they were furious and imagine! A company that has a Union, and the workers strike.

They say, "There's a problem. What's going on here? Something is happening." So, they realized that their mistake perhaps was that they didn't have Hispanic representation when they should have had it. So, Jim Lewis at that time was forming a group of people and this group had to do with the problems that exist in the poultry processing plants.

And I went to those meetings, the same as people from the international Union. Because that was his achievement, that today the organization that he formed which is called Delmarva Poultry Justice Alliance comes to be, that was where everything was initiated, after that strike. And so, I attended those meetings. And I explained the situation of the community. And there, there were important leaders of the international. And there, well, I don't know, they saw me, they liked me, I don't know. And another thing, Jim Lewis also spoke to them about me, and he told them that, well, they had to change, they have to make the necessary change, so that the members had a voice, and I would be a good candidate to work with them.

And after a certain time, I don't remember, they asked did I want to work for them. Since I didn't work at that time, I told them yes and I accepted the work. And here I am.

Maria Lopez

I met Maria Lopez at the Summer Migrant Education program at North Georgetown Elementary School on July 17, 2000. A graduate of the program herself, she now works as a recruiter in the summer months. The rest of the year, she's a teacher's assistant at Project Village, a Head Start program in Selbyville. Maria invited me to go to the Bridgeville Apartments to check for newly arrived children.[83] On the way, she explained that she had come to this country when she was 12. Originally from Zacatecas, Mexico, Maria followed her father to Milton in 1980, where he had found work in the King Cole cannery five years before. Although her parents had little formal education, Maria emphasized that they encouraged their children to study hard. She and her four siblings all finished high school.

We stopped at the Bridgeville apartments, and by chance a young man with a boy about three was leaving the main office. Maria asked him it he'd just arrived, and soon the two were engaged in lively conversation. The young man explained that he and his family had arrived three days earlier from Phoenix, where they had lived for five years. He was looking for work, maybe in a nursery or harvesting corn. He invited us up to the apartment, where we found two young women and two toddlers. When Maria asked the mother if she'd like to enroll her older child in the summer program, she expressed some nervousness, but readily agreed. We joked about the boy wanting to imitate his older friends and go to school, while Maria took information from the boy's birth certificate and vaccination record.

As we walked out with the boy, the young mom explained that she had been in Delaware before when she was 12. Later she left for Phoenix and Mexico with her husband. She is originally from Michoacan and he is from San Luis Potosí. We belted our young charge into the car, while the parents waved goodbye from the sidewalk. Maria calmly explained where and when the bus

---

[83] Built by Delmarva Rural Ministries, these apartments constitute model housing for migrant workers.

would be dropping him off later in the afternoon. We headed back to the school. What impressed me was the ease with which Maria worked to identify and enroll her young charges.

On a subsequent visit, Maria agreed to give me her life story as well as that of her father, a very important person in her life. We began the interview without the benefit of a tape recorder, so some of this material is direct quotation, while some is my summary, indicated by brackets. Later, Maria agreed to tape her story, and I provide here, selected parts of that conversation.

Maria's Father

My father was the youngest of six children. He didn't know his father, because he died three months before he was born [in a fever epidemic that swept through Mexico]. So, his older brothers were like his "father figure." They sent him to work hard in the fields. He planted honeydew, watermelon, corn. He worked all day in the fields. My grandmother brought him lunch. Well, he did that for many years from the time he was very small.

He married at 18. He came here to the United States in 1970, because he came here after I was born [1968. On the first trip he spent about eight months. He came back for two years, then went North again]. He didn't want to keep working in the fields. He wanted to leave Mexico in search of better opportunities.

He suffered a lot. On his way up again, they caught them. The Coyote who was bringing them told them to run. [He had come up with another young man, and they ran off together. They got lost in the desert and wandered around for three days without food or water. Finally, her father asked God to deliver them, and a short time later, they came to a highway. Dehydrated, they threw themselves upon the ground and were ready to die. Maria says her father remembers that several cars went by without stopping.]

A man in his forties and another in his twenties came up. They stopped their truck and took them to their house. They spent several days recuperating there. [The family gave them showers, clothes, food, a place to sleep and cared for them for a week. After they recovered, the family, who were Chicano, offered them yardwork. So, they were there almost a year, in San Antonio, Texas.]

He missed my mother a lot. He went back. He stayed for a while, a year, and then he decided to come here again. My mother tells us that it was two or three years, and then he came back. He went to work for the same people, three or four years. Then he decided to look for something more. The same man he had come up with [that first time to San Antonio], told him that there was a cannery in Delaware, and that they gave you as many hours as you wanted and they paid better. That's when he decided to come here to Delaware...

He just came to Milton, Delaware, but he didn't know where the company was located. He didn't have the address. He didn't know what to do, because he only saw American people. Luckily, he [met] Raul. The man knew where King Cole was, and he showed him. They went to King Cole and applied and they gave them work.

My father worked from 4:00 in the afternoon to 8:00 in the morning. And sometimes more. Because in those days there was a lot of green beans and broad beans. Since at that time there were a lot of those vegetables, father says, sometimes there were twenty trucks to wash. [People picked over the produce and threw away the bad pieces]. He worked there for many years. The last time he worked for five years. He worked there and sent money over to Mexico and from that my mother saved some of the money and used part of it for us.

Papa told her to save—to buy material to build a house little by little. We were able to build a house of cement block with two rooms and a kitchen. After five years he didn't want to live alone in Delaware anymore. So he sent for us to come from Mexico to the United States. He went to Mexico. Before coming to us, he went to San Antonio. He visited that family that he had met that first time. [He told them that he was going to bring his family, but he needed help. They said they would help him.]

The Crossing

We went to Laredo for two days. So that man had the same children as my father had—three boys and two girls. So, it was night. We were sleeping in the back of his truck. And they showed their papers, saying that we were their children, but we were sleeping. They were Chicanos, born in San Antonio, Texas. My father and mother stayed behind. They waited. They crossed as wetbacks. My father wanted to accompany my mother, but in crossing, the "migra" caught them and they sent them back all the way to Rio Grande, Zacatecas. And my mother lost hope. She cried and told my father to call the man and tell him to send back her kids.

When he called, the man took my father to task. He said, "But tell me something, who wears the pants in your house?" He said he would return the children if that's what my father wanted, but if my father wanted to bring everyone to the United States, he would keep them and they would have to try to cross again. My father wanted that, and so even though my mother was very afraid, he insisted. He became very firm.

She had never experienced anything so terrible. Because mother says that the Coyotes are very bad. They yell at people, they pack them together…then they arrived in San Antonio, Texas. It was three or four weeks [later]. The family was really good to us. They gave us a lot of attention. When they arrived, I didn't want to go.

"You go, Papi, but I'm staying here. I'm not going." I was twelve.

My mother said to me, "I brought you up, I killed myself for you. No, no you're not staying behind. You're coming with us."

And from there we came to Delaware. I never went back to San Antonio. I called the wife of that man grandmother. She told us not to call her, not to write to her, to erase that family from our memory. Maybe she was afraid, but I don't know. Sometimes–

Packing Corn at the Papens Packing Station
Kent County, Delaware August, 2000
(Courtesy of Katherine Borland)

like, for example, about three years ago, one of my brothers married. We went to Mexico. But by then I didn't know the way to the house. How well that family treated us! I would like to write them and thank them.

Delaware in the 1980s

Well, when we came here to Delaware, we arrived and well, immediately after—two days later I imagine, it seems like it was two or three days later, a woman came, a very nice woman—I remember her, I will never forget her—her name is Sister Kathy— and she showed up to help us, to register us at the school.[84] Because my father didn't know how or where to go. Well, he knew where the school was, but he didn't know how to speak English. So, well, the woman, I don't know even now–don't know how she knew that we had arrived at the King Cole camp and all. She took my brothers and sister and me to register at the school. And that's where I met–it seems like there were like five or six students who were Mexican, of Hispanic origin, and they helped me. That is, how to do the lessons, well, because the teachers talked to me and tried to help me. But, I didn't understand, well, I didn't understand, because I didn't know any English. And those friends, well those Hispanic girlfriends I had, knew a little English, not much, right, but what they knew, they told me…

After I got out of regular school, I entered the program called the summer school[85], well, and in that little summer school—I really loved it, because there were even more Hispanic students who were in the same position I was, who didn't know how to speak English, and couldn't converse with the teacher. Well other students, it's true that there were non-Hispanics, right—

---

[84] Sister Kathy worked at Casa San Francisco, which at that time, provided services for Hispanic immigrants. Maria attended an after school program there to help her learn English and manage her schoolwork. Casa San Francisco now has fewer Hispanic clients and provides services mostly to families in crisis— with a shelter and soup kitchen.

[85] The Migrant Summer Education Program, a federally funded program.

like Koreans, Haitians—and well, they were there for the same reason. And they were really nice. Well, we got along super, with the teachers as well. They—it was like they gave us more attention, and they helped us a lot in everything we tried to do—the work or anything—they were there to help us.

Then from there, I, well, I went back to the regular school, in September. And so, I went back and I put in a lot of effort, right, because now I knew that it wasn't just a few of us, right, who had the same problem of not being able to communicate with the teacher, but there were a lot more, right, although they didn't live close by. Well, I still knew that there were more of us...

The first two years was like, well, there weren't very many people. That is, when one went to the supermarket or to the shops or simply to the Laundromat—one would go and well, the people would be—staring at you as if to say, well, where did you come from? Who are you? (laughs) Right, the American people. Well, one would just stare back at them too. But then, like two or three years later, then was when we noticed that there were more and more arriving. Well, up to right now the percentage of Hispanic people who are arriving each day is even greater, more immense, compared to years before...

Well there are American people who do accept us, because I've noticed that a lot, that there are people, Americans, who do accept us. They like to talk with the Hispanics even when they don't know the language and it's as if they try there in one way or another to communicate with each other, and besides that, they find ways to help us. Nevertheless, there are other people who just seeing you tell you everything, right, that you aren't from here. You shouldn't, you shouldn't be here. You need to go back where you came from. Well, I've been in those, well, like you say, positions.

[When we first arrived in 1982] there was no Spanish Mass, there were no Hispanic shops, totally American, I remember—not dances, not soccer, nothing like that. We came here and I remember that well, we came. There wasn't any chile. There weren't any tortillas. And well, they mentioned to my father

Summer Migrant Program
(Courtesy of Rocio Flores)

that there was a store, right, that in Dover there was a store of, what are they called? [Dominicans?] No, they weren't Dominicans, where the woman who had all those shoes [Filipinos?] There you go, Filipina, that's it. (laughter) There was a Filipina store, and they sold things that were more or less like Mexican things, right? And we went, and yes, there was where we found the Maseca, the flour where we make tortillas. And we found cilantro. There was chile. There was cheese. There were giblets. And it was from there that each weekend, well on Sundays, we went all the way to Dover. We bought three or four packets of Maseca for the whole week. Then we bought chile for the whole week. And well, cheese, when we were doing alright, you know, when what my father made, his little check was more or less, right, we would buy cheese to make enchiladas, the giblets for giblets, the soup...

I remember that there was a *quinceañera*.[86] It was like four years after we came here. And we didn't know how to react, if it was truly true, that they were going to have a *quinceañera* here. I said, "But where are they going to get the ladies in waiting for the *quinceañera* there? Where are they going to get the musicians from? And where are they going to get the people to come? Because I didn't know many, right, of those there in Milton. And well, they had their *quinceañera*. There weren't more than—no— I'm going to say that in that *quinceañera*, there weren't more than 50 guests. That, and all those people came from different places. They came from Milford, Dover, from Maryland also. But it wasn't a lot of people, well, very simple but very pretty that *quinceañera*. The dance was with records, with—how do you say—with a sound system. And well, it was very pretty, yes. I was included in—I was one of the ladies in waiting and well, it was very nice.

After that, then more or less one saw more dances. But with sound systems only. It wasn't like now that the Cadets come, the Veleros come. Like those big groups, right that are well known. But before, nothing. There wasn't any of that.... After I

---

[86] An hispanic rite of passage for young girls marking their 15th birthday, similar to a sweet 16 party.

left school, I would go home, I ate whatever there was, and then I helped clean the kitchen. Because at that time, there were five of us, well, children, well my sister and my three brothers, my father and my mother in one room—yes, in an apartment with one room, at that time it was one room and a kitchen. We all lived there and well, I helped my mother pick up the house...

Yes, it was the same King Cole, and from that same place, they came, they charged part of the money, well, the rent, they took it out of my father's check. And so, we lived there for about four years I imagine, three or four years. From there, they began, well, they closed it, and we had to find another place to live.

And well, my father met a man, who is a very good man. He helped my father buy a little trailer here, and the little trailer had two rooms, the kitchen and a living room. So from the Camp we moved to a trailer. And it was right there close to the store and the workplace and all that. Well, we never moved to a place farther away. We were always close to that same place.

...I don't remember how many years later, well, my mother decided to go to work at a chicken plant. To Perdue. And well, my father remained in the same work. He loved it, well, from the time he stepped foot in King Cole, he never left. I imagine he never missed one day. And he lasted like 20 years, 21, like 21 years. But that man never missed a day, he was always there, at his King Cole. He never wanted to leave until recently, they closed down.

And well, then, not my mother, right. She also wanted, well, to get out of King Cole and work somewhere else. And so that's what she did. She looked for the way to do it, and she found it. She worked in Perdue in deboning, I believe, yes it was light deboning. She worked there and well, she earned more, and the hours were about the same, right? The schedule didn't change.[87]

When I turned 16, I decided to work also and help my father and mother. And the way we did it was that I began to work

---

[87] In the canneries the work cycle is tied to the agricultural cycle. Therefore, when the harvest comes in and the product needs to be processed, the hours can be very long.

in the Milford cannery, it was called Clifton Canning, something like that in Milford. And I worked there for a while. And then, that is to say, I worked all during the summer. Well, and then after the summer ended, I started at King Cole. Then I worked in King Cole together with my father. And I began at four in the afternoon. After school started in September, I began to work, from four to eleven at night. Well, it's that it was hard, right: learn English in the afternoon, help my parents, work, and all that was hard. And then my father, well, sometimes I said to him, "Papa, today I don't feel like going to school. I'm really tired, really sleepy. Let me stay home. I want to rest."

And he said, "No, child. You have to struggle. You have to go to school and learn," he said, "because in that way, it's the only way that you will be able to overcome. You'll be something when you grow up." That's what he told me.

"I don't want to see you killing yourself in a company like I'm doing. I want to see you do something for yourself," he says.

He told me, "I want you to go and put more effort into school." And well, yes, that—what he told me, right, was what I always kept in mind. "I have to go to school. I have to go to school." Every day it was the same thing…

And yes, that's what I did for two years, I think. Two or three years, until I left school, that is, I graduated. That is, I always—as I told you before, right—struggled to continue my studies and get my diploma. Because my father and mother, as I say, never let me—leave school.

[My father] never had the opportunity, because he always worked as I told you before. He worked from 4:00 in the afternoon to 8:00 in the morning, and sometimes later—it depended on the product that they had to run that day. And well, apart from that I believe his goal was to work hard so that we had bread on the table, right? And so we could continue with our education…

And he never, never said, well, "No, I'm going to leave work for five hours so that I can go to learn English or improve myself." No, he always—"I'm going to work hard, and I'm going to have the food there, well, enough money to give my children food, clothing, whatever..."

[My mother] never studied. Well, she studied for one year, but my mom says that she didn't learn much in the first year that she went to primary school. Well, first grade. For the same reason also, she was the baby of the house. Her mother, my grandmother, died when she was fifteen. So she also suffered a lot with my grandfather. Because my grandfather was, as they say, very hard on her. Also, he always liked to worked in the fields a lot—to plant corn, squash, beans. There were a lot of things that he planted, right? My mother always had to be there behind him, as if she were a little man, always. She, well, went riding on the mules, watering the vegetables there, the corn and all that. He always told her, right, "Why do you want to study if you're not going to learn anything anyway." He never believed in that. And that's why Mama never went to school.

Until she was now already, well—it was when, after she was already married—then my father came north, and he sent her letters, and she had to look for a person to read them to her. And so she made the effort, well, she says there were some classes. They had some classes in night school for parents who needed help in reading, for literacy. And then she attended and she made the effort to go, and well, that way she learned to write her name, because she didn't even know how to write her name. So it was after she was already married that she learned. And she still writes, right, but not very well, you can understand it, but she was able to do it, right, and well, you know. She doesn't know how to write much, but she knows how to read. And all because she went to that class and learned the alphabet. You see the Mexican alphabet is easier, easier to read, right?

Yes, my family and I straightened out [our legal status] with that amnesty that came out in 1987, I think. I don't remember exactly, but, it was through that amnesty that came out in those years. And well, from there, they gave us permission for ten years. And then after those years, I had to put in an application for another ten years. And then after, I think that it's five or ten years after that you can obtain the visa or permanent residence. And then from there apply for citizenship, which is what I'm doing right now. Trying to well, well yes, to become a citizen.

Maria's Worklife

Well, I worked as I said in King Cole, in Clifton Canning, which is a company like King Cole. I worked in the poultry processing plants—I worked on the line, and yes, that work was really hard. And then one day I said to myself, "Well, I went to school. I know English, well, I don't know it perfectly, right, but I know how to manage. I have my diploma, my High School diploma. I can do something more. I can't, well—my father said that he wanted me to be something. That's what I wanted, right? Then what am I doing in this chicken company? And from there I left. I went, I applied to college, for that financial aid. From there I began to take classes in college. And while I was in college at the same time I was working full-time. I worked in a day care, and I worked in the day care preparing the meals, preparing the lunches for the children. And from there, well, I became pregnant with my fourth child, when I worked in the day care, and I left. I had to leave, right, because of the pregnancy.

And after I had my baby, I met Maria Mendoza[88]–I don't know if you know her–I met Maria Mendoza and she said, "You know what, Maria, I know a person who is looking for a bilingual person who has cooking experience." And I said, "Oh yeah?" She said, "Yes. That woman is going to open a new day care in Georgetown[89]," she said. "She's looking for someone to manage the kitchen." So, I said, "Okay. Fine." I told her, "Give me the telephone number, and I'll call that woman." And yes, they offered me the job, and I accepted it...

---

[88] See personal narrative of Maria Mendoza this volume

[89] The day care, *Primeros Pasos*, was the first bilingual daycare to open in Sussex County and was established to meet the growing need, especially of Hispanic single mothers in the area.

From left, Nancy Soriano and Maria Lopez, recruiters for the Summer Migrant Education Program
(Courtesy of Katherine Borland)

So I worked there in '95—it was like in October, like in October I think when they opened. I worked there October to March of '96. So, from there I said, "I like to work in the kitchen, I love the children—what more can I do? I have to look, to keep on looking for those little pinholes. I have to do something more." Like something was telling me, there's something more for you, or, there's something out there for you. So, one day I said, "Tarran! The schools! I would love to work for a school."

And yes, I called the school in Selbyville, and well, I spoke to them, I spoke to a woman, and I told her then who I was and the type of work I was looking for. That I worked in a kitchen, I'm manager at the *Primeros Pasos* Day Care and all that, and she said, "Okay," the woman told me, "Maria, Maria, the name Maria sounds like it's Spanish or Hispanic." I said, "I'm Hispanic. I'm bilingual." She said, "Ah," the woman said, "Yes, I have the perfect position for you." I said, "Oh yes?" The woman said, "Oh yes." She said, "Right now we're opening, well, or a program is now in process for four year old children, which is called, Project Village." And so, I said, "Oh, yes." She says, "Yes." She says, "Would you like to come for an interview with Mrs. Susan Bunting," and I said, "Sure," I said, "right now if you want." And then she said, "Good. Not right now, but let me—I'll speak to the lady, and I will tell her to call you." And yes, immediately, I don't imagine it was more that an hour later that woman called me…

That was in '96. Well, I loved it then. Well, my work there is Teacher Aide, or Assistant Teacher, but it's not, well, my work is combined. How can I tell you? It's a mix. I work with, well Hispanic people. Well, I help them to get the services that they need. And apart from that I help the children who are there in the program, the Hispanics right? Also the others, or the American race and Blacks, well. That is, I get along really well with those children, and well, like I try to help them so that they like the little school, so that they continue going to school and all that. And well, I'm still there today, well, I love my work…

One day when I was working at my regular work at the little school in Selbyville, the Project Village Program, the Nurse

Beverly Evans went to give us what is the vision exam for the children. She was a volunteer. She went to do those exams for the kids. And I said, "I know that woman." "Where do I know her from?" And I asked her, or, I went to her and said, "I know you." And she said, "Yeah," says, "What's your name?" And I told her, well "I'm called Maria Bailey, but years ago I was Maria Lopez, Maria Guadalupe Lopez." The woman says, "Well no," she says, "Were you in the Summer Migrant Program?" I said, "Yes," I said, "Ah, you're the nurse, you were the crazy one"—because she was the one who liked to play a lot. She says, "Yes, Maria you are"—there we got to talking and all that, right. I said, "By the way, are they still doing that program every year like before?" And she says, "yes, sure" she says. "Oh, good," I got to thinking, ah. And so after finishing the exams, giving them to the children, she went and spoke with Susan Bunting, and she said, "What do you think? I just met an ex-student of the Summer Migrant Program." She said, "Uh huh and who is it." "Who do you think, the one you have working for Project Village. She says, "Yes, well," she said, "Let me—I'm going to talk to her.'

And then from there they gave me this work and since then—this is the third year that I've come to work and all. Well, for me it's a pleasure. To come and return each year and work, right. To see those beautiful children who are here. And well, it fascinates me—and you'll see, when I go to the cafeteria, I simply go walking—you'll see the children, they say—Maria. And that's very nice, to know that the children know me and that well, they know that I'm the one that helps them go to the clinic or any little thing, right?

And apart from that, well, Mrs. Susan Bunting invited me to go to a national conference. The first one was in—where was it? Little Rock, Arkansas. We went there for five days. Well they paid for everything, the plane, the transportation. They paid for the food, the hotel. Well, stupendous (laughs). A vacation that you waited many years for (laughs). But it was really nice. I enjoyed myself a lot with her.

We went to the conference and in that conference we had to do like a workshop. Well, and in that workshop we had to talk, well about the program, what the program is, the students, and well, that was the job of Mrs. Susan Bunting. And Mr. Tim Core, Mrs. Beverly Evans, and so they were telling all about the work. Listen, apart from that as well, Mrs. Nancy Soriano was included. And well, they left me for last, or, so that I could tell my part. Well it was about what my experience had been as an ex-student of the program. And well, I told it, and the people were enchanted, and well, really nervously I told about all of it, in front of a great many people, and well, they were enchanted, and they even applauded me. But it was, or it was a very nice experience, and well, I was enchanted and here I am…

In the future that is something that I want to continue doing—I want to keep on helping people. And apart from that, well, my education is another thing that also is up there very high. It's something that I want to accomplish still, to go to school and expect even more of myself, to develop myself.

Maria Martinez family:
Top row from left: father, Manuel Robles, mother, Evangelina,
baby Jose Angel, two friends of Evangelina.
Bottom row from left: Mario, Victor, Sandra, Federico and
Little Maria at bottom
(courtesy of Maria Martinez)

Maria Martinez

I first met Maria Martinez and her family at her apartment in Selbyville in the summer of 1999. Maria had been involved in the wildcat strike at Selbyville's Mountaire plant in 1996, and subsequently went to work for the Local 27 Food and Commercial Worker's Union, as a union representative. Maria has eight brothers and sisters also working in the poultry plant, some in management positions. Her aging father was working in a local peach orchard for several months out of the year. He said he preferred orchard work to the factory, but Maria was worried about his physical condition. Meanwhile, Maria's mother was living in their home in Matamoros. The Martinez family explained that union activity was in the family: Maria's father had been a union representative in Monterrey before he joined the migrant stream.

The next summer I was able to tape record Maria's life story at the Local 27 office in Georgetown. She was born in Monterrey, Mexico, a large industrial city, in 1965, and moved to the border town of Matamoros when she was six. Her father worked in Matamoros for a while and then, following his father, started doing seasonal labor in the United States to support his 12 children. Maria remembers he worked in Washington State, California, and Florida before coming to Maryland's Eastern Shore. Maria graduated secondary school at 14 with a diploma as a bilingual secretary. From that time she worked in offices in Matamoros. Maria's family follows one common pattern of Mexican migration to the United States, where the father migrates first and then is followed by his adult children. Yet, the Martinez family is special. Following their father's example, they fight for justice wherever they find themselves.

Life in Mexico

There was a time when [my mother] was working at a restaurant in Brownsville [Texas]. We lived in Matamoros, and she went to Brownsville almost every day. But they paid her very little. And since she was almost always pregnant, pregnant, pregnant (laughs), she hardly worked. It got to the point—we were so poor that it got to the point that we went to the blood banks to sell blood in order to bring a little bit of money back home. The situation was that difficult. I remember, and my brother and sisters and I remember, and we cry. We feel sad. Not for us—we—I don't think that I suffered or had a bad time—but I think that my mom must have suffered more seeing that she couldn't do much, and all of us were very small. However, she did everything she could, even selling her blood in order to bring back some food to the house. It's that it was difficult. But thank God, all of that is now behind us. None of that can make us bitter now. My mother's fine...

All of us send them a little bit of money. Well, my dad has his social security check. They send him a monthly check. Well, we can't complain. They have a big house now in Mexico, all that they need. It's not like before, nothing like. That little house with only two rooms that they built and the two pieces of land—they are already very small compared to the big house that they have built now. Well, all of us built it for them. Now they're even about to tear down those little rooms, get rid of them and put something bigger—a bigger patio, a garden, whatever.

The Crossing

When I was 15, my parents decided that they had to bring us here to the USA. So, they applied, but since we were so many and they charged a lot of money for all of us—to process all of us—they only got the passports for the eldest. I was included. When I was 15, my parents got my residence card, the resident alien, as they call it...

My mother made the application there at the border, at the INS office, at the border in Brownville, Texas. That's where she got the applications. Then right there, they gave her an appointment at the American consulate in Monterrey, Nuevo Leon, Mexico. We went in August. They didn't accept us, because there was information missing: check slips from my Dad, showing that he worked in the United States. Then we were given another appointment for that same year in October, 1980. Then, we went there again, and we took the papers that we needed, and then we took care of it in that year, in October of 1980.

But since our youngest siblings weren't processed, well, we couldn't come. My Dad kept coming, but he brought with him my eldest brothers in order to work with him, to help him. My brother and my dad could buy some land there in Mexico, two pieces of land, to build a little house, a wooden house with two, two rooms only. I was working from the time I was 15 years old—16, 17– and I got married at 19. So, at 19 I was already a resident. My husband lived in Texas. So, we went to live in Texas for a while, but, but we couldn't make it. They charged a lot of money for rent and all. We returned to Matamoros, to Mexico. And, then, well, the situation was also difficult in Mexico. And one day we decided to come work with my dad and my eldest brothers...

Delmarva

We arrived in Maryland, working at a job where we grew little trees, pine trees and those trees.[90] I came here in [1987. I was pregnant.] That was my first daughter. I had her here in Maryland, in Salisbury. I worked there with the trees. They gave us a house there, and they paid the rent, the electric, the gas–it was very cold. And well, the job was fine, but–and for several years, I think we were going there two or three years, but only during the summer, because it was a well, a seasonal job...

There were about three families, four families no more than four families. The rest were rooms where only single men lived

---

[90] Maria and her family worked at a nursery in Showall that no longer exists. There are nurseries throughout the Delmarva peninsula that rely on Hispanic labor, either through guest worker programs or by hiring documented immigrants who are already residing in the area. The demand for labor varies with the season in this industry, so many Mexican workers spend part of the year here and then return to their homes as Maria did.

who were working that job. And I was working there. In 1987 my daughter was born—1988—and 1989, but in 1989, they closed. Either the company went bankrupt or they closed it down, I don't know. Then, we moved to work in Ocean City, Ocean City, Maryland, at a restaurant, which also gave us—housing and electric and the work. So, we were there for two years…

I worked there in the kitchen making salads. (laughs) Yes, I liked my job. Well, I worked alone, and I didn't have any problems with my employers. They liked me and trusted me a lot. Well, there was a year, one year in 1990, when we stayed there. The lady allowed us to stay [through the winter]. It was just that in 1991, I got pregnant with my second daughter, Marisol, and I left that place. And I went to Willards, Maryland. My husband was working cleaning floors in the big stores. I didn't work then, because I was pregnant. So, well, when my daughter was born, after nine months I started working at a chicken factory, in the line. In Mountaire, there in Selbyville in 1991. Later I separated from my husband in 1992.

Ah, we just had a lot of problems. He was–he was (laughs), he was a good person, but he was very irresponsible. He never mistreated me or he never did anything horrible that I couldn't stand, but he just was very irresponsible. He didn't care for the family, he just stayed with his friends drinking and he did a thousand things but never took care of his responsibility. That's why I divorced him when my daughter was one year and some months old.

And so, I went to Mexico, to Matamoros, for a year with my dad and mom, working. I was living in Matamoros and working in Brownsville in order to make it, with those two daughters. And well, that year was very hard, but in any event, now it's passed. Later I came back again. My dad did a great thing. He bought me a car (laughs), and he helped me a lot.

Papa was coming here to work picking peaches by then. That year, he didn't come, because it was when a trailer killed my grandpa. It ran over him. So, he was fighting through the court, because he said—well, that it was going to just be left like that, and he didn't want it to be left like that. Because he says, they hadn't killed a dog to leave it like that as if nothing had happened. And yes, he sued and he finally won...in Brownsville, Texas. There a trailer ran over my grandfather and they killed him right there. They killed him. My dad brought that case to court and he won from the trailer's insurance company the money that was owed the family, not only to him but to all my grandfather's children.

One day, after having been in Matamoros for a year, I decided that I wanted to come back here again, because I couldn't be there. That is, I couldn't make it with the money that I earned. And I didn't like to live in Matamoros and every day to cross the border, the border, the bridge, every day in order to go to work. It was very tough for me–to take my daughter to the school also in Brownville, since she was American. They asked me to stamp her birth certificate in order to give her a special permit to study in Mexico, and I didn't want to. It was better to put her in Brownsville to study. She was just starting first grade. My daughter was six. And I said, "No, I'd better put her in Brownsville," but it was very tough for me always to take her, so they could watch her in a place where the bus could take her and drop her off, so that she could go to school in Brownsville in the United States, in Texas. And then, in the afternoon to go pick her up and then, finally go home in Matamoros. It was very tough. I spent a year like that, but then I said, "No more."

And it was better for me to come back here again. Where I worked, at the poultry plant, my supervisor liked me a lot, despite the fact that I had a lot of problems with him. He liked me a lot. He gave me the job very quickly. I hadn't been here for a week, and right then he gave me the job. In the same place where I was working before. And well, time went by. I was working there, in 1994, in '94 I think, I started working there in Mountaire. No, in 1993. I started working there again, and then, well, with all the problems that a single mother always has, right–small children. You have to take them to the doctor, or they get sick in the middle of the night, or you don't have anybody to take care of them. The common problems of a woman with children who doesn't have a husband. I always had problems because of that in the poultry plant. They never let me go. They never let me stay at home to take care of them, or like that. They always gave me pretexts. And well, so, then time went by, and one always finds somehow the solution for everything.

The Community

I remember that—not when I started working—but when I arrived here, Mountaire—well Mountaire was just nothing. You didn't see it in the town. Nor did you see Hispanics. That is, I went there to Selbyville, and you saw those great big houses with many windows but no people. The town looked like a ghost town. It's true. It didn't—we have the shopping center that we have there at Selbyville, that is Food Lion, Right Aid, Dollar Store, and all those businesses which have just started, that are starting to open there—we didn't have anything. There was only a small store at the end of the town, which sold things at very high prices. We had to go to Salisbury, to a market at the mall, where they sold food a little bit cheaper. They didn't have Mexican food, either. Nothing, nothing, nothing. Nothing. We went and bought what we could eat more or less, because in Mexico food is different from what one eats here.

...in 1987, I got to know all of that: Selbyville, Delaware, Showall, Salisbury, Ocean City. I noticed all those towns, all of them very far one from the other. And there were no Hispanic people in 1987.

I met a few people but, no—well I think that I almost knew the whole community, because the guys played football. They got together in an open lot and played soccer with other Hispanics who got together, but there were very few. They formed just one or two teams to play. My brothers were the ones who started this, even my husband, my ex-husband, because they started with a, what do you call it—a tournament in Ocean City. They started having soccer tournaments in Ocean City. And well, but there were many

Americans. Well there were more Americans than Hispanics. I think that there was only one Hispanic team. All the others were Americans.

And from then to now, everything has changed. Selbyville is no longer the ghost town it was before. Mountaire isn't either. And you know, at the soccer games, how many teams there are!...It is an Hispanic league. That is, all the people playing are Hispanic, and it's odd to find someone who isn't, maybe one or two, I don't know how many, well, Americans. I know this because I have gone to the games, everything has grown due to the Hispanics. It has a lot to, well, the poultry industry has given a lot of work to the Hispanics. And they have grown, that industry has grown. And the Hispanics as well, the number. By 1996, there were already a lot.

The Wildcat Strike

And one fine day at the poultry plant in 1996, a young man cut his finger off at work. And, well the guy–I knew him a little bit, not very much–but the one I knew was his mom, who also worked there. Later, well, one day, when he cut his finger off, I think one or two days later, I came across his mom in the store, and she started crying. She told me that they had gone to the hospital to fire him, that a woman from Human Resources had shown up there, the secretary. And she had told him that he was fired.

So, then all the Hispanics were angry, because they had done that and I don't know what else. And then, we all came to a decision, and one day we all left work. Well, not all of us but a good number. And the plant had to stop working–Mountaire. And well, from there my career with the union started, not just because I was in the strike. There were many women who were angrier than me, but they didn't speak English. So that was the problem, and when they asked for a woman who could speak English, then all of them pointed at me. And I speak a little bit, but I manage any way I can.

Soccer in *Georgetown*
(Courtesy of Rocio Flores)

And so, the television reporters were there, and what I said was on T.V. that we were treated like animals there, worse than animals. And actually, I have always thought that, because I, I have seen American houses, no offense to anyone, right—I've seen American houses. They're very big and really pretty, and one or two old people are living there with a cat, a dog, or animals, and they care for them as if they were children. They take care of them better than they would a person. They don't have anybody else to care for or to love. And well, up to a point, everyone has their own reasons why they do that. But we as human beings, right, working very hard, and doing our best, paying taxes, doing all that one should do, are treated like that, so badly. That is, that guy had his finger cut off, and they fired him.

Another woman was hurt in her arm, and she was cleaning the tables of the company. And she couldn't move her arm–it was developing gangrene. And, and well, at that point, I said, "Well, what is happening here? Or where's the balance here? This is a very fair and free country, so what is happening?" And so, it made me angry, and that's why I said what I said. And I think that's why I got noticed...

The Union

I didn't know that there was a union, an association to defend workers and their rights. I didn't know, because after the strike I went to–since they told us that all of us were fired, I went to the employment office. And in the employment office they told me that if I was working at Mountaire, that Mountaire had a union. Therefore, I had to go and talk to the union negotiator in order to see what he could resolve first. And if he couldn't solve anything, then I had to come back to them. That's when I found out that we had a union. I didn't know anything. And so, from then on they started working very hard, because they realized—not so much because people didn't know, but because of the language barrier. It was a very big barrier...

And from there, they looked for me, I don't know if it was a year or less than a year. They came to my house to look for me, the people from the union. One of them was Pilar,[91] and they asked me if I wanted to be a union representative for the company in Mountaire. I told them yes. And I started as union representative, and everything went well. I had many problems with the supervisors, but people liked me a lot, they trusted me. They came to look for me, from the two shifts, the morning shift and the evening shift. And later, well, one time they had a seminar for the representatives, and well, there I was given a certificate for being part of the union. I started well, I started well.

Later, well I had my goals. I wanted to work in the same plant but as a government inspector, checking chickens. Then I started studying in order to be an inspector. I started studying the GED, or the high school. And so, I started taking classes, and I took them for two years in order to get my citizenship, because I have to be American in order to [get that job]. Yes, so I had to get my citizenship, and I had to get my GED. Then I started working on the two, and I got both things almost at the same time: the citizenship and the diploma. But, I was already deeply involved with the union...

Well, my work is mainly to listen to people's problems, to see if they are justified under the contract. And if there's a way to resolve them with, with the supervisors, well, I would solve them. Otherwise I would have to go higher up, or I would call an office representative from the union to come and resolve it. But almost always, well they were resolved right there. There was never the need to call. It was almost always when they fired a person unfairly. This is the ordinary work: to see if a person was paid his holiday check, or if he is being paid the extra time, or if they are taking time off his timecard— all those things that happen—if he is sick, that they did let him go, or if he has children that he needs to go and care for, that they give him permission. Things like that which always happen. Or if they need light duty, as they say, light

---

[91] See Pilar Gomez's life story, this volume.

work, that they give it to him, or that the nurse is giving him. That is, that there shouldn't be those unfair things that are always occurring...

Around 1997 I started being a representative. I had my problems and all that, but I liked my job. I liked defending the workers and being taken into consideration, being respected, something that I hadn't experienced before. And yes, I succeeded. Many people, actually all of them respected me there in Mountaire. They knew I was speaking seriously, that I didn't play around. They knew that I was doing my job seriously, and I wasn't playing or lying, and yes, they respected me a lot. And I also had a lot of power with people. They supported me a lot, and they stood behind me, with all their problems, because they trusted me.

[The man who lost his finger] was fired. No, he wasn't given his job back anymore. According to what I heard, he was fired because he was illegal, and that was the reason why he wasn't given his job back, because when he was working, he was working under one name and when he went to the hospital, he registered under his true name, according to what I know. And so, when Mountaire called the hospital in order to see how this person was doing, they said, "we don't have anyone here." Because he had given another name, his true name, and not the one he worked with. And that was the problem. That was the reason they didn't give him his job back. However, they gave him a lawyer. They paid him worker's compensation, and he was paid what he deserved to receive for the finger that he had lost...

The union—they gave me the post of vice president of the union. After we had a convention in Chicago where I had a, what do you call it?—a speech of five minutes, a five minute speech. But that was so that they would give me the vice president post— with a speech of only five minutes. There was an audience of about 3,000 people. And from there, the president of Local 27 told me that they were going to give me that post. Actually, he didn't tell me, the executive vice president simply came here, and he told me that they were offering me this work. That there was a person who had already retired, and that the position was vacant, did I want it?

I told him yes. And then, well, as union vice president, as secretary of the Office of Health Benefits for poultry plant workers, and as—and well, I am not a union representative any more, but I am part of the union. I am still paying union dues, and I am part of the union.

And I am not a representative, but I do have a lot of pull, because now since I started working there,[92] the secretaries' contract expired. We also have a contract. Every three years we had it.

And I asked them if they had negotiated the contract, and they told me no. Twenty-three years of having a union, they had never negotiated a contract. They simply took what their boss gave them. And so, I told them no. There had to be a negotiation and we had to go on strike there, because they weren't giving us what we wanted. And we went on strike, the three secretaries. There were only three of us. Well, we are four, but one of the secretaries didn't want to participate. So the three of us were on strike for four hours. The strike lasted four hours. (laughs)

But I told them, "You, we are Americans. We can shout and demand. We have to do this, we have to set an example for the people who cannot do it, to see that they can do it also." The secretaries were a little bit afraid, because they were already old. One of them was going to retire. She's got three years left before retiring, and she was afraid. She says, "They'll fire me." And I said, "Here they are not going to fire anybody. It's the union that is supporting us." I said, "No." If the union told us, "No, don't do it. No, because well, that is good and all, and one could make improvements over there." But they supported us. I say, "They're supporting us! We have a strong union, and no one is going to fire us."

And yes we struck for four hours, and they negotiated the contract again. They didn't give us what we wanted, but they didn't give us what they were going to give us. They gave us a little more. And well, that was something. And so, that's the good

---

[92] At the office of Health Benefits for union employees in Millsboro.

part of my work—as part of the Union. I like people to fight for their rights to get ahead.

The Delmarva Poultry Justice Alliance

I think of it this way. The government cannot do much for us, because the poultry plant is a very good taxpayer. It is paying good money. The day that they start having problems because of that, they will move. They'll go to Mexico or they'll go to another country, I don't know, some other country. So, they don't want that, because the money is very good, and many people get very good employment. So, they don't want it because of that, and that's why it is difficult for the government to put itself very much against—or in favor of the workers or against the industry. It is difficult.

But little by little, through the Alliance, I don't know if you have heard of the Alliance, The Delmarva Poultry Justice Alliance. Because, I am part of that Alliance, and through that Alliance we have been able to get many things... Through the Alliance, we have gotten the word out that there is much more involved than just a very cheap chicken. There are many things within it, and that is a great advantage, that people start noticing it. Because when people realize–when they are going to buy a chicken—to realize, then, they must talk and ask for a change in the conditions of the people. Because there are many people, people who have morals and respect, and I think that they should treat [the workers] equally—with respect.

And we have achieved that through the Alliance. Several Congressmen have talked with workers through the Alliance. And it even got to the point that a chicken catcher spoke with President Clinton in order to let him know the conditions under which those who catch chickens are working. And they were able to organize. The chicken catchers got a union at Purdue.[93] It hasn't been easy.

---

[93] The Perdue Chicken Catchers made union history in August, 2000 by being the first group to unionize ever at Perdue.

Poultry Worker's Clothing
Emilia Alvarez with her children Johnny and Josue
(Courtesy of Allison Burris)

The strike was the beginning of everything, the spark that lighted the fire. After the strike, around one year later, the Alliance started, with Jim Lewis and several other chicken breeders and workers and the union and people from the churches, a lot of people. Bay Foundation, organizations like Bay Foundation and like that...

I'm a person who is very timid about speaking in front of a lot of people. But when I speak, you have to catch it, because I don't say some foolishness or talk around the subject. I say what I have to say. I was with the ...what's his name? The director of the U.S. State Department, the Department of Labor? In Washington. I was talking with that man. Sure, I went with an executive committee of the Catholic Church supporting me. So, they had to listen to me, even if they didn't want to. And I questioned the man, a very well educated man and very nice, he's the new director, they just appointed him—the government. And he said that they were going to do another investigation of the poultry plants. And well, they did. They did. I don't know, I think this month we should have had some findings, in July. But well, they know that Maria is going to be there to say what the truth is.

An investigation because they're not paying—they're robbing time from people in the poultry plants. That is, not for overtime, but the time when one arrives and has to put on the net, the gloves, well, the helmet—all that is plant time. We have to be there like 20 minutes before, to mark our timecards, get out the coats, go to the locker, get dressed with all the equipment we need to enter the plant. And they don't pay us until the first chicken starts to come out on the line. And when it's time to go, it's the same. We have to go, wash the gloves off, the boots, take them off, go to the locker and take them off, put them away, and go to the coat room and leave them in the coat room. And then punch our timecard. Then there were twenty minutes more there. It's almost 40 minutes. And so, well—they don't pay you for that time. But it's our time that we have to put in there to be able to enter the plant. If not, you don't go in. If you don't have all that on, you don't get in.[94]

So, he says that they did—in '97 they made an investigation. Kim Bobol told him, I don't know if you know Kim Bobol. She's a representative of the Church in Chicago, who is fighting for the rights of the workers in the whole country. She isn't from the Catholic Church. I don't know what church it is, but she's a religious leader. And Kim Bobol went in the vestibule. She asked what the results had been in '97. And so, he said, that they had found various anomalies in some plants. Sixty percent were at fault. Forty percent okay. And so, I told him, "If you made an investigation of the poultry plants—I work in one—yes. But I never knew that you made an investigation and what the results were." I told him. "And you would think, right, that the workers should have received that. And we didn't know anything. Not even an announcement, nothing! Nothing, nothing, nothing, nothing, nothing. And, that is, I would imagine, something for the workers, that you should have informed them."

And he says, "We're going to make another investigation."

"When we have the findings, we'll begin to send them out to different organizations." They were going to find the way for the people who were working in the poultry plants to know what was happening.

Future Plans

I would like my daughters to have something, a better job than [the line]. All women in United States work. So, I would like them to have a better job than that, and for that, they have to study, I tell them. And I say to one that she has to be a lawyer and the other, a veterinarian. But in the end, they are going to do what they wish. But I want them to study, and I don't know how I am going to manage it, because it's so expensive, but we will see. God is first.

---

[94] January 2001, the U. S. Department of Labor concurred that standard practices in the Poultry Industry resulted in underpaying workers.

Maria Martinez and her two daughters
(courtesy of Maria Martinez)

Yes, I wish them to have a better life than the one that I had. Well, they are already having that. Well, when I was a kid, we were very poor and all of that–they don't lack for anything, they don't lack for anything. Thanks to God, who has helped me a lot, I don't complain. I have given them, not much actually, but I have given them a lot more than I had. And thank God, they are healthy, they are healthy. And that's the most important thing to me, being able to give them what I didn't have. And well to be a model, as you said, to set an example for them to get ahead, to go to school, to be someone who doesn't live on or depend on anyone. Because I am like that, I don't like depending on anybody. I don't like to live off anyone.

Maria Mendoza

I first met Maria Mendoza at an organizing meeting of El Centro Cultural, the volunteer cultural arts organization for the Hispanic Community that is responsible for putting on the Hispanic Festival in September and the Christmastime *Posadas*[95]. Later, I visited her at her new house on the outskirts of Georgetown for a tape-recorded interview. Maria is the "ESL person" at Del Tech, a job that entails recruiting, teacher assistance, materials development, counseling and a host of other tasks. A graduate of the program herself, Maria just finished a degree in Human Services from Del Tech after three and a half years of hard work. She is adamant about the importance of learning English, but sensitive to the difficulties that prevent working immigrants from attending classes. In her own case, Maria spent her first five years in Delaware with no English. The birth of a daughter with Down's Syndrome was the trigger Maria needed to enroll in school.

Maria was born and raised in the border town of Rio Bravo, where she finished school and worked as payroll manager for a department store, before marrying and accompanying her husband north. Rather surprisingly, she went from office work in Mexico, to migrant fieldwork in Delaware. From there she worked in the poultry processing plants, and finally, after leaving work to attend school, she has found her niche in the ESL program. An extremely competent individual, Maria has been featured in magazine articles about ESL and successful budgeting. Maria became eligible for U.S. residency through her own and her husband's family's migrant work under the 1985 general amnesty for foreign agricultural workers.

---

[95] An Hispanic tradition of reenacting Joseph and Mary's journey to Jerusalem and the birth of Christ.

Arrival in Delaware

I was born in Rio Bravo, Tamaulipas, Mexico in 1967. I am the youngest of five children, and I came to the United States approximately twelve years ago. I came with my husband, newly married. I didn't have either of my two daughters yet, and we first came to Delaware, like migrants, like field workers. Yes, we came to work on a farm where they grow cabbage, and corn, and chile, and cucumber, and I don't know what else. We worked for a season–a summer, and at that time I was pregnant with my eldest daughter. And so, after the fieldwork ended, we stayed. Better say I decided we should stay. I didn't want to return because of the fact that our job ended around September and my daughter was going to be born in October.

My husband had already come here to Delaware before with his sister–before we two had married. He had come here some years before, but it was the first time that I came, and neither of us knew anything. He only knew the farms where he had worked, and until that moment we only knew the place where we were living. Anyway, I wanted to stay. He told me it was fine for us to stay. He started working in a poultry plant. It was ConAgra then. Now it's Perdue in Milford.

And he worked there for a year more or less. Later, I went to work there also. When I got day care for my daughter, still a baby, I also started working. We worked, and for housing reasons we had to move to Seaford. So, the trip from Seaford to Milford every day for work was very long. The house where we lived in Seaford, [is] a farm. The owner of the farm allowed us to be in the house, he rented us the house, but we had to work on the farm in summer. And so, it was convenient for us. We said, "Okay, when summer comes, we'll leave the job at the poultry plant, and we'll stay and work on the farm."

And that's what we did. We worked that season, that summer on the farm in Seaford, and later the season ended, and we started working at Purdue, Georgetown. Closer, once again to the poultry plant.

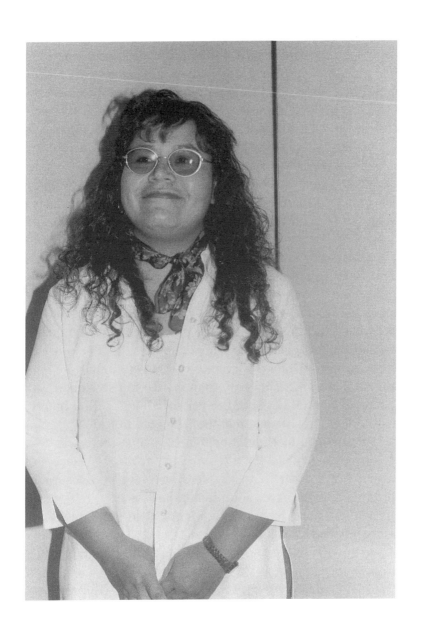

Maria Mendoza July 2000
(Courtesy of Katherine Borland)

His sister, my husband's sister and her family [were also there]. We were two families living in that house. And we both did the same–we worked in the farm during summer. The summer ended, and we went to work at Purdue, in Georgetown. We were working there for a long time, and when the next season came, I said to myself, "I don't want to go back to working in the field," because if we were there, we had to work in the field. When the season came closer, I said "No!"...

From sunrise to sunset–if it doesn't rain–it is a whole day [of] work. It's quite isolated. Apart from the fact that at that time, there weren't so many people like now. And yes, one feels very isolated. In fact, you feel isolated just by not speaking English. I consider that I am a person who doesn't talk much. I talk only what's necessary, but when I didn't know English, I was even afraid of going shopping. Because if I understand, and I say "Oh, yes," later they would ask me to talk [more], and I was afraid. For example, going to a McDonald's. Once I went to McDonald's, and I asked for chicken nuggets, six pieces, chicken nuggets, you know, and the girl gave me six boxes. After that I said to myself, "I won't go to McDonald's anymore for a very long time" just for fear of another thing happening to me, and I felt so embarrassed by not being able to tell her "I didn't ask for all that." So I had to take them all (laughter). It's just that the feeling is so bad...

Well, since the condition for us to live there was to work there, I said to myself, "We'll have to look for a place to live, because I don't want to work there anymore." Because in the poultry plant, you have your health insurance, your vacations, things that you don't have working in the field. We bought a trailer in Georgetown, where many Hispanics live... It is in the outskirts of Georgetown, close to 113, where the trucks go to Purdue. We lived there for eight years. We bought a Chevrolet. We continued working in the poultry plant for a while. Later, I got pregnant with my second daughter. She was born in 1994. The only thing that had changed was our housing. Neither of us spoke English or anything. We always looked for someone to help us to get our electric–we survived like that.

So in 1994, my youngest daughter was born. And that was when I stopped working. By then I wasn't working at Purdue any longer but in Allens, another similar poultry plant. I just changed places, and we were still living in the trailer park. When my youngest daughter was born, I didn't return to work. It was then when we had a lot of problems with her health. We had to go to the doctors for a long, long time after she was born, and we had a lot of problems. That was when I decided that we couldn't depend on anybody else, that we had to do something.

So, we talked and I told him "Okay. You work. I will go to school, or I'll work," but it didn't seem good for me to work and for him to go to school.

"It's better if I go to school and you work. If you work, work work for the two of us," because the money we both earned was very necessary.

And he said, "Okay. Good. So I went to school, I entered school and he, well he had always worked, but he was trying to work more hours.

Apart from the fact that he said that he didn't like school very much. He never liked school much. And, well, I always liked going to school. In Mexico I finished my high school. I did a technical career. I worked in accounting. I always liked school. But here it became almost impossible for me to go to school, because of the English...

Of course, if I had gone to a language school to learn English in Mexico, I would surely have learned it, but the English we are taught in school is only supplementary. It's like the Spanish you are taught here, it is not a lot. So it's the same situation there. It was six years, with English being taught two hours a week. I thought that I knew English, because I passed all my English classes, but when I came here I didn't know anything. They talked to me, and it seemed they were speaking in Chinese. For five years, I was–we behaved like dumb people...

317

English Classes

So since the first thing to do was to learn English, I looked for an English program, which is the one where I am working now. But at that time it was much smaller. It had only one teacher, and it had 12 to 15 students, a single class. So, that's when I registered and started going to classes in the summer. So, you know, it's a long term thing.

Because I wasn't working I sometimes wondered, "Will this be worth it? Will I be learning?" You never know if you are learning because it is something long–that you cannot see in the moment. You are acquiring it and practicing and all that. And I always sat and said to myself "Ufff! Will this be worthwhile for me to be–?"

Ah, by then my daughter, the eldest one, was going to a summer school, because she was old enough for school. She was about six. Because I started in summer. And I had to put the little one in day care, so that I could go to school, because my husband was working. He worked like one and a half people.

Well. Now I had been taking classes for two or three months. I got along very well with the teacher, the one who taught me English, and she motivated me a lot. Elba.[96]

The teacher taught her class three times a week, and the more advanced students stayed for another class, like for grammar, a little bit more advanced. When I had been attending the class for several months, she told me to stay. It was as if I had gone up one grade (laughter). But once she asked you, "Could you please stay? I think that you are able to follow this…" I think it was for one hour, one stayed twice a week and did more grammar, in a little more advanced way. And when she said to a student, "do you want to study?" it was as if you had passed from primary to secondary school!

"Now I can!"

---

[96] Elba Guiles, an instructor in the Del tech ESL program and resident of Lewes, Delaware.

Allison Burris, ESL Class, April 2000
(*Courtesy of Allison Burris*)

So I continued. I was attending classes for almost a year, pure English, ESL. Apart from the fact that I went, when I didn't have class, I went to the library for books, and I read. I had to take my daughter to the day care every day anyway. Because you don't pay only for the time you take your daughter, but you register her for the whole week. Then, since I had to take her, I took advantage when there weren't classes. I would go to read, or—to try to take advantage of the time...

[After a year] I said, "Okay, if my teacher is saying that I can, maybe I can." So I registered [in college], and I had to take basic classes, of course, because of my English. What I had learned in ESL wasn't enough. And during that time, after I had started my classes, I was offered a job in the school.

It was the first time that the school had a federal program which was called Americorps Vista, and they were looking for six people to work–there were different areas. This program works with low income people, in budgeting, housing, education, reading, to help people who don't know how to read. And they were looking for several people, and one of the areas they were interested in was that one for people who didn't know how to read. The students entered there who are unable to read English. They were in ESL. And so, they needed someone bilingual. I wasn't that bilingual, but I applied, and they called me. Maybe I was the only one who applied for that...

And that's how I started. I was working for a year in GED and the ESL because they went together. So for GED–I was working for a year in the GED classroom, preparing things for the GED students and preparing things for the ESL students, who were in the next classroom, everything. They are separated, but under the same program, so if you had to deal with one, you had to deal with both, testing and helping my supervisor. With the ESL, I did things by myself. I started getting my hands in there and doing it by myself. And they told me, "Do whatever you want."

The first [task] was how to attract people. And also to keep the people there. In the second semester after I started working there, the ESL enrollments surpassed the GED enrollments for the first time. Many people started going. I started doing flyers. I started going to places like La Esperanza, the churches. I started visiting people, meeting people, calling people, looking for the priests within the churches, taking my flyers to the restaurants and laundromats, to the banks. The first time that I saw a flyer about the classes–when I registered–was in a bank. So I knew that the people could see the flyers, because I saw that one. So I started making a lot of propaganda–wherever I was needed to speak, I went. I didn't know how to speak to people that well, but I told them what I could. And I think that it worked because they came.

Many people started coming, many people. They had to get another teacher. They had to hire another teacher. Because there was only that one teacher. So now there were two and also evening classes. And the number kept growing. After that, I didn't make a lot of effort, because now it was known. Once one knows about it, then what's called word of mouth [takes over]. It works better than the newspaper. Of course, later, when it came– Ah, I used the radio station many times, the Hispanic radio station...

So, a little more than two years ago we were given a building in the school, the building where we met? Ahah. This even brought more people. People there feel it's their place. And we don't have Hispanic students only. We have students from Asia and Haiti. There are lots from Haiti... people from India, Brazil, from everywhere...

But yes, the poultry plants try to offer this to their workers. Many times I have spoken personally to department supervisors— I'm in the middle—yes, because they have their job and what do they care if the student goes to school? They are also working, and they want their work done. And I don't know if people are very hard workers and that motivates them to try to help them. I have called them when there is some problem with the class schedule and their work schedule. They say "Okay, if he is going to class, I will give him permission to come half an hour late," or things like that.

Rafael Orlando Dossman, Radio DJ
Radio Exitosa July, 2000
(Courtesy of Katherine Borland)

My husband is working at Purdue. He is in mechanical maintenance. He is now in a slightly better position than the one when he started on the line, working with knives and all that. I don't know if you have been explained how the work is done inside. It is very tough. He is still working there in Purdue, Georgetown. And he is also going to English classes. Only he says, "Ah, I learn more slowly than you." I say to him, "What happens is that you are less interested." But he is taking classes...

Reasons for Emigrating

During all that time that I was working in the fields and the poultry plants, it was as if that wasn't me. As if the one who came here wasn't me but another person. And now I can say this is me. Once I entered school, once I started to learn English, simply by sitting there in the classroom, I felt again that that was me. All that time that I was working in the fields, when I had never worked like that in my life–that's why I didn't want to go back later. It is nice, but it is very tough. Any work is decent, but it is very tough, and you cannot have the goal of working there all your life. You will have to do something to stop doing it, because one day you will be unable to do it. And I thought about that from the very first moment. I said to myself, "I don't want to do this forever, not me."

I just wanted to survive here. Truly, we didn't know what we were thinking. And the difference between working there and coming here—well, I didn't expect what I saw here. When I came, I came recently married. And I just wanted to be with my husband, my new husband (laughs)...

And I worked for two years in Mexico after I finished studying, in an accounting department and it was a very nice job, in an office, with air conditioning. I worked in a big shopping center, like Wal-Mart, but I worked in the payroll department. There wasn't a big difference between the salary of a person working in the accounting department and a person working cleaning the floor. In the work there is, because it is not so physical, the hierarchy of the work is better. But actually the important thing–to pay the electric bill and all that—there wasn't much difference. I wanted more, but in Mexico that is difficult.

There are many industries in Mexico, in Reynosa. Many people from Rio Bravo, from the town where I am from, worked in those industries in Reynosa. Those industries are a little bit like the poultry plants here. Many people work there. It's one of the biggest sources of work. And [my husband] worked there in one of those plants. He worked there, and he was studying. He didn't finish. He only got to the first year of high school. He didn't finish. He didn't finish, and he kept working, working. He says he never liked school very much. That's why when we decided who was going to the school. He said "you," and I also said, "me."

A Child with Downs Syndrome

Also another thing. When my daughter, the youngest, was born, she was born with Downs Syndrome, and for that reason she had a lot of–fortunately, she didn't have complications like most of the children, but tests and examinations and all that that the doctors wanted to do because they knew that it carries a lot of complications. They took us to the doctor, the hospital, the Children's Hospital—DuPont, they took us to this place and that. To doctors in genetics, and well, it always seemed as if they were talking in Chinese, because when the child was born, even in the hospital when she was born, the doctor–they tell you immediately.

My pregnancy was normal. It was when she was born, when they told us that she had Downs Syndrome. It was like–I had just given birth, and then to have someone come and tell you something like that, and you don't know English, you don't even know what they are telling you. You know that it's something bad because of the expressions–awful! awful!

When the doctor came to explain–this and that, I don't know what he told me, because I didn't understand him. The only thing I could understand was that there was something wrong. I guessed that he was telling me that my daughter was blind, because the only thing I could understand was the eyes. She had some of the characteristics and one of the main ones was her neck and her eyes. Her eyes were a little bit slanted.

And I said "Is she blind?" (laughs) I don't know, "I think my baby is blind." I didn't know what he was telling me. So I asked my husband to bring a friend of mine, a bilingual friend, and when this friend came she told me, "No, what he is saying is that the baby has Downs Syndrome."

And then I asked, "What's that?" (laughs)

And she didn't know much Spanish, and she said (in English) "I don't know, I don't even know."

After we left, well, that was just the beginning. Later there were doctors, and I don't know. Awful. And of course, having to look for people to translate for me, interpreters. Letters and letters came to me, and well, I didn't know how to read them. And that was when I said, I thought, I told myself, "We have our daughter and we are going to have her during our whole life, thank God, if he lets us, and we cannot have people here with us, depending on them." And so I said, "I have to do something."

I didn't know exactly what it was or why she had been born. They explained it to me a thousand times, but when there is an interpreter involved, you don't get even half of what you are being told. At least the interpreters that I had. (laughter) Often they are people who don't know how to speak English well or maybe did it with good intentions. It's so important that one has to do something in order not to depend on anybody else. Nobody could care more than us. So, after taking her to the day care, when I didn't have class, and I went to the library, that was what I read about, about Downs Syndrome, about doctors, about theories, about what they were—updates. What they were doing.

I found many things in a national association. I could never go, because I was always having classes in the summer. The last one was in Dallas, Texas, but I did get in touch with a lot of people. They sent me the reports. And they sent me the whole package that the people attending got, and since I couldn't go, they sent it to me. Information about workshops and all that.

325

And yes, I keep struggling, now with special education because I am more focused on education. I am not interested in learning any more about Downs Syndrome, because with the information I could obtain, I know about it. Now the thing is special education, because she has to go to the school, and this is what I am more interested in.

The first things that [Jennifer] learned she learned in a regular class. She was always going to Easter Seals. After she left there–she couldn't go anymore because it goes only to age three–I enrolled her in the Child Development Center at the college. And they have a very good teacher in her class. My daughter was the the only special child. All of the children are regular. It was more than one year, almost two years.

Later, she had to receive therapy, and it's always a problem. It's a headache, let's call it that. Every time that the parents of special kids have an audit. Well, there are a lot of factors, because before the audit, they make an evaluation. A psychologist comes from the school district, makes an evaluation, with which I have never agreed, and they know that it's not a hundred percent accurate. Because my child has never seen this man in her life, and she sits like you are seated here with me. Of course, I am an adult, and even though I first wanted to talk, I felt like I couldn't. Imagine if a man comes, whom she doesn't know, carrying a lot of things in order to test her, she just simply looks at him and doesn't want to do anything.

So they say that that's the only thing that can be done, and that's how they do it. And I don't like it, I don't agree much with this. It's something that I always raise as an issue, and I suppose that many people don't like it. But they always say that we parents have to talk, and then when we talk, they don't want to pay attention …

Views on the Community

From my own point of view and from my worksite, where I see differences in the community, people are trying to educate themselves. It's very difficult for them to acquire it. I am trying to help them from my worksite, because I experienced the same situation on my own without getting any help, and I know that if there is someone there to help you, it makes it less burdensome. And if you want to quit, you won't do it if there is a person there to tell you, "No, no, no, look." I had this teacher who told me, "Come on, go on." Just hearing somebody telling me, "You can do it, go," I believed it.

What a benefit it was to be able to pursue a career in my own country and study, because it helped me a lot. Otherwise, I couldn't have done it in the time that it took me. Most of the people here, the ones that I see…I am not saying that all the people come here without an educational level, let's say at a secondary school level, but most of the people I see, the Hispanics at my worksite, the level of education is not very advanced. And that has great repercussions when they want to move on in education. They are going to take more time to learn, because they don't have that training in absorbing knowledge and practice. Apart from the fact that having a family makes it more difficult, a family, your children, sometimes even transportation.

There are very few women who start and continue. Most of them start, and their children get sick or something happens. The intention is there, but it's that there are many factors. There are many things that come first before–saying "I want to educate myself, I want to do something else than simply work and work and work until I can't anymore. Instead, I can study and I can practice a profession and my children are going to see me. And they will"— But this does not happen so quickly. Many, many students come and register but not many finish for many reasons, and to retain them is the most difficult thing.

I sometimes call them and ask them how we can help them. If we can, let's try. If not, then we'll see if there is any way for someone else to help you. Either they have another job, or simply they are postponing. They say, "I wanted to start, because I only had one job, but now I have another one, I have two jobs." People here work a lot. The Hispanics work a lot. Often they don't think about the long term. And often they do think and they have the intention and they begin, but a problem confronts them, and ya! It stops them.

So it requires a lot of work on the part of the people who supposedly are able to motivate them, people who can tell them, "Look, I have resources. If you need transportation, let's see if we can look for a van." I have talked a lot with Allison, Allison Burris. She and I are doing a lot of projects together and we sometimes talk about transportation. We have said, let's go with the Esperanza Van to bring them to the ESL building. Let's see what happens, because this transportation thing is giving us a lot of problems...

Many male students cannot drive to school, because either they don't have cars or they don't have a license. They don't have the license, because they don't have a social security number. Or they had their license—how wonderful that they had it–and they lost it because of something they did: a ticket or something, some infraction that they committed, they've lost their license. And they are forbidden to drive. There are many of them like that.

[The single men] have very few friends, the only thing they do is work. And I am not justifying them or anything, but I can see a reason, at least for the people who are alone. The people who have a family have a different problem. Because I think that they are alone, and they leave their families behind, perhaps their children, their mother, father, their friends, and they are here by themselves without anybody to cook for them, without anyone to ask them how things went at work. I think that they get depressed, and the men don't find any outlet besides drinking and forgetting themselves for a while.

And the bad thing is that it becomes a vice and it has repercussions. When they are out of beer, for instance, have to go for more and a policeman stops them, or they have an accident, which is the worst thing. I find that a lot or they go there, to those centers, those places that are being closed down now, those places where they go, to dance—Hispanics are very into diversions [like

Allison Burris with Jennifer Lopez (1998)
(Courtesy of Allison Burris)

that]. The bad thing is that the diversion is linked to liquor. There are many things.

These people, although they drink, go to work every day. If it were otherwise, they would be fired. They know they cannot risk losing their job, because many of them either don't have transportation and their workplace is conveniently close, or a friend works there also, and it is convenient for whichever of the two sides you view it from. But you don't see very often that they quit their job, because they don't go to work, because they drink. Because they do go to work. The problem is that they end up having more problems.

Yes, we [Hispanics] have that stereotype, that we don't take [the traffic laws] too seriously. We think "Oh, never mind. If I pay the electric bill, so they don't cut it off, or the telephone, the house rent–which is the most important, to pay the rent and electric, because if you don't they evict you from the house–the rest doesn't matter so much." But it does. That's what we take time to learn here. It really matters a lot, because it is a crime not to carry insurance on your car. And it is hard to learn that. And the authorities know that. So, what do they do? If they see a car— they stop you, even if you are not doing anything, they check you. They will find something.

It is discrimination, sure, because they say, "I'll bet that there's something wrong." And I think that they are right. Most of the time, unfortunately, they are right, but why do you stop them? Why? There have been a lot of cases like that. Yes, there is discrimination.

Look, when I used to live in the Trailer Park, the police patrols would be there at the exit on Saturdays, on Saturdays sometimes. Yes! Several times I was stopped. That is, anyone who passed was stopped. Out of ten cars, I think that seven had something, or better put, they didn't have something–the license, or it was suspended, expired insurance, something. There was always something, unfortunately, and they know. But I think that that is discrimination, even if they know. Because if you haven't done anything wrong, well then it is what you said, harassment, trying to see what mistake you commit to net you.

It's difficult to gather the group and keep it formed. It is similar to when you group your students and try to keep them in their groups. Once this is achieved, you cannot believe it. When you call a meeting, if everybody attends, you can't believe it. I am alluding to the community people, people who go to work everyday and say: "Well, today I asked for a permission to arrive a little bit late to work, because I have this meeting." It rarely happens.

Protest in Washington, D.C. to close the School of the Americas.
(Juan's banner is behind the seated crowd.)
(Courtesy of Katherine Borland)

Juan Perez

I interviewed Juan Perez on two occasions in the Spring and Summer of 1999. His life story is rich and evocative for a number of reasons. Juan is one of the few Guatemalans in Georgetown to have received political asylum. He had direct experience of persecution during the 1970s and 1980s, whereas many Georgetown Guatemalans would have been children at that time.[96] Juan is also a self-taught artist, musician and actor. On arriving in Delaware in 1995, he quickly became involved in Phyllis Levitt's art exhibition, *Collage of Cultures* and received some recognition for his work. Later, when Georgetown Guatemalan contingents attended a march on Washington (1998) to protest unfair immigration policies for Central Americans, and another to demonstrate against the School of the Americas (1999),[97] Juan provided compelling banner/paintings that helped identify the group. Juan's paintings evoke both nostalgia for a vanishing indigenous way of life and the horrors of the war years in Guatemala. His perspective on indigenous culture is highly self-conscious, since Juan grew up at a time when the community was undergoing rapid change, and he himself has had the opportunity to move beyond his community and to represent their experience to outsiders. A man between cultures, Juan has developed a critical perceptiveness and a unique vision that sets him apart from others both inside and outside the community.

Juan is also a community organizer. When I interviewed him, he had just given up the relatively carefree life of an artist in order to take a job as a community outreach worker for Children and Families First. His limited English and abhorrence of

---

96 While younger community members witnessed many of the assassinations and kidnappings of indigenous community members, they themselves would not have been targets of persecution.
97 The School of the Americas is a United States training institute where Guatemalan soldiers were taught Vietnam-style counter-insurgency techniques, which were employed to decimate the Maya indigenous communities in the highlands from the 1970s to the 1990s.

paperwork have made this job a real challenge. In the summer of 1999, Juan and Pilar Gomez[98] were providing recreational activities for grade school children from Kimmeytown almost every evening in the summer. Yet by the end of the summer both were frustrated by the lack of parent involvement and participation in this effort. Juan is a member of OGAM and had hoped to have this organization sponsor children's recreation activities. By 2000, Juan had purchased a home in a quiet residential area on the southeast side of Georgetown. Every Christmas, though, he returns to his childhood home in Guatemala to visit his aging parents and to restore his soul.

Memories of Indigenous Life

The place where I was born was a marvelous place, a fantastic place, where nature filled everything around you and the song of the birds, the animals, the trees and all this. And though our life was a very poor life, the area where we lived was encircled by nature. For example, the agriculture and all that, the plants that one grew, one had to share them among the animals and among ourselves. But sometimes the animals won and didn't leave much for us. [laughs] It was very interesting because also–now I'm going to relate my story from when I remember things, from when I first understood...

Everything was around the house. Because the custom that existed among us was that we did the work of one family, and then we did the next and the next and the next until everyone's [planting] was finished. They gave to one and the other and the other and the other until they finished with everyone. It wasn't with everyone in the community, not all the people, but only the people living nearby–the people with whom one had more communication, closeness, family. One did everything among family, friends, and all that. That was the way we worked...

---

98 See Pilar's story this volume as well.

When I was a child, I don't know how many houses, perhaps [there were] about sixty or seventy houses, maybe more. And all these people communicated with one another. Some because they didn't have time, or they weren't at home, they didn't show up for a family or community activity. It was very interesting. Because all the people were united. They split one job among everyone. And they even shared what was the food. They shared the experiences of the people. And we who were children saw everything, all the changes that happened more than anything.

Before, when they began to tell the story of our grandparents, the ancient ones, it was more surprising than the life we were leading, and we asked ourselves, well now, why isn't it that way now? "No, because things change," and then religion arrived and everything changed and changed and changed, and the community began to separate more and more, due to religion. And now they're even more separated. In the place where I was born, I don't know how many churches exist. Churches everywhere. And now [people are] united by their religion, they're not united by tradition or custom.

We didn't learn one hundred percent what is our language [Pocomam], neither that of my mother nor of my father, because my father didn't speak the language with my mother, his language; nor did my mother speak her language with my father. They spoke more in Spanish. And the little that we learned, we learned when my father's friend came or other neighbors came, so they began to speak in that language. And when my father said something to us in that language–that we should go get something or do something, we didn't understand. And we ran to ask our mother, what did my father tell me? And she didn't understand him either [laughs]! And so, that's why our language became mixed–better say it died out. Because all the neighbors, the children who lived close by who were my age–the father and mother spoke the language, and they all learned to speak both languages very well. Because my father didn't speak Spanish very well, neither did my mother. Where I learned some Spanish was in Mexico.

Yes, our language was lost in our family. So, the other families, due to the jokes that the *ladinos* told about us as indigenous people, for that reason the typical dress disappeared. Yes. Because the children of the *ladinos*, who were townspeople, the women wore dresses. And in our family it was always with the typical dress. And we [men] also with typical dress. So, they laughed at us. They yelled even at our parents, our grandparents, "Dirty Indians" and everything–the discrimination, the racism, all that, the persecution of the Indian lands. Every time we had to go farther into the mountains, farther and farther. At that time all the land belonged to the farmer, it belonged to the indigenous people. But then came the Germans, English, Japanese, Spaniards, North Americans and all those–they took control of all the fertile lands. They began to make coffee plantations, raise steer, cotton, sugar cane–all that. And so, we, all the indigenous people, they sent us to all the places where the land doesn't produce. Stranded out there in the mountains, where there are a lot of rocks, or where it's all a desert even now where not even the sheep grow. The animals, now there aren't any. And so, in that way they gradually pushed us out, and that's how we were persecuted and there are even some people who've died out completely. For example, where I was born, if there are five men who use the typical dress of the men, it's a lot.

When we were children, everything was beautiful. Everybody went with their typical dresses to the town, yes, yes. But the young people used them more up to the age of 17 or 18 years. Now from 20 years old those of my generation started to discard them. And then the older people also discarded their typical clothing, because there wasn't anyone who made them anymore, and if one bought them, they were very expensive. There wasn't the money to buy them, and then there weren't many who made them. Because my grandfather, my dead maternal grandfather made his own typical clothing. Yes? He wove them and all. He had his loom and all. And other people came and asked him to make typical clothing for them, but all those people came to an end later. People weren't using the clothes either, so the looms were destroyed or fell out of use...

They began to modernize and the cloth arrived, then, and it was easier to go and buy the cloth than to be there all day weaving. One has to take care of the animals, one had to go and leave dinner, one had to do all that, all the household chores, one had to take care of this child, and then when was one going to weave the clothing for the other one? And so, it was easier to go and buy the cloth, cloth that wasn't for typical clothing, and it was being lost...

[The mill] was something that came down from my, I don't know if it was my great-grandfather or my great great-grandfather, but it's a long story. And so the mill was given to my father by my grandfather. Perhaps they didn't leave it to my father, but it was my father who was interested and who wanted to take care of the mill. Because this is very hard work. My father's brothers probably didn't have any interest in taking care of the mill, because my father is the one who made the great rounds of stone in order to grind the wheat. To make wheat flour. But over the years, as the years pass, the stone is used up. One has to make another. As the stone wore out, one had to make another. And he was the one who made them. And it was a little machine that always brought in a little money. Almost every day. There were days when people didn't come, but on Thursdays and Fridays they always came. Because he was the one who made the flour for all the bakers in the town. Those who sold bread, people lived on bread. The people went and sold bread and from what they made they bought the corn, they bought sugar, or they bought what they needed. And all those people came, always on Thursdays and Fridays to the mill, and that's how the money fell into my father's hands. And they plant a lot of wheat there. Everyone plants wheat. Yes, because the tradition in Holy Week is to eat bread. And so, in some way or other, I don't know how much they plant, but everybody grows wheat. Partly for food and partly from the custom of eating bread during Holy Week...

Working on the Plantations

The first time that they took me to the plantation with them, I believe, I think I was six, to pick cotton. Yes. And on arriving there–well everyone, my mother, my father, and all of them, the mill was closed up, the house was closed up. They took us all to the plantation... We had to walk three days. Three days we had to walk to get to that place where we were going to work. Yes. Walking with the rooster under your arm, the dog behind. Everything that was in the house went with us. We had to take the animals with us. I remember, well, because it was the time of the thorns and the great heat. I'd never gone down into a place that was so hot. And cutting cotton, well you're right under the sun. And the thorns. All of us, everybody there, no one wore shoes. Everybody went barefoot. The food was horrible and all. It was a place that was very isolated. I believe that's when I started to realize–because from when I was born they always took me to the plantation.

It was seasonal. Three or four months. And the plantations where we went most often were the coffee harvests. To pick coffee. We would go partly to plantations in Guatemala and partly to plantations in Mexico. So in Mexico, we went, all the family together as well, to cut coffee and all. But today, it's very sad, it's horrible. Because in the plantations they put us in *galerones*. They are roofed areas only. The house doesn't have any walls. And there all the families are together. And the food is made by the plantation that's paying the workers. And so, at times a rat or a cockroach or ants would show up on your plate, or bats, or it would smell like gas because the lamp was there close to the pot of beans and it fell over. And lots of fleas and lice and ticks. Do you know what a tick is? All that stuck to you and there was a lot of illness. That was just the food.

Now as for the work it was more difficult. Because we as children, not just the children, my parents too, went barefoot. It rained. Everything got muddy and you began to get infections in your feet. And then the mosquitoes. Some flies arrived and began

338

to bite, and since we were children we scratched and scratched, and we got infections. When we returned home it was with scars on our legs and on our faces. But this has never been put right. It's still going on.

For example, where I'm from many people still go down to the plantations. With the whole family still. And those who don't go, who don't go to the *finca*, it's because a child is in the United States. Yes? And so, it's a very hard, very difficult situation. And all the money we had to save and save and save in order to maintain ourselves again in the summer. One bought corn, one bought beans, one bought everything that one needed to eat. And this went on every year, every year, every year, and so. Well, I was one who wasn't going to endure it. Yes, I was one who wasn't going to endure it.

My father, when he was a boy, experienced the same life situation, and even worse than what happened with us. We were living a life that was perhaps more modern. Because my father said, "No, at least now we have a roof. The house doesn't have walls, but at least we have a roof. When we came to work, they didn't even give us a place to live. We had to make our houses with leaves and under the trees. Yes."

And the owner had to force them to go harvest their crop. They paid them badly. They treated them badly. But for me, at least, each year, as I grew older, it was worse. For me it was very sad. When the time came to go to the plantation, I couldn't find where to go, where to hide. But it didn't help. My mother, my father, all my family–there wasn't any place for me to stay, I had to follow them. We're seven brothers and sisters. We were more but the others died. From what I understand, two girls died. A sister of mine died at 23 or 24 and another died at 2. She died of malnutrition. She died of malnutrition, but all of us, we experienced the same thing...

As indigenous people that we were, if we studied in the community, there was a list in the teacher's roster, but we weren't registered with the secretary of education. They never recognized us. So, when we studied in the town, among all the children of the *ladinos*–it's something humorous now that we saw it this way, but what could we do? The teacher had a list of the *ladino* children that was separate from the list of the indigenous children. Yes? So, first they went down the list of the *ladino* children. "Is John Doe present?" and then they took the list of the indigenous or country people and then they would go down our list. For us, the school year in Guatemala begins in January. But in August–the 25th or 28th of August is when everyone starts to go down to the plantations. And the classes end in October. And so, my father would say to us, "Well, kids"–it would be the 25th or 28th of August—"we're going to the plantation. Forget about school." And all of us would go to the plantation. We'd come back the next year. Well, they'd pass us without our having taken exams, whether we knew or didn't know, but because we had to keep going. One would come–If I was the first to go to the plantation and I was in first grade, the next year they put me in second. They passed me to third and all. I never had a report card, because I never went to the final exams.

[My parents] don't know how to read. I believe two of my sisters don't know how to read. The one who died didn't know how to read, and the two older sisters don't know how to read. So, those who know how to read are only my older brother, me, and then all the younger children. The others don't know how to read. My father and my mother, never. They never knew how to read. Because at that time there was no school (laughs). There wasn't any school (laughs).

When we went to the plantations in August or September, all the cornfields that we'd sewn were small, no? And when we came back, they were almost dried, and with lots of flowers under the corn and all the birds because that's the change of season, the alterations of the vegetation–it was very, very different. And all the people began to come back again and the people/town became happy again. Because when the people went to the plantations, the only people who stayed behind were old women or the old people, people who couldn't handle going to the plantation anymore. And so they say that the people/town remained, but sad, sad. And so, then, the people began to arrive and it was after Christmas or after the New Year there. In January, the people began to arrive. The Festival of the Virgin of Guadalupe, I think traditionally is celebrated at the national level I think in Guatemala and Mexico the 12th of December, but in the town, in the rural area where I was born, they celebrated it on the 25th of January, I think. And on the 25th of January, they started to celebrate the 25th of January, because if they celebrated on the 12th there wasn't anybody around. Nobody was there! And so, they put the date back to the 25th of January. They celebrated the festival of the Virgin of Guadalupe. Because then the people had returned from the plantation, everyone had returned from the *finca*. They arrived and they set off fireworks, *marimba*, *tamales*, bread, food, and everything, and the older people danced. A gathering of the people but very tranquil, without authorities–there wasn't any authority present, everything tranquil, everything peaceful. There weren't any arguments, nothing. Everything very calm, and it was a festival that they enjoyed a lot. There were horse races, potato sack races…

And so, and this–well, there was a great change in everything, from the moment that one returned again to our house. It was one's greatest pleasure to be recommended and living and eating the cockroaches in the plantation. And on coming back, perhaps one would go and eat corn on the cob, eat the very plant that was coming up in the cornfield. You eat the bean greens, we also ate the leaf of the bean plant. We still do. The flower of the squash, one ate the flower of the squash and many other plants that were around. So, it's a great change. And I believe that when one came back from the plantation was when one started to recuperate.

Because in the plantation what they gave to you was only beans beans beans beans, every day. There was one day that they gave out beef. But they bought I don't know how many little pounds of meat and they put more water than anything, and they were pieces of bones that they gave out. And the people were content with that. But it was once a week! And, alternately, when one came back to the house, well, there was a great change in everything. And things were not as we had left them by the time

Youngsters Performing at the Festival
(Courtesy of Rocio Flores)

we came back. The edible crops were all fresh, and so one ate all these fresh things–vegetables that were there.

Indigenous Traditions

Because in the community there were traditions, celebrations. For example, they knew what day, what hour, what type of eclipse there would be. Yes? So, what did the wise men of the community do? These were people who didn't know how to write or read or anything. Who knows where they learned this from? And they alerted the community. On such and such a day, at such and such an hour there's going to be an eclipse of the sun or of the moon. So, they put the warning out, if you're going to look at the sun, don't look directly at the sun, put out some big tubs of water outside and there you can see it. And if it's lunar, you can do the same. And then, they gave a ceremony to the moon or to the sun. They played *ambotes*, plates, guitars, violin, but each one in his house. And the horns of the bull–because this would be if you–or shells, they played conch shells, all kinds of music, all kinds of instruments, even if it was just a bottle, whatever. Everybody played and yelling everyone from his house at the eclipse that was passing through. Something that doesn't happen daily. And there are many people who didn't even come to learn what it was that was going on, but since it was a tradition, that this is what one had been hearing for many years, so–and if the *aldea* was playing bottles, making a big noise in the night or in the day, it was because there was an eclipse. And so from there they began and they did it and did it and did it until the eclipse had passed. And then everything was tranquil again. And this was something general that the whole community did.

And also, there are other traditions, for example, the festival of San Juan, San Juan el Bautista, and I don't know if this comes from religion or not, I imagine so. So, the Festival of San Juan, the 24th of June is the Festival of San Juan. Also, what they do–they go to adorn the springs–you know what a spring is?–it's where the water is born, purified water from the hills and all. They go to adorn them with lots of flowers and everything. And they make a ceremony to the water. And all the people do this at the springs where they go to drink water. But they also make a general one each year which is that each family has to do it on a certain year. For example, I have to go and sign a list and they say, your turn is in 10 years, that's your turn.

Then sometimes they made them–but more than anything they did it in the *arroyo*, the wells or the springs, no? And the festival they do in the house. And at 4:00 or 5:00 in the morning, everyone who is in the festival and even the marimba they take out to the spring, and everyone washes his head. The water is cold. But what do you call him–the wise man of the community has to be there. Because he's the one who has to make the prayers, pray for all the people, to do the ceremony. He's the chief of the ceremony. And in this and in everything–for example, even when we were going to pick the corn–because there were several in the community–so, for example, my father, or someone from the family would say, "You know what, go and call John Doe, to come and make the ceremony, to come and collect the corn," because we had already collected it. But we had to store it, we had to ask permission and thank the earth, the sun, the water that what we planted is for us, it's the product of the earth that blessed us with it. Because they said, "we should give thanks to nature to the four fundamental elements of man's life." And so they said that one should give thanks to the land, because "the mother earth watches us when we are born, she watches us when we grow, she gives us food, and with her open arms she awaits us again." Yes. That's what they said. So, why should we not give thanks to the mother earth. Because we're also, as human beings, part of the earth. We came from the earth and we will return to the earth. And they say that we are like the grain of corn. It's not we who are going to decide what we will do after death, but it is the earth that decides what will flower from us after death. Yes.

Because in the sacred book of the Maya, *Popol Vuh,* it mentions and puts the example–and this I read about very recently–and my grandfather, the people from before, already told us that in the prayers or in the conversations they gave us to educate us, the education that we should carry with us is our culture or race. And so, that's how it was passed down! From the older men, the wise men of the community.

Afterwards, over time, the religion began to come. It was like a dislodgement of the community of our race. Because I remember very well when my dead grandfather said to me, "Listen, son," he says, "they say that now there's another God. They say that he's a single God. A God that's in the skies. A God," he says, "That when we are dying they say we have to tell him stories about all our sins. We don't know this God. We didn't know him. And they say we have to go and sing to him! We don't know him. And we don't know that God." But then, the young people enter in. They were being filled with the idea, the idea filled the people, and the mentality of the poor was being changed.

They came. People from Spain. People from North America. People from–I don't know, people from other countries. And the *Ladinos*. The *ladino* people who communicated with our community and all. And they pushed in more and more, and they gained more people and they formed little groups, little groups. And there are people that came out against even our own traditions. "No, you're celebrating–how are you going to celebrate festivals of corn? How are you going to be giving thanks or making a festival to the water? How are you going to be making ceremonies to the sun. These are things of the devil, things that aren't true." And the people left this. And they began giving them other ideas, abandoning what is truly our tradition and our culture, no? Yes.[99]

Those who came to be the leaders of the communities knew or divined or foresaw things and told them, and as they said they would occur, that's how it happened, everything, no? Because

---

99 Juan refers here to Catholic Action and other missionary projects that began in the rural areas after the fall of the Arbenz government in 1954. See Kay Warren, 1978, *The Symbolism of Subordination: Indian Identity in a Guatemalan Town* (Austin: Univ. of TX Press) for more on this period.

they even said, "At such a time, or on such a day, or in these months, the storm, the rain will be very strong, that such and such will happen, that there will be a great wind, that we'll see–that a certain illness will come that we don't know what it is and all this." They'd tell the community, and the community–that's one thing. The other is that they only had to look at you, and they'd say, "you're sick. You have such and such an illness. You must take a certain plant, you must do this and this." And they told you. They gave you a mountain of prescriptions and without even touching you, without looking at you, true? And they did all those things, and the people recovered. So, they had this talent from childhood. But there came people who rose up, only to deceive people and rob them of their money. Afterwards.

And they charged. For example, you felt sick. And you know that I'm one of those that cures people. But I began to cure people when I was already grown up. I went to learn from another person who taught me. Yes? So, you come, and I tell you, "Bring me so much money, bring me a rooster, bring me a mountain of things." And in the end, all this that you bring is for him to eat. So that he eats and gets money and all. It wasn't like what the people did before. And many of those appeared. And it was when those people began to appear, that my father didn't believe in them anymore. "No, that one's a charlatan, that's a liar, that's a shrewd one," and many people began to say that about the other people. Because now the grandfathers were dying off. They were dying off. On one hand. On the other, religion began to gain on them and it changed their mentality. They lost their traditions. They lost a lot, everything that was our culture. Because I remember when I was a boy there were hundreds of crosses in the patio of my father's house. Those crosses had been there for years. They came celebrating the day of the cross. And the day of the cross is the day of the four fundamental elements of life. And for this reason, there's the cross, the cross exists that one part is shorter and the other is larger. Those little *granzitos*. And it's that the longer part from top to bottom–the part on top is the sun, and the part of the sun, the distance of the sun to the earth is long. And after, this one is the water and the air. And they make what is the cross. The Mayans painted in the middle of the cross–well, this is what we saw when–maybe it's because of one of the wise men of our culture, or I don't know, but they always painted what was almost a skeleton in the middle of the cross. Because, they said, "They are the four fundamental elements of life," they said. "We have the sun, but if the earth doesn't exist, there's no life." "We have the sun, we have the earth, but if there's no water, there's no life." Yes. "We have the sun, we have water, we have earth, but if there's no air, there's no life." So, "when in your body one of those elements runs out, now there's no cross, what exists is death." There's death because one of the elements of the four fundamental elements of life is lacking. And so, they celebrated, once I don't know how many years, but every year, I think, they celebrated this and in the hills under the rocks there were thousands of crosses.

And all this ended. Now the people of today. Well, now there's nothing. There's nothing. And if there are a few places that they still are, they pull them up, they throw them out, they kick them. They don't respect them. The respect for this ended. And that's how the [traditions] died out. And nowadays, perhaps there are still a few old men, but they don't pay any attention to them. They laugh at them. They laugh at them. So, now there's no one who pays attention to them. Because now, more than anything they go to Mass, they go to church, they go–now it's a very different world, a world from where, we don't even know where it's from.

Leaving Home

So, at an early age I left my parents' home, due to the same situation that I didn't want to live anymore. That is, every year having to go down to the plantation, every year, every year, which for me was a great torture. So, what I do is I go to another place, far from my parents' house, [at 13] with the aim of continuing my studies in another place. Because the situation we were living in was difficult. My parents didn't have very much money for us to continue studying. And I was already grown. And so, I leave my parents' house and I go to another place, and the place where I went, perhaps I fall into a worse situation, because... It was right there in San Marcos. A place that was called Malacatan.

And so I go there, and I present myself at the school and what they ask me for first is a certificate that shows what grade I have gotten to in school. And I tell them, "Well, I don't have one. I went to school, but they didn't give me anything. I don't have any paper." Well, so, I couldn't, I couldn't. Until at last, I believe it was the director of the school who took pity on me. So, he said, "you can't come and attend all the classes, but you can choose two or three areas that you want to take," he said. "We'll give you an opportunity. But you're not going to be matriculated in the school or anything. You'll just come as an auditor, because I see that you are interested in learning something." And I said, "well, okay."

So I go and I take physical education and industrial arts and plastic arts. Those were the three areas that I took. Because that's what I wanted. I said, "Well, physical education, that has to do with my health, the organism and all, ...know a little more. Industrial arts, that I could get to do that better, and something else, because, I had seen where I was brought up, and I had seen other towns outside where there were other things to do. And so, I began to think, and I say, "How strange, I'll go for what is called industrial arts." And I also took what is called plastic arts, because in plastic arts I could do, even painting, sculpture, and everything, no? And then, not much time passed before I went to another place and in that other place I began to have problems and all. And the time came when we were thrown out by the army itself.

Political Persecution

We were 35 sons of indigenous people, who were in Malacatan in that school. They formed a student group in all the schools. So, I was able to enter into what was the student group, but not playing musical instruments. Yes, they played musical instruments, but it wasn't the reason I joined. Because I liked comedy a lot. And there were three of us who were comics, who did sketches, we sang, we did comedies and all that, but the comedies that we did were comedies about how they treated the indigenous people–we made people understand our real life in theatrical works. Yes. The songs that we did as well were songs about the injustice towards the indigenous person, the mistreatment of the indigenous people. And we made music and we sang and all, and many people didn't like this.

There was a teacher who was encouraging this but all the works that we presented, those arose from us...But then we said, "now we have the power. We're going to demonstrate what our reality as indigenous people is. And we're going to demonstrate how they treat us as indigenous people. And even though in the society they realize this, we're going to do something humorous so that the people laugh, but we're going to make them feel what one feels, what the reality is." No? Yes. And that's what we thought. And that's what happened.

But at this time a political party arises, which is the PGT, the Guatemalan Worker's Party, and they begin to make propaganda all around the town, no? And even the walls of the school showed up painted, the bathrooms and everything. And so, they began to accuse us of having done this. Because we sang protest songs. We did protest sketches. We presented protest comedies. Yes. All our works were in protest. Protest. Protest. Protest, no? And so it fell on us that we were the ones who handed out the propaganda, who did all that. And they began to persecute us.

But now, it got harder and harder for us when they killed one of our schoolmates. Of the three who did songs of protest–the one who sang the protest songs, they took the boy from his house. They took him and they took his father. And they turned up dead. And after that, a note showed up where it said, "This is how we will get rid of the others." And the others, well, that was us. Yes. And so, the guard began to pursue us. They went to look for us where we were living. They told the people that they were going to kill us. And I don't know what else. And so, what we did was we separated. Well, the other one left the school and I did too. And all the others–many of us left [school]. Because that was when the kidnapping started, people started disappearing. And so, before we disappeared, we had to get ourselves out of there. We had to leave.

I'm talking now about 1978. And in 1979 I decide to go to the zone of Ixcam. The zone of Ixcam is a jungle area. Where we had transportation, there wasn't any road, there weren't any cars, there wasn't anything but one little plane, nothing more. We had to fly 45 minutes to get to where we had been in the town. And the plane was only for 3 people–the pilot and two more. That was all the plane could hold. It couldn't hold any more people (laughs). That was my first flight in the little plane. So, I arrive there. Of all my friends, I had just left school. I had a much broader vision and a more developed understanding. And I had gone to a bigger town. Where I'd been studying was a larger town. There were roads, there were bicycles, there were cars, there were stores, there was cinema, there was everything. And then, with the others who were in the mountains, what was there? There wasn't anything! Yes. And so, I began to tell them, "Why don't we begin to do a program? Let's give classes to the children. Let's learn about health. Let's learn sports. Something that we can amuse ourselves with. We have to learn something. We have to do something so that we can excel." And the cooperatives already existed, already founded cooperatives. So, we were like facilitators for the cooperatives. And I was there working, well, for a long time.

Then in 1979 they began to kill the directors of the cooperatives. All the country people who knew a little about other things, the well-being of the community, they killed them. They disappeared. All those catechists who strayed a little bit, speaking of the reality of our life situation of how we were living–if it came to the ears of the authority, they disappeared. The priest who spoke in favor of the indigenous people–disappeared. So, everyone, everyone was being brought to an end.

And so, in 1980, it got more difficult, and in 1982, that was when they started the bombings with the airplanes. How those men decided to bomb the people! And one Sunday, the market people–the town was really small, but there were a lot of people, no? More than 2,500 people in the little town, yes. And so, and it's the day that everything is exchanged. You go to buy, you go to sell or you're going to amuse yourself, or you're going to go play soccer or you're going to church. The Catholic church was full of pure Christians, the Methodist church was also full of people from that religion, no? And the Charismatics. But with no compassion for anyone, they dropped bombs on those churches. And the army surrounded the people and all the people who wanted to escape, they went to kill on every side. And the helicopter up above, then we heard it go bon, bon, bon. And they killed more than 840 people, yes more than 840 people in two hours. Yes.

And so it was during that time that I was still there. This story that I'm telling you now is a shortened version. It's really long, imagine, detail by detail, I even remember the dates, everything, no? Yes. I was 23 years old at that time.

[We knew] that it could happen. What are the people going to do? They have to live. We have to live in one form or another. Because it was a place where the community was oppressed. And so, at that time, everybody of those who remained alive went to escape. They left for Mexico. So, the first refugee camps in Mexico were those who arrived in Chiapas. And so the Mexican government sends them to Quintana Roo, to Campeche and I think to Yucatan as well, I don't remember. We brought a lot of people over, we brought a lot of people to the border with Mexico.

In Mexico

And after that I stayed in Mexico. I was working as well. I even had to go back to the coffee plantations in order to be able to survive. And then I began to work for my life, for my own self. I went into photography, painting, into everything. I'm half electrician, half carpenter, half plumber, half cook, half taxi driver, half everything, because I went into everything in order to make a living in Mexico. And not only that, but I saw the life of the community of people in Mexico, also, in different places. Because I became acquainted with almost the whole of Mexico from 1982 to 1993, when I came to the United States. I saw almost all the states of Mexico, and the people's life situation in those places as well.

But so, in Mexico, what I always did was try to find a way to become legal, because I couldn't always be living illegal. So, I went to different government institutions and all. I set my problem before them, and what they always ordered me and told me to do was to go to the refugee camps. So, I said, "how am I going to go to a Guatemalan refugee camp, when at any moment they might send us back to Guatemala from those camps!" As it happened in the Caravan I think of 1982. They sent, I don't know whether it was 400 or 4,000, I don't remember. They returned the Guatemalans to Guatemala, and where did they end up? They ended up once again in military detention, controlled by the military army. And they killed off the young men. They assassinated them again, and they disappeared. So, imagine me. I go to a refugee camp to fall into the same thing, they return me! So, I looked for a way, at various institutions everywhere, and they always ended up saying, "look for a Guatemalan refugee camp. That's where you need to go. There you will be safe. There you have"—and I said no...

But in Mexico I lived some off of the arts. I worked in photography and I painted. And all the paintings I did, whatever they gave me for them was okay. Well, I never got to paint a painting the size of the ones I'm doing now. I always made them very little on coconut shells, on stones, on glass, on wood, on bricks, on disposable plates, on whatever. That was my material, because I got all the material for my art work in Mexico in the streets. I found it in the trash. The only thing I didn't find was the paint, so I had to buy that...

I lived there on my own. In Mexico it's easy to live, something that here you can't do. Here we're in a developed country, a big country and everything, but you can't live. You can't live if you don't work, if you don't have a house to live in. Whereas in Mexico, no. In Mexico, with the little that you can make, you can live. You can live a life even without a house. Because, I lived under the bridges. I lived in the street. I spent a long time sleeping in the central bus station. I always went with my suitcase, and the people thought, "oh, you're going to travel." And as soon as I woke up, I went some other place. I went to make my living again, selling something, doing whatever work [was available].

Because I began to pay for a house or for a place to live only when I got to Mexico City. Yes. Because there it is very difficult and very dangerous to live much in the street. So there I began to pay for a place to live. But in the states in the towns and such, I never paid. Because I lived in the mountains, I lived in the trees, I slept in front of the store, wherever. And you can–I ate the fruit from the trees in the roads or at the edge of the rivers, the plants by the rivers. Yes.

I lived for a long time on the land itself in Mexico, because I was also hiding from immigration. Sure. Because without documents! You're traveling in a car from one place to another, and there's immigration, "give me your papers." I don't have any. So, what I always did was I went walking from one place to another. I stayed for a while in one town. Then I asked how far the next town was, and then I went walking to the other town, and the next. And it took me a long time to get to Mexico City. Yes. And that's the way I came to know part of the Mexican culture. And after that, well I familiarized myself with the people of Mexico, taking on the tone of speaking or having more friends, more friends who could tell me now, do me the favor, say, "no, this guy is from where I live, what happened is he didn't bring his papers, he forgot and all." And that way I could also travel from one place to another. By bus or by car or something.

There are days when you eat and days when you don't eat. Yes. As a man said last night, he says, "our life, we've led our lives like ducks," he says, "there are days when you swim and days when we don't even drink water" (laughs). But it's a very long story. But half the time has already gone by. You should understand that all that's left is the memory. It's not the same as when one is living it, when one is suffering these things. Yes. Now everything is different. But you can be sure that I won't forget, and I won't forget it ever...

If that hadn't happened where I was living, I would have made my life [there]. I wouldn't be here now. And many of the people who are living here would not be here. Yes. Many of the people who live here are here due to the situation that happened during those years. Many of them lived it themselves. Many, the young people, their parents lived it. Because there are many Guatemalans here. And most of them are young people. But they weren't born in Guatemala. They were born in Mexico. Yes. And they don't stop being Guatemalan. Because being in Mexico, for one reason or another, we couldn't register them. Yes. And there are many who are illegal. They aren't Mexicans or Guatemalans. They aren't registered. So, many suffered themselves, and many, their parents suffered. So, there are some who, even if they wanted to return to Guatemala, for example the young people who would like to return to Guatemala, and what are they going to do in Guatemala if the grandfather and the grandmother, the cousin, the uncle, were all killed. They abandoned their lands, they abandoned their houses, they abandoned everything and some of them are stuck in refugee camps, and others are definitely slaves of the Mexican landowners' plantations. Yes. They aren't recognized as Mexicans or as Guatemalans. And there they are. And what do these poor people do?

The Decision to Come North

Some people told me, "why don't you go to the United States?" There you can ask for asylum, you can explain your situation, your problem and all, and maybe you can win." And since one heard that a lot of people came here, and that they were given political asylum. And so, for that reason, I decided to come here, so that I wouldn't have to continue living illegally in Mexico. Because I couldn't establish myself in one place...

So, there wasn't any other way than to come here to the United States. And on arriving here, now it was just about when the law tightened up, immigration. So, when I believe that, I don't know under what law I came but a few days after I got my working papers was when they stopped giving out working papers. So, my goal in coming to the United States illegally was that if here in the United States they gave me or I obtained political asylum, well I would stay. And if I couldn't get political asylum here in the United States, I didn't know what country I was going to go to. Because I wasn't going to return to Guatemala. So, that's the reason I'm here in the United States.

And the situation that one comes to live here in the United States, well imagine, everything is different. The language, the food, the work, the pressure of the work, and everything. It's a great change. Even the climate, the weather affected me. My enclosed world. Because I was accustomed, for example in Guatemala or in Mexico, to see the children running in the street, the people running around, the dogs, the animals throughout the land. And here one comes and doesn't see anyone walking in the street. If you see one, it's an Hispanic. Well, one wonders what's going on. And you come and everything's new. You're grown up but it's as if you've just been born. (laughs)...

So, for me it was easy to get to the border. And once I was at the border I had to inform myself about all the movement there in the border, how people crossed. And well, my best information was to communicate with the boys who were there. There were even young men who helped people cross the border, but they handed them over to the coyotes, charging money. In other words, they sold us. As one says, "I have three people or four people. Give me so much money and I'll bring them to you." So, I informed myself about everything, everything–what it was that they did, at what time the immigration changed guard and all. They told me the hour. And so, I then, from the hotel began to watch the hour and the movement on the other side of the border.

And then when I saw that it was one in the morning and all the patrols that went along the border were quiet, that's when I jumped over the wire and I crossed over to the other side. And then I went to a McDonalds that was close to the border...

What I had imagined of the United States was like what I had seen in movies and all–huge cities and all. But I hadn't thought that one could find places like this, no? Small towns. Places with few people. But coming here makes you see things completely different, because the lifestyle is more uncomfortable. Yes. Because, you come here. There are people to speak Spanish with, no? But what you wish, what you want to be is difficult because of the language. And so, coming here for the first time, imagine. You don't know anyone, you don't–how are you going to obtain work, how are you going to pay all the bills that you have here. In Mexico it's very different. One can live adventuring, because I lived that way for many years. But if I wanted to live that kind of life here as in Mexico, I can't. Here you have to pay your taxes, you have to pay for a place to live, you have to pay for everything. And you can't live in the street here. Yes. Because it's something that's illegal. They see you living in the street or spending a night in front of a house or in front of a store, well, they pick you up and take you to the police. (laughs) Yes. It's true.

Within a week of my arrival, I found work. I was working in the fields, and meanwhile I had to apply for asylum and permission to work, and months later my working papers came, so then I could work in a poultry processing plant. A poultry factory. Then I began to pay for a place to live, and then I began to work, and then I began to meet more people. I began to have communication with the Hispanic people, [find out] who here speaks two languages. I began to meet people also who had an interest in Art. And in that way I went on, I went broadening [my horizons].

And so, now, when I went to work also, what I did was I began to buy my art materials. Because when I had just arrived, I was a few days, it was months that I was almost without money. Because all the time that I was here, well I had to borrow money, I had to borrow money to be able to eat, to be able to pay the rent, and I also owed money. And so, I didn't have enough money to cover my art materials. And that's why I began to paint on paper plates, wood, pieces of rock, and all that. And then afterwards I began to buy my art material to be able to paint formal canvases. I began with very small ones, I've only recently started to paint large canvases. Because I didn't have any money. And I almost never have now. Yes. (laughs)

Because I have to send money to my parents, and I have to maintain my art and all the costs that are necessary to live. Because, at least for me here, what has always happened is that the only money I have is what I have in my pocket. Always to eat. But now money, let's say, to have savings, I never have enough. Because the pay here is a pay that goes in line with the prices of things. So, because the pay that one earns, at least me when I was working, is minimum wage. So, it's not to make money with.

There are a lot of people here who make money to send to their family to buy their things there, but they work 15, 16, up to 18 hours a day. Yes. And I, well, I don't, more than anything, I didn't come for that, well. Because, there are times I say to some people, "I didn't come here to work lots of hours, or so many hours, as they do sometimes. Because I came here to live. And I try to live in a way that's more, not so overwhelming in my life. Because now I also have political asylum, my residency, and all. Now that's a great advantage for me, so I'm not physically destroying myself.

Political Asylum

I don't remember exactly the date. But I think it was in 1995 that I got political asylum. And after my political asylum card arrived, one year after I received the political asylum card, I had the right to apply for permanent residency. And after the year, after having applied for permanent residency, I think it arrived six months, seven months later. Yes. And besides that when, for example when my appointment for the interview comes and all,

Study of Guatemalan life by Juan Perez
(Courtesy of Phyllis Levitt)

they either give you asylum or they deport you. That is, all that time I lived, well tense, with fears and all, and if, given the case that they didn't give me political asylum, they denied me and all, well I had my doubts. If I didn't get it, I didn't know either what country I would go to, because I wasn't going to return to Guatemala. Even if they deported me and all, I wasn't going to go there.

I don't know why they gave me political asylum. Because, well, almost all the people who have working papers, all of them applied for political asylum. But I believe that perhaps the proof that immigration asks for, they don't qualify or I don't know why. For example, I gave them a minimal part of the history of my life, what happened to me in Guatemala. And what happened to me in Mexico wasn't very much of what I gave them in my account. But of Guatemala, the account of Guatemala, yes I gave them some of the story. And everything was the real thing, what I had lived, all the time. And well, I wrote an account and I gave it to immigration. Yes. And also, there were many people who helped me. There were many people who helped me, because they sent letters of recommendation to immigration. Perhaps that was what helped me. Or perhaps it's the art. I don't know what it was. They had pity on me, perhaps. (laughs)

The Poultry Plant

After I had working papers, and more when I had political asylum and all, well all that time I was working in the poultry processing plant. And the truth is, I didn't like it. I didn't like how they pressure the people, the treatment that one receives, the free time that they give to one—it isn't enough time and all. Inside the plant it's a very uncomfortable place, because they use a lot of chlorine. This bothers your eyes. It bothers your throat. And a lot of ammonium. A lot of ammonium. And all the time where you're working, well all the time there's water, yes, because they're washing the floor with water. And all that humidity, you're absorbing with chlorine and ammonium, and who's knows what other acids they use in the plants. And a lot of people begin to get sick, and the treatment isn't good, and the pay isn't good either, yes. So, they exploit one too much, they steal hours from one, and if one claims one's rights, they don't pay attention to you. And all those injustices that I saw inside the plant, I was also living myself. So, I said, "Well, I've got my papers now. I can yell. I can complain all that I want with no fear."

So, there are a lot of people who work in the plants–they don't complain about what they're doing to them, because they're afraid that they'll fire them. And they think that being out of the poultry plants, they're not going to find work. And so, because I always complained, complained, all that. Even the hours they didn't pay the other people, they did pay me. Yes. Because I wrote down at what hour we began to work and at what hour we ended. And I wrote it down in front of the supervisor, and with the supervisor's clock. And so, at the end of the week, I counted up how many hours I worked, and then in the check, those hours didn't come out. And so I complained and said, why, if I have it written down and even more the supervisor knows very well at what time we began to work, and here it is written down. So, and they paid me in cash. But they stole 15 minutes, 10 minutes from all the people. Imagine if you steal 10 minutes, or only 1 minute from one person, from one person and there were 700 people working on the shift. That's 700 minutes, no? And all that money. Now, when they robbed 10 minutes, 15 minutes–there's a man that they stole 18 hours from once that they never paid, because he stayed to work double shifts.

And so, I always complained about that. And I complained for the others, but the others didn't back me up in my complaint. And so they didn't pay them. And they paid me in cash in the office. And this almost always happened. Every week. And so, on seeing that I always complained, what they started doing was to cut my work hours. And they would say, "you know what, now there are a lot of people working, why don't you go home and come back tomorrow." And when the next day came, the next day, they told me, "Look, uh, work four hours and we're going to pay you the other four hours, because now there isn't any more work. Go home and tomorrow come back again." And so I said, "What's happening here, what's happening?" And so, they went on cutting my time. And there were days when they said, "Come tomorrow," and when I arrived the next day they said, "You know what, there's no work for you today. Come back tomorrow." And so, they had me, they had me, until I said, "This one doesn't want me to work anymore, so, I better go." Because alone I couldn't do anything, and the other people didn't support me. I said, "okay." And so, I left. I decided to leave. And what I had as well was the painting. And so, I sold some paintings there, and some other jobs from other places came along, and I received a little work. And I got along that way without working in any plant in any place, for a year and a half. I survived. I paid my rent. I paid for my food. I paid for everything. Yes. And well, afterwards, well, I decided to work again, because, really art only earned me enough to eat, but now to send money to my family or my parents or other friends who needed help in other places, I couldn't.

And so, I found myself obliged again, and I began to work in a restaurant. I was working in a restaurant, and after that I worked in construction. But no, that is, I didn't find it difficult to stop working, because I also had a way to get work—art, painting—although I didn't sell much, I earned enough at least to eat. And if I didn't, then I had to borrow, and in one way or another I found the money. And that's how I lived and that's how I'm living. (laughs)...

Community Organizing

[As a community outreach worker for Children and Families First] what I do now more than anything is I work for the community—that is, observe the problems, the necessities of the community. So, there are many people who know the services that exist in the community, but [they don't utilize them] due to the fact that the people are illegal or they are afraid. And the fear that they have wasn't created here. The people always bring their fears from there, yes? And here, living here, the situation is more difficult. And they are people who carry the fear. They are people who don't know how to read, and they are people who also don't worry about communicating with others in the community. So, now what? And many of us, many of the people don't know truly the laws under which we are living. We don't know. And so, that's why a lot of people don't have all the information. So, what I'm doing now, more than anything is letting the people know and understand that each country or each state has its laws. And so, we have to adapt ourselves to the laws of the place where we're living. So, for this reason I also have to be well versed with the rest of the people about what the law is where we are living. What is it that we must do and what we must not do.

And for the people who have special problems, what I do is orient the person and take them to the institutions, the organizations or agencies where one must resolve the problems. And also I have to be always available to the people, observing their problems, and what problems are occurring in the town/people and take them to the community. Because I'm working from house to house. Because I'm also looking at the quantity of children who are being born here in the community. Because what we want is that in time when those children become adolescents and all, well, that they all have an education.

What's happening now is that many adolescents have arrived here. Their parents were someplace else and they moved here, or children who came from Guatemala with their parents, and on arriving here, they took them to the school. So, and the school each year passes them from one grade to another, every year they're passing their grade, whether they know or don't know. And this is one of our greatest worries because in all the schools here, the high schools, there are a lot of students. There are a lot of Hispanic children. And we have learned that these children don't even know how to read. Yes. And so, each year, as they pass through the grades it becomes more difficult for the student. Because the grades are higher, they're older. And so, what has been happening–they leave school. Because many have dropped out. And so, and they think and they say, "Now, what I'm going to do is go and work in the poultry processing plants."

And once they are working in the plants, poultry processing plants, they discover that the work is hard, it's difficult. Because they didn't work in Guatemala. They didn't experience working in Guatemala, and on coming to work here, and the work their father does and all is very hard. It's a difficult job. So, what happens? They leave work; they don't go to school or work. What do they do? They hang out in the streets. And over time they're going to fall into alcoholism, they're going to get into drugs, they're going to get into vandalism and they're going to have confrontations between the children of Hispanics and either the African Americans or the youth from here. Now they're going to form groups. And if they say that we Hispanics have a lot of community problems now among the older people, no? Now the concern exists with the new generation, what can happen. And that's what we don't want.

But here it's more difficult, it's more difficult to organize people. Because a lot of the people who have come from there, sure, they've suffered. But the suffering here is a different kind, it's a different kind. The people who suffer in Guatemala–it's the tension, tensions in the situation that they live. It's a very poor life. And besides that they are people who were hit in the war years and all. And so they are people who've lived with a great fear, and within the problems that they lived, they've resolved their problems and all. And so, there what the people were organizing for was to work together for the well being of the whole community...

Here in the community there are very few older people. The greater part of the community is young. And the young people have little experience in what you call getting involved in organizing. And the young people are the ones who are the most productive workers, yes, and that's why the company has more of them. And it's a new generation of workers. And there're many people who are always moving to another place. They leave here and others come from other parts...

Because the time comes when they get bored; they get desperate with working in the same place in the poultry plants. There are many here who've worked in all the poultry plants. I only went to one. And so, in all the plants, it's the same treatment. So, then they get bored, they get desperate, they go to the fields, I don't know, they go to other jobs, and in a short time, they come back. It's a circle.

OGAM

OGAM arises when there was the first March on Washington. The information comes to us that there would be a march on Washington, and so, each person, from his own initiative began to announce that there would be a march to the people. We went to announce to the people that there would be a march, a march, a march. But there was no one to direct it. There wasn't anyone to direct the march. And so we found out who the people were who were announcing the march, and everything–there were people who were interested in supporting the march and so, we decided–we got together and we decided that it would be better to announce to the community that there would be a general assembly to see there what would be decided, or who would be the director of the march, no?

So, we put up announcements and a good number of people got together in the church hall, and they laid out what was going to happen, why they were going to have a march and all. So, the community, the people who came began to say, "why don't we form a committee? Or a group?" Because we first formed as a committee, at least it started out as a committee that was going to direct the march. How we were going to organize to transport people. What we were going to do, where the trucks were going to be, and all of this with the help of *La Esperanza*. Yes. And that was how OGAM emerged. OGAM got its name a long time later, I don't even know who gave it that name, no? Yes. Who put that name, OGAM. And well, now there we are working for the community. There are many committees within the organization, and now we're legally recognized by the state, and we have the support of other organizations, other institutions, and we are in communication with all the immigrant organizations that exist in the United States...

There we have to learn. In step with what we are doing. The responsibility of each one of us. And since we are working together, many of us bring ideas, and we propose them in the meeting, and there in the meeting is where it's decided which ones we're going to do and what's good and what's not. In other words, it's a gathering of ideas. And depending on the ideas that are brought, depending on responsibility of each one of us.

A work plan exists for the community here in Georgetown, yes, for the community. And within the community there are short-term plans, medium term plans, and long term plans. And we also have plans for Guatemala and for Mexico, for other countries. We more than anything need to concentrate ourselves here in the community first. And we have succeeded in organizing the community here, in this way, we can start in on the plan to help Guatemala, because what we have to do here, more than anything is form the base first. The plan now is more focused here in the community, and to resolve the problems in the community. Because there's a lot to do within the community.

Juan Perez with a painting of his at the Dover Art League
(Courtesy of Phyllis Levitt)

Youngsters playing in Kimmeytown at Pedro Ospina's Park
(Courtesy of Dana Long)

Olegario Capriel

I first met Olegario Capriel in the spring of 1999 at a Sunday afternoon meeting of OGAM, the Guatemalan Mutual Aid Society, in Georgetown. OGAM had been actively organizing the community to attend protests in Washington regarding unequal treatment of Central American immigrants under the law and to participate in local street cleanings in response to negative stereotypes about Hispanic lifestyles. When Hurricane Mitch devastated Guatemala, OGAM, led by then president Julio Herrera, actively worked to send hundreds of boxes of relief aid to the victims. However, when Herrera resigned from the presidency, the organization faltered and has been relatively inactive since 1999.

Olegario is the current president, but work, family and school keep him from investing the necessary energy to revive the group. Olegario is also the only Guatemalan member of the Board of *La Esperanza*.

As one of the first Guatemalans to arrive in Delaware in 1992, Olegario's migration account reveals the sense of adventure that brought many of the young men and women here. He remembers that in 1992, the large red apartments on Race Street were full of Blacks and Haitians. Now they are almost one hundred percent Guatemalan. In that first year, Perdue was offering $100 a head for people to go to Florida and recruit more workers. Olegario used to go down on the weekends to areas like Indiantown where Guatemalans had concentrated. He'd arrive at the main store, and, once the word was out, people would line up to speak with him.

Olegario is not, however, from the same region as most who live in Georgetown now, and, as he explains in his narrative, he is often mistaken for a Mexican. Like Juan Perez's story, he grew up speaking not Spanish but the Maya Quiche language. Olegario's account of his early life reflects the destruction of indigenous religious practices with the arrival of Catholic Action and other evangelizing groups to rural Guatemala in the 1960s and 70s. Though he acknowledges that the erosion of indigenous culture is linked to schooling as well, Olegario is an ardent student and supporter of education as a means to personal and community advancement.

Early Memories

I was born in a rural settlement called Tierra Blanca in the municipality of San Bartolo in the Department of Totonicapan, which borders Quiche. I was born there 28 years ago. I left Tierra Blanca when I was about fourteen, and that's when I started to learn Spanish, when I left the settlement for the city of Quetzaltenango.

We Capriels–there's an indigenous group called Capriel like my surname. There were about, well before, six families there. And the six families were united. I'm talking about thirty years ago, when my grandparents arrived at that place, Tierra Blanca. They were spread out, but when they arrived, they arrived together. Just one household, they had just one house. When all the people, their children arrived there–they were like brothers–and after that, the family expanded. We all dispersed. But those who arrived were there for a long time, like fifteen years together, living together in the same house...

So everyone worked to feed everyone, and they did everything together. But it only lasted like fifteen years, because the family grew. It grew and grew and grew, and that was when they said that they would divide up and that each one should look for a way to live. Because now there were too many to have all together, and that's how we dispersed. And now the Capriel family has maybe 300 or 400 Capriel families. And many people ask me about why my name is different from the rest, the Garcias and the Rosarios. Capriel–I don't know how to explain why it is that the surname Capriel arose, but today it exists and there are Capriels in our country, Guatemala. I don't know where, where it came from...

And the tradition that the family carried, they say, was, how do you say?–like doing witchcraft. I don't know how to say it, but they burned *cocal*. It was like a tradition that one had to continue. Because they were the roots of our grandparents and great grandparents, one had to keep doing that. But I think that was also lost. My father practiced it, yes. I would go with him when I was little to pray to the–it was, I remember, how do you call?– that he believed a lot in the gods that he prayed to, and I only know in my language, I don't know how to say it in Spanish. But there were different gods that they worshipped...

And that's what my grandparents and the older people wanted their children to inherit–to do the same that they had done, but Christianity began to arrive, and many people began to change to different religions–Catholics, Charismatics, Jehovah's Witness– and so, all that resulted in witchcraft being lost. Witchcraft or, well, the indigenous religion. I think that eighty percent have some religion. Now nobody practices that. Perhaps there are two or three families who continue...

And all the children my age, most of them are here. Not exactly from my family. My father's parents have thirteen children, and my mother's parents have eleven. That's to say that I have 12 uncles, and of those twelve uncles no one is here. No one. It's the same with my mother's family. None are here. Other families are here but in my family, only my brother and I are here. They live in Quetzaltenango, Huehuetenango and other places. They maintain themselves as itinerant merchants. They sell different things–they have shoes, jewelry–not quality jewelry but costume jewelry...

We have land, but it's a little difficult to cultivate, because they are very dry places where it's difficult to get by with the harvest. What it mostly gives is peaches, avocado–there are a lot of fruits, but I don't know the names, pomegranates–have you heard of pomegranate? Well, there are also *anonas*. I think so. It's the only thing that serves in those places, because they are stable trees, for a long time. And now the corn only grows once a year, because the place is very dry. It's not a hot place, but it's not very cold either. It's a cool place.

My paternal grandfather makes baskets, and now my father makes baskets. And my maternal grandfather makes wax, that is candles. Well, he used to make them, [but] he doesn't make them anymore. None of my maternal uncles or my paternal uncles learned to make what my grandparents made–baskets and candles. None of them, no one practiced that...

Leaving Tierra Blanca

When I finished sixth grade of primary school–it was when I was sixteen, fourteen, fifteen, sixteen, yes–because when I was in third grade I went to school in the city, and I continued studying until I finished primary school. Then, I had the opportunity to continue school, but I didn't get the scholarship. I didn't qualify for the scholarship, and I went to a private institute, wanting the great opportunity to be able to pay for my studies. But it was impossible to continue, because it's too much money, and I didn't qualify for the scholarship. And the institute is called, Adolfo B. Hall, which is the institute that teaches you so that you can continue in the Polytechnic if you want to be an army officer. That was my dream, and that is my dream that I have. I want to be in the Army. And I wanted to continue that here too, but it is very difficult. And so I didn't continue, because it was very difficult to want to be an army officer. It was difficult to continue studying that profession, because of the fears that there were between the guerrillas and the army all the time. But maybe I would have continued, if I had had economic resources. But there were no resources, so I didn't continue.

We weren't exactly [affected by the fight]. In some places, yes there was quite a lot. People came to kill whole families. That was the only thing we experienced. But no one from my family, no one from my family was persecuted. There were problems. There were threats, but they never came knocking on our doors. They came knocking to ask for water or food, perhaps. But not the

370

army. The guerrillas came to our house, they came, but they were very familiar, they were very respectful. They were from other places. They were always respectful. I don't like to speak ill of people who didn't mistreat me, who didn't mistreat anyone.

But the army, when they came, yes. We were more afraid of the army showing up than the guerrillas. They were two very different groups. When the guerrillas showed up, we felt different from when the army showed up. When the guerrilla showed up, they chatted, they told jokes, they played with the children, or they played with us, but they never, never, never made us feel bad.

When the army showed up, the first thing they looked for was arms, shoes that they used or those caps that cover your whole face, ski caps. Well, that's what they looked for–it was shoes, pistols or firearms that we had in our houses. They were looking for them. They went all around the house. They went upstairs searching. So when they showed up, there was that fear, because they threw everything they wanted around, and then, the families left. We were more afraid when the army came than with the guerrillas.

We were afraid, but it never affected us. I say in the place where we were, it never affected us. In other places in other rural settlements that were more isolated than where we were, it did. Where we were, it was two hours by car and a long time walking to get there.

When the army began doing that it was about fifteen years ago, more or less, in 1985. I knew what they were doing was bad. The idea I had was to change the system of the army. I was very small. But my idea was to change, to make the army different, because I didn't want to be a soldier. I didn't want to be a lieutenant. I wanted to be a lieutenant colonel, who directed the army. That was my dream. So when I enrolled in the private institute, thanks to my father who gave me that chance to be there for a year, I wanted to totally change them. And if I could have changed them that year, I would have, but I had to study to get to that point. I had to study a lot in order to be able to do what I wanted. But it was five years of preparatory school, three years more in the polytechnic, and from there, every two years if I didn't have any problems–they would promote us and then– It was sub-lieutenant, lieutenant, and then lieutenant colonel I think, and then colonel. And it was so difficult to get there, but people have done it, and I said, "I'm going to get there, I'm going to get there." But at that time I was sixteen, more or less, and it was difficult. It is difficult, and it was difficult.

A Business

What happens is that very few of us had the opportunity to study. More, our parents demanded that we work at eleven or twelve years old. You're already working, and they paid us half the fee that they paid the older people. But we were already working, and what I wanted to do and what I did was to look for a business, establish a business, and study at the same time. But a business without capital, or without the money already established in the business is difficult. It's difficult to continue with the business, because the business is only [dealing] with credit. So, one has to sell and pay the suppliers at the same time. But if I had had a proper business. For example, with 50,000 dollars, I have a business with 50,000 dollars, and I ask for a 10,000 dollar loan. I, what I sell every day, I would take out and save in order to be able to ask for more.

But no. What we did was, I had like 10,000 *quetzales* of capital. I had 20,000 in credit, and I had only 10,000 to cover the credit. So that was what didn't help us in the business. And that affected my studies a lot, because the supplier comes next week. I have to study for exams. I'm thinking about how to pay that man. I'm not selling. Business went down for some reason. There are days when you sell very well and days you don't sell very well. The supplier is not going to wait for his money until I can get it together. The supplier will come on the date that I told him to come. How am I going to pay? I don't know. The only thing I know is that I have to pay that money.

So, that has a great influence on school. It takes away our morale to keep on studying. One can't focus on studying. Nevertheless, my father studied that way. And I wanted to keep on studying like that. So, I had that short opportunity to continue studying and working at the same time. But it's difficult, very difficult to continue studying. And for that reason, I didn't continue like that. It was so difficult to keep going.

My father only got what is preparatory and is high school [sic]. He got his high school diploma [sic] and that's it. His dream was to read and write. It was the only thing our parents, our grandparents wanted. If the child knows how to read and write already, that's it. He knows everything. There's no reason to invest more money, because there isn't any. I only remember my grandfather saying, "there's no reason to invest more money, because there isn't any. It's enough for him to know how to sign his name." That's what they told us. That we should know how to sign our names, that's it.

My mother doesn't know how to write. My grandparents learned how to read and write by themselves, but they didn't have the ability to give their children lessons. For the same reason, because they didn't have the money. Perhaps it was also because the schools were quite far from where we lived. They had to walk two hours to get to school. Two to get there, two to return. So, it was difficult. It is difficult. But now I think that there are different ways one can study. Now there are teachers in our rural areas who can give classes. So the world is changing...

English Classes

I think that the one who cries is suckled. It's that if I am interested, if I put my desire, my great desire into studying, I will meet my goals. I know I will meet them, because I'm living it now...

What happens in this country, what most damages us is the loneliness. Many people ask themselves, why are the Hispanics such drunks? Why do Hispanic men run after so many women? Why, blah, blah, blah?

In the first place, the reason why we're such drunks is because we're homesick. We forget ourselves with beer, or we relax. We think of our families, think of our wives, our children. We'd like to be drunk every day to be able to think of them, to satisfy, perhaps, our desire to talk about it all. Because sober it's hard to talk to you about what I have inside, what I feel inside. But drunk, one satisfies, one let's that out by talking with another person. So, that is what makes us like that here. If we had our families here, perhaps one would study more. But I come to the same thing with the children here–the problems of adolescence, the problems with school, problems, problems after problems, we wouldn't study.

I have a son here, and my son sees me pick up my workbook. He picks up his workbook also. But many parents don't do that, having their children here. Instead of picking up a workbook in front of their child, they pick up a cigarette or a beer, and the child is learning exactly what the father is doing. And now, what I do is I pick up a workbook, my book or whatever, and my son is going to paint. And I say, paint, and he starts to paint. And I say, draw, he starts to draw. Because I'm doing almost the same thing. We're doing almost the same thing with him. So, I think that having the interest, one learns, some way, any way, one learns. And God first, this semester I'll get my ESL, and next year I'll keep studying…   And if someday, God gives me the opportunity to return to Guatemala, why shouldn't I say, I have my GED in Spanish, and I have my GED in English, which are the two things at the same time. But if I were to go to my country with the GED or with a profession from here from the United States, the language–whether it's English or whatever language it is–I have my profession here, and I go to the country of Guatemala, I can use that profession there. Yes. Completely. But if I bring that profession from my country to the United States, I can't use it. My profession in English serves me better even if I take it back there…

The Crossing

I left Quetzaltenango at 16, I think, or 17, and I went back to Huehuetenango at 17—18, I believe. I was on the border between Mexico and Huehuetenango and Guatemala. There was when I began to see a lot of people who came from here to there with new cars, everything. That is, young men who were different, who were ambitious, and it was ambition that impacted me. Their ambition impacted me, and it was when I was around 19 that I came here from there...

When I was in Huehuetenango, I was there with my father's consent. I was at the border bringing Mexican candy to Guatemala, like a trader but underground. There Mexican candy shouldn't go [out of] Mexico [sic] without paying tax. That is to say, you can trade, but you have to pay tax. But if we paid the tax, there wasn't any profit. So we looked for a way to cross the border without them seeing us.

Contraband. The *Maseca*,[100] candy–mostly it was *Maseca*, clothing and other things. So, that was when I began to do business that way. I had my friends who got it from Mexico to this side. They knew when I would arrive and what I wanted. So, that's when I started there. I was there for about a year. After that I asked my father if I could come to this country, and my father refused. He said, no. We aren't made for that, and you will not go to the United States. My mother, the same.

The reason was, he didn't want the family to disintegrate, he didn't want our family to be divided. His vision was always to be together as a family all the time. Perhaps not in the same place, but we had our customs. On all the festivals in Guatemala, that is, Holy Week, Christmas, New Years, the holidays, our whole family got together with my grandparents. I'm not exaggerating, we were sixty-six grandchildren. We are sixty-six, I say, now we're sixty-six. But before we were like fifty-one, but the number has risen. So my grandfather has sixty-six grandchildren. So all my

---

[100] A popular brand of corn flour used for tortillas.

grandfather's children and grandchildren, all came to spend Christmas with them. They all spent Christmas with them. So, we were exposed to that.

We were accustomed to be with our grandparents on those days. If I came here, my grandparents and uncles and aunts would have to know. My whole family would have to know that I was coming to this place. So, what happened was this: I wanted to come–I came like in April or May, I don't remember very well but there was a festival there with us called the first ashes, the first Friday [sic] of Lent–so, during that festival my parents gathered my aunts and uncles and my grandparents and there was a meeting, a luncheon at my house, my parents' house. So, then he explained that I wanted to come to this country. And they asked me if I had that desire. Why did I want to come here if I had everything. I told them, "No, I don't have everything. I don't have a car. I don't have a house. And the business that I had was very ambitious–there were times when I was selling; there were times when I wasn't selling. I had to buy, I had to buy in order not to lose." So, I explained that I didn't have enough money to be able to do what I wanted to do. So my grandparents said, "We give you the opportunity, but well, we just want there to be one condition. When you get there, call us, send us money, keep your parents in mind, and we will think it is reasonable. And I have done that up to now. God has helped me to be able to communicate with them and all. But they gave me the means to come, and now I am here.

So, I came in April of–I don't remember the year. It was about nine years ago. In 1991 or 1990, I believe. So, I came, and I messed up on the way. Mexican immigration caught me and I went back. They sent me back to Guatemala. So, the first thing I did–many of the families or many of the friends that came in those days said, "No, let's stay here at the border and look for work here and then later we'll get some money and we'll go again." And I said, "No, I don't want to deceive [my parents] or myself either." They told me, "If you are going to fail, you have to go home." And what I did was I went back home again, saying that I had failed. And all of them learned that I had failed. And they said, "Are you going to continue trying?" And I told them yes.

And that's how I came the second time, and the second time I did get across. From that time to now, I'm here. So, I cross the border between Mexico and Guatemala, and then I had to go from there to the border between Mexico and the United States...

I had some friends who already specialized in that. So, it was through them also that I decided to make the venture. They brought people here. And that was what helped me, basically, get here. Now it's a business. Now they charge $4,000 or $5,000, even $7,000 to bring an individual from Guatemala to the United States. Before it was, "because you are my friend, I will take you," but not now. Now it's a business, but it wasn't before. It began to be a business after 1991, from 1994 on...

Travels in El Norte

I was in Los Angeles for a week. I was there one week. I didn't like California, because it seemed like Guatemala to me...I arrived on a Friday. Saturday and Sunday I was there, and all my friends, and all those who we hadn't seen for a year, three months, two months, I found them there. We went to a soccer game, and they had Tierra Blanca. They had Buena Vista, which were the rural settlements that were close to us, El Achac, which was another settlement close to us. They had their own teams from the same settlements where I was, that is, from where I'd been in my country. They had their teams where everyone knew each other. They were all cousins. I went to work. All the opposing teams that we had played yesterday worked in the same factory in Los Angeles.... It was making pants, swimsuits, all that. So, the work was a little easier, because it's pure machines, all by machine sitting down there all day long...

So, I said, "I wanted, I wanted to see the United States totally different." I wanted to see 'gringo' Americans," as they say in my country. So, that was what I wanted to experience. Well, sure, the city is totally different from our city, but the people, the

377

workers were the same. So, then there was this crazy idea. Four of us said, "Let's buy a car between the four of us." And I didn't have any money, so I said, "Put money in for me, and let's go to Florida or to Texas." First it was Texas. Well, when we got to Texas, we passed the exit. Since we had a map, "No, well, let's go to Florida. I've got a friend in Florida." So we went to Florida.

We got to Florida, and it was a little different, the place where the people from Totonicapan were, people from San Miguel Huehuetenango, where all the Huehuetecos were. The branch of Huehuetecos here spoke *Mam*. There was another branch of Huehuetecos who spoke only *Migueleno*–yes–*Cajobal*. There was another place where [people] lived—[who] only spoke *Solomero*. So there were three different languages that they spoke plus ours, which was *Quiche*. The new people all got together in a place called Indiantown. The other one was the Blue Camp and the other one, the White Camp. Well, all the languages were divided in lines at work. So, it was almost a competition. Because we worked in different areas of work in the fields.

Those of us who spoke *Quiche* didn't understand those who spoke *Mam*. So we joined together in the field. Everyone was either *Mam* or *Quiche*, and we didn't understand anything of what they said, unless they spoke to us in Spanish. Among ourselves we spoke *Quiche*, and among themselves, they spoke *Mam*. And the other group did the same. It was amusing, because when they spoke and looked at us, we knew, we felt or we had the presentment that they were talking about us.

So, when we saw that they were laughing at us and all that, we started to talk about them and now totally–because we knew now that they were talking about us, we felt that they were talking about us. And so what we did was we talked about them. We talked, but in our dialects. They didn't understand us at all. And we made a party of it like that. When we needed something from them, we spoke to them in Spanish, and when they needed something from us, they spoke to us in Spanish. So it was! The field was so different, so rough that it just–there were tomatoes, lettuce, onion and all that. We didn't mix as much with the

Mexicans, because the Mexicans, what they liked was the orange orchards. That's what fascinated the Mexicans. Not us.

So, one day, another crazy idea. With the four men we came from Florida to here. Now it was just two of us. Two went back to California, because they didn't like agricultural work. And two of us stayed where that friend was...In Florida we worked under the sun, under the rain. We got wet. We felt thirsty, we felt all that. It was perhaps a little more money, and we worked seven days a week. Seven days a week, and we worked from six in the morning to six in the evening. And one day I remember, one week I remember, when the work began to overlap, because the chile was ready then, the tomatoes were ready then, the onions were ready then, the squash was ready then, everything was ripe and ready to pick, and there weren't enough people to do it. And so they asked us to do this: to work from six at night, I mean six in the morning to eleven at night. And we did that one week. I'll never forget that check, it was so immense and big! That week I think we put in almost 120 hours. It was too much. So we worked from six in the morning to eleven at night, and what time did we have to rest? We didn't have any break. We got home, we bathed, and at 12 midnight, we were sleeping. One, two, three, four, and at five we got up to get ready. We made our food to take with us, and to work once again...

And I have never, never in my life worked like that. But it was juicy, perhaps, it was our ambition that we had, and we decided that that time is the first and last time [working] that way. I worked eleven months in all in Florida illegally. I didn't have working papers. It wasn't necessary in the fields. And I got together with another two, another four people–that person who came from California and two from Florida, and we got it in our heads to discover the United States, not to stay all the time in Florida. And we wanted to come to Virginia. But peninsular Virginia, or this side of Virginia, I don't know. The thing is a friend of that man had come to Delaware. He was in Delaware when we left Florida. So we said, "Let's go to Delaware. Let's see

what it's like there, and then from Delaware, we'll go to Virginia."
And that's how we came here.

Arriving in Georgetown

Then when we got to Delaware, we slept in the parking lot,
the one in the circle. We arrived one Friday morning and we
stopped to sleep there, and how cold it was! In Florida it was hot.
When we got to Delaware we were freezing in the car. We got
there and we called where the man was, and they told us he was in
Lewes. When we got to Lewes, there were seven of them living in
a trailer. So, there wasn't any room for us. And we ended up
sleeping in the car for two weeks. We spent two weeks in the car,
and we began to look for work. That was in 1992; yes, in April of
1992 when I arrived here in Delaware. April 17th, if I'm not
mistaken, I got the vaccination to work. Unfortunately, the
vaccination tested positive. I had to wait a month more in order to
work, and none of the four of us were working. We didn't have an
apartment. We didn't have any place to stay. We didn't have
anywhere to bathe. We didn't have anything. And we didn't have
family here either. We stayed in our car for two weeks.

That 's when we learned of the *Casa* San Francisco, we
learned of the Christian Church, which is here in Georgetown.
They gave us food there, because we weren't working. We didn't
have any place to stay, either. And they didn't want us here,
because it was just for women, and they didn't have one for men.
So, we decided to remain in the car. So, we went to Mountaire, to
Mountaire in Selbyville. They took us there. They didn't check
our vaccination, I don't know how. We started working there. So,
we stayed in the parking lot. We put in an application in the
Roxana Apartments, and they gave us a one-room apartment
finally for the four of us. Now we had a place to bathe, cook,
sleep, and now we were okay.

But the work we got was in the cold. We weren't
accustomed to work in the cold. In the first place, it was another
adaptation. We got sick with colds, with everything, fever,

because we'd never worked in the cold. We'd only worked in the heat. So, our bodies didn't bear the cold. [One] man was allergic to the chicken water, and he started to get a rash on his body, and another guy started getting a rash on his face. So, the other one said, "Let's go back to Florida again. We were fine there. It doesn't get cold there like here. This work is no good." So, we paid $295 in rent just for that room without a living room, without anything, just that room. So, "Let's go," they said. And I said, "No. I'm going to stay here."

I stayed, but it was so sad for me to remain without those others in the apartment. Because I didn't know anyone. I didn't have any friends. I didn't have anything, anything, anything. I was motivated simply by the fact of staying. I didn't want to be like those who don't like to work. I was accustomed to working in whatever. I was accustomed to rough work, to hard work, and I wasn't afraid of anything. If it was with the language, I invented ways to get them to understand me. It wasn't strange for me to have to bow my head because I didn't understand what they said to me. I did it so that I could get ahead. So Roxana. And then I began to [meet] some Mexicans and I got together with them...

They were saying Townsends, Townsends, Townsends, more money. And I decided to change companies to Townsends. I had the address already, and I went to apply at Townsends. I told them I wanted to work. And they gave me work. They gave me the same thing I was doing in Mountaire. I started over at Townsend's. But now Roxana was far away. So, I said, "I'm going to change apartments." I moved to Georgetown. I moved to Georgetown because of transportation. And it was easier, because now the friends that I had were mostly here in Georgetown. Afterwards, I didn't like where I was living, because my friends drank every weekend. It was like a fiesta that they had there in the apartment, and I was the only person who didn't drink. I drink but only on holidays like Christmas or something. But I'm not like the other people who get drunk and all that. I've never liked doing that.

So when I saw their ways, I said I can't live with you anymore. That's when I left and moved to Motor Home—Vetches Motor Homes, do you know where that is? Well, I lived there for three years. That's where I completely changed to live with more Mexicans. I lived three years with Mexicans. And that's what changed my language even for other Guatemalans. They all took me for a Mexican so my own people said that I was Mexican!...Then I got together with my girlfriend. I formed my family, then, and she's Mexican. So her friends thought I was Mexican as well. So,...

For two months I've been in supervision, and thank God, I've left the line. But this is also work, because I administer 105 people. So it's not easy to work with 105 people. I would say it would be easy with twenty or thirty, but it's difficult to work with 105 of them, God willing. If it please God to give me a lot of patience to be able to get ahead. My dream doesn't stop here. I can be someone more, and perhaps it won't be in a poultry plant exactly, but to continue studying. I'm going to continue and I'm going to dream of being able to continue. I have various projects. But before that, I need to get my ESL. And then after that, there will be some other work. But for now I'm satisfied with what I have. But in the future, I will be something a little better.

OGAM

We organized OGAM, which is the Guatemalan Mutal Aid Society, three years ago in 1998. Sadly, it is now inactive, but when I began with that, there was one called Julio, who also had the interest. I said, "Let's get together." He said, "We can get together, but we're five people." I said, "No. If we get together we five, we can't do anything. Let's get together, but we should bring the people together." And we began to bring people together.

I have experience [in this]. My parents—my father more than anything: potable water, the school, the road. What else did they do? They made telegraphs. There are four things my father

[did]—he is part of the committee. And the last committee that my father formed was for electricity. He was involved in the committee for five projects. So, I know how difficult it is to form a committee. In the long run, it's beautiful. Those organizations [that exist] weren't formed like that. It was years and years. They had to go through thousands of things to be where they are today. *La Esperanza* is the same way. That wasn't formed in the blink of an eye. Many obstacles had to be overcome. It's the same with OGAM. So, my first project was here with OGAM. I am not satisfied, I don't feel fulfilled, because OGAM is not moving forward. But it's one of my goals to have it move forward. So, I carry that from my birth. My parents have always done that, they like [community] projects. So, that's what motivated me to create OGAM also.

But to do that, in the beginning it was like, people thought that OGAM was going to do everything for them. That's what our people are used to. If I'm the leader, I have to do everything. They just have to listen and know. Here we all have to be leaders. We all have to give our point of view. And our people don't think like that. Our people think that I'm the only intelligent one amongst us, that I'm going to direct them. That I'm going to say to them what they have to do. In this country, no. Over there, yes. But here, no. Here we all vote, and we all decide that's what's going to be done, it's going to be done like this.

We had a street cleaning. The people helped us. They were with us, but what happens? They left. If we had said, there's another cleaning tomorrow, the day after, two or three are going to show. Because, I say, "Hey, in Georgetown we need a street cleaning. Let's do it, but all together, no?" I have to go and tell them to do it. They don't do it any other way. That's our people and that's how we were raised. So, I hope that OGAM still grows, and I have hopes.

They say, "if Julio[101] isn't here anymore, now it won't go forward." If Julio left, everything was Julio. I wanted to reform it.

---

[101] Julio Herrera, former president of OGAM, who stepped down for personal reasons.

From left: Judy Lewis, Sister Ascension, Olegario Capriel and Gonzalo Martinez.
La Esperanza Board Meeting, 2000.
(Courtesy of Allison Burris)

And because I was also studying, I didn't have the ability to be with the people either on Sundays. What's more, my exams were on Mondays, or on Fridays. So, I have to do three things: my studies, my work and the organization. I don't want to neglect OGAM. I don't want to neglect my work, and I don't want to neglect my studies. But well, I have to neglect something…And that's when I said, "Okay, I'm not going to move, I'm not moving. They're not looking for me, so why do I have to go looking for them?" And I also got demoralized, because people didn't help me when I needed their help. After two or three months, after I already said, "I'm not moving at all, until I do well in my studies," then they said, "What happened to OGAM? What happened to OGAM?" They should have done that when I was struggling, telling them, "let's do this. Let's do that."

La Esperanza

Well, I have to thank my teacher, Allison Burris. She had confidence in me. She more or less knew who I was and what my interests are, and she recommended me to the Board of *La Esperanza*. I haven't done any work yet for *La Esperanza* but, God willing, I will begin working with them. I don't want to just be part of the Board and sit there and warm the seat and that's all. No, I want to do something. And I'm thinking of a lot of things that I'd like to make happen at *La Esperanza*.

And I'm motivated by the simple reason that there's not one Guatemalan who represents our Guatemalan people in *La Esperanza*. Who are the beneficiaries? It's the same thing I've been saying again. We are used to receiving everything, but we don't do anything to make *La Esperanza* capable of growing. No one is interested in what it is that *La Esperanza* needs. They have a jar there where it says donations. If we leave a dollar, it's good. Well, so, I think that it's not just the economic [support] but also morally *La Esperanza* needs us. Without the Sisters there wouldn't be an *Esperanza*. Without Jim Lewis, there wouldn't be an *Esperanza*. So, there are people who truly are interested in us, and we are the interested members in this. Before [*La Esperanza*] was small. Very soon it will be large… And as I say, thanks to experience, to my mistakes. If there are no mistakes, there's no experience.

List of Illustrations

Youngters in traditional Hispanic clothing vi
Mountaire Chicken Processing Plant, Sussex County 6
1ˢᵗ Grader Johnny Alvarado 20
Midfielder Dribbles Past Defense............................... 22
Pedro Ospina in Kimmeytown, art work 26
Tamales, Tamales 29
Festival dancers.. 31
Two governors 35
Ground breaking at *La Esperanza* 43
Photo of Carmelite Sisters 55
Sister Rosa and Maria in Washington demonstration.............. 60
Sister Rosa with the Cervantes family 65
Alicia Sosman 67
Map of Guatemala.. 78
Father and daughter in Tacaná................................. 81
Son Jorge Luis Perez in Tacaná................................ 88
Festival of the Virgin of Guadalupe........................... 91
Perez Family in Tacaná... 94
Wilbert Perez, with tools and turkey.......................... 101
Sister Maria Mairlot.. 114
Unidentified girl on soccer field 116
Photo of Race Street, Georgetown.............................. 121
Yanitza with children.. 126
Photo of Dancers at the Opening of Gomez International......... 132
Representative and Actor Olmos, Summer 2000.................... 134
Carmen Garcia and Sister Rosa 140
Marta and her daughter Marisa................................. 147
Watching Soccer with friends................................... 156
Joe's Market, Georgetown.. 172
Nevy Matos 181
Map of Mexico... 184
Hulisis Perez, August 1998...................................... 186
Beautiful dancers performing at the Hispanic Festival.......... 195
Rosario Hernandez and her daughter............................ 210

Two photographs, Opening of the Gomez International 220
Family Literacy Class 226
Photo of Margarita Gonzalez 228
Comet Baseball Team 248
Pilar Gomez in the Local 27 Office on Race Street 250
Two Year Olds at *Primero Pasos* 264
Regular Soccer Match 266
Garden Project behind Twin Cedars 268
15th Year traditional ceremoney 270
Packing Corn at the Papens Packing Station 281
Summer Migrant Program 284
(From left) Nancy Soriano and Maria Lopez, recruiters
for the Summer Migrant Education Program 290
Maria Martinez' Family 294
Soccer in Georgetown 302
Poultry Worker's Uniform 308
Maria and her two daughters 311
Maria Mendoza 315
Allison Burris' ESL Class 319
Rafael Dossman, Radio DJ 322
Allison Burris with Jennifer Lopez 329
Protest in Washington to close the School of the Americas 332
Georgetown Hispanic Festival 342
Study of Guatemalan Life 358
Juan with his art in Dover 365
Youngsters playing on art forms of Pedro Ospina 366
Olegario at a meeeting of *La Esperanza* 384

Bibliography for Further Reading

American Friends Service Committee. Sept. 1988. **In the Shadow of Liberty: Central American Refugees in the United States.** Phila: AFSC.

Black, Jan Knippers, ed. 1998. **Latin America, Its Problems and Its Promise: A Multidisciplinary Introduction.** Boulder, CO: Westview Press.

Bodley, John. 1999. **Victims of Progress.** 4th Ed. Mountain View, CA: Mayfield Publishing Co.

Bodnar, John. 1985. **The Transplanted: A History of Immigrants in Urban America.** Bloomington, IN: Indiana Univ. Press.

Booth, John A. 1993. **Understanding Central America.** Boulder, CO.: Westview Press.

Borland, Katherine. 1999. Hispanic Arts and Narratives: Fieldwork January-July, 1999. Delmarva Folklife Project Final Report.

Burgos-Debray, Elisabeth, ed. 1984. **I, Rigoberta Menchú.** Trans., Ann Wright. New York: Verso.

Coutin, Susan Bibler. 2000. **Legalizing Moves: Salvadoran Immigrants' Struggle for U.S. Residency.** Ann Arbor: The Univ. of Michigan Press.

Delmarva Poultry Industry, Inc. March, 1996 **Delmarva's Poultry Industry: Facts, Figures, and other Material About Delmarva's Poultry Industry.**

Dublin, Thomas, ed. 1993. **Immigrant Voices: New Lives in America, 1773-1986.** Urbana: Univ. of Illinois Press.

Escobar, Arturo and Sonia E. Alvarez, eds. 1992. **The Making of Social Movements in Latin America: Identity, Strategy, and Democracy.** Boulder, CO: Westview Press.

Fouse, Matthew J. 1998. **Immigration and Immigrant Policy: Guatemalans in Georgetown, DE.** B.A. Thesis. Univ. of Delaware.

Gjerde, Jon, ed. 1998. **Major Problems in American Immigration and Ethnic History.** Boston: Houghton-Mifflin Company.

Grimes, Kimberly M. 1998. **Crossing Borders: Changing Social Identities in Southern Mexico.** Tucson: Univ. of Arizona Press.

Gutierrez, Gustavo. 1973. **A Theology of Liberation.** Maryknoll, NY.

Herrera-Sobek, Maria. 1979. **The Bracero Experience: Elitelore vs. Folklore.** Los Angeles: UCLA Latin American Center Publications.

Horowitz, Roger and Mark J. Miller. 1997. Immigrants in the Delmarva Poultry Processing Industry: The Changing Face of Georgetown, Delaware and Environs. Paper Presented at the Changing Face of Delaware Conference, University of Delaware, September 11-13, 1997. Reprinted as **Julian Somara Research Institute Occasional Paper No. 37,** Michigan State University, East Lansing, Michigan, 1999. A version of this paper also appears in **Migration World Magazine** 1998, 26: 15-18.

Jones, Maldwyn Allen. 1992. **American Immigration.** Chicago: Univ. of Chicago Press.

Jordan, Rosan Augusta. 1975. **The Folklore and Ethnic Identity of a Mexican-American Woman.** Dissertation. Bloomington, IN: Indiana Univ.

Lowell, B. Lindsay and Rodolfo de la Garza. June 2000. **The Developmental Role of Remittances in U.S. Latino Communities and in Latin American Countries: A Final Project Report.** Washington, D.C.: Inter-American Dialogue and The Tomás Rivera Institute.

McWilliams, Carey. 1990 [1948]. **North from Mexico: The Spanish-Speaking People of the United States.** NY: Praeger.

Namias, Jue. 1992. **First Generation: In the Words of Twentieth-Century American Immigrants.** Urbana: Univ. of Illinois Press.

Payne, Jessica. 1995. **Hispanic Cultural Traditions Survey Final Report and Recommendations.** Delaware Folklife Program, Delaware Division of Parks and Recreation.

Portes, Alejandro and Rubén G. Rumbaut. 1990. **Immigrant America: A Portrait.** Berkeley: Univ. of California Press.

Public Justice Center. 1998. **The Disposable Workforce: A Worker's Perspective.** Baltimore, MD.

Public Justice Center and CASA of Maryland. 1999. **Unequal Justice: Barriers to Justice for Latinos in Maryland.** Baltimore, M.D.

Rosenblum, Marc. 2000. U.S. Immigration Policy: Unilateral and Cooperative Responses to Undocumented Immigration. Paper presented at the International Studies Association. http://www.columbia.edu/dlc/ciao/isa/rom01.

Rothenberg, Daniel. 1998 **With These Hands: The Hidden World of Migrant Farmworkers Today.** NY: Harcourt Brace and Co.

Simon, Jean-Marie. 1987. **Guatemala: Eternal Spring, Eternal Tyranny.** New York: W.W. Norton.

Stinson, Craig M. 1999. Delmarva Folklife Project: Latino Cultural Survey 1998-99. Delmarva Folklife Project.

Torres, Gabriel. 1997. **The Force of Irony: Power in the Everyday Life of Mexican Tomato Workers.** London: Berg.

U.S. Census Bureau. **Profile of the Foreign-Born Population in the United States: 1997.** Current Population Reports Special Studies P23-195. [Also see the University of Delaware Website for statistics from the U.S. Census: http://www.cadsr.udel.edu/

Warren, Kay B. 1978. **The Symbolism of Subordination: Indian Identity in a Guatemalan Town.** Austin: Univ. of Texas Press.

Westerman, William. 1998. Central American Refugee Testimonies and Performed Life Histories. In **The Oral**

History Reader. Eds., Robert Perks and Alistair Thomson. New York: Routledge: 224-34.

Williams, William Henry. 1998. **Delmarva's Chicken Industry: 75 Years of Progess.** Georgetown, DE: Delmarva Poultry Industry.

Yeoman, Barry. July/August 2000. Hispanic Diaspora. **Mother Jones**: 34-41.

Newspaper Resources

The Hagley Museum. Hispanics in Delaware Archive. [Curator, Roger Horowitz] A collection of newspaper articles and unpublished theses about Hispanics in Delaware.

Baltimore Sun, 1994-2001. see especially Fesperman, Dan and Chris Guy. 18 Apr 1999. Hopes of a Better Life Take Root in Delmarva: 1A, 10A.

Central America/Mexico Report: Bimonthly Journal of the Religious Task Force on Central America and Mexico. http://www.rtfcam.org/report/

Christian Science Monitor James L. Tyson. 30 Nov 1998. A Holy Alliance: p. 15ff.

Delaware Coast Press, 2000-2001

Delaware Communion, 1994-2000

Delaware Wave, 1994-2000

National Journal n. a. 14 Aug 1999. Delaware's Hispanic Peace Corps: p. 2357-58. [Part of a Special Issue: Beyond the Myths: Hispanics in America.]

New York Times 6 Oct, 1999. Priest vs. 'Big Chicken" in Fight for Labor Rights: p. A12.

Sussex Post, 1994-2001

Washington Post, 1999-2001 see especially:

Special report by Peter S. Goodman, entitled *Poultry's Price: The Cost to the Bay.* Three articles on environmental impact running Sunday, August 1, 1999: A1ff; Monday, August 2, 1999: A1ff; Tuesday, August 3: A1ff.
Special reports by Lena H. Sun, Gabriel Escobar, Peter Pae. Four articles running Sunday, Nov. 28, 1999, On Poultry's Front Line; Monday, Nov. 29, Immigration Transforms a Community; Tuesday, Nov. 30, Poultry's Price: Hidden Identities; Wednesday, Dec. 1, Chicken Plants Open U.S. Doors for Koreans.
http://www.washingtonpost.com/w...metro/A44096-1999nov24.html
Wilmington News-Journal, 1993-2001.